Empire by
Treaty

Empire by Treaty

Britain and the Middle East

in the Twentieth Century

By M. A. FITZSIMONS

UNIVERSITY OF NOTRE DAME PRESS 1964

TO
FRANCES

PREFACE

In *Empire by Treaty* I present an account of British policies in the Middle East. The title is intended to suggest the characteristic form of British relationship with many Middle Eastern countries. By treaties Britain sought to gain the assent, notably of Arab rulers, to concessions and bases that Britain believed to be essential for the protection of British interests and the maintenance of a British order. The antecedents of the Treaty Empire, a half-way house of British imperialism, go back to Britain's early impact on the Persian Gulf sheikhdoms. The Empire itself is mainly a product of the interwar years. Since the Second World War the Treaty Empire has been in retreat, and since 1958 a changing Britain has been compelled to deal with a new Middle East on new terms.

The author of a work based on research incurs so many obligations that a preface to a scholarly work often appears to be a listing of the co-authors of the volume. For myself I have realized since my college days how greatly any achievement of mine is dependent on others. This understanding first came to me when upon reading *The Meditations* of Marcus Aurelius I imitated his pious practice of recalling the things I owed to predecessors and contemporaries. The great indebtedness, so much investment to produce so few scriptural talents, was overwhelming. In living with this sense of indebtedness I came to appreciate that it was the happy and inescapable condition of man as a social animal.

Here then I can but acknowledge some special debts: to Mrs. David Fowler, Mrs. Frank Dietrich, Patrick V. O'Dea, and David Schlaver, among others, for typing the various *avatars* of this manuscript; to George E. Kirk, Elizabeth Monroe, and John C. Campbell, who read and most helpfully criticized an early version of this book; to Father Theodore M. Hesburgh, C.S.C., President of the University of Notre Dame, for his warmly understanding help; to my colleagues, Father Thomas T. McAvoy, C.S.C., and Thomas J. Stritch for their encouragement; finally, to Professor Stephen D. Kertesz, Head of Notre Dame's Committee on International Relations, whose example is perhaps even more helpful than his wise counsel.

M. A. Fitzsimons

CONTENTS

Preface   ix

1 The Postwar Setting   1

2 Britain's Middle Eastern Interests   4

3 The Interwar Years   18

4 Britain and the Middle East in the Second World War   36

5 The First Postwar Years   49
   A. Palestine, the Arab-Israeli War, and Israel, p. 58; B. Jordan, p. 68; C. Iraq, p. 72; D. Iran, p. 76; E. Egypt, p. 92

6 The Baghdad Pact   117

7 The Hardening of Lines   136

8 Nationalization and the British Effort to Regain the Past   161

9 The Aftermath of Suez and the Iraqi Revolution   193

10 Britain and the Contemporary Middle East   207

FRANCE SWITZ. AUS. HUNG. Budapest RUMANIA U. S. S. R. ARAL SEA

Belgrade Bucharest
YUGOSLAVIA BULGARIA
Rome Sofia
ITALY Tirana ALB. BLACK SEA CASPIAN SEA

ALG. Tunis Athens Ankara
TUNISIA GREECE TURKEY KURDS Teheran AFGH.

MEDITERRANEAN CYPRUS SYRIA Euphrates Tigris IRAN PAK.
Tripoli SEA Nicosia Damascus
Benghazi Beirut Baghdad
LEBANON IRAQ
ISRAEL Amman
Tel Aviv-Jaffa JORDAN KUWAIT
Cairo Kuwait

LIBYA U. A. R. Neutral Persian Gulf Gulf of Oman
(EGYPT) Zones BAHRAIN QATAR TRUCIAL SHEIKHDOMS Muscat
Riyadh MUSCAT AND OMAN

ALG. RED SAUDI
SEA ARABIA

NIGER Nile

CHAD Khartoum San'a ADEN PROTECTORATE
Fort-Lamy Ta'izz YEMEN
NIGERIA SUDAN Blue FR. Aden Gulf of Aden
CAMEROON Nile SOM. Djibouti INDIAN

CEN. AFRICAN REP. White Nile Addis Ababa OCEAN
Bangui ETHIOPIA
CONGO REP. OF THE CONGO UGANDA KENYA SOMALI REPUBLIC

MILES

Maps on this page and the following one show the Middle East with Great Britain reduced to positions on Cyprus, in Aden, and on the Persian Gulf.

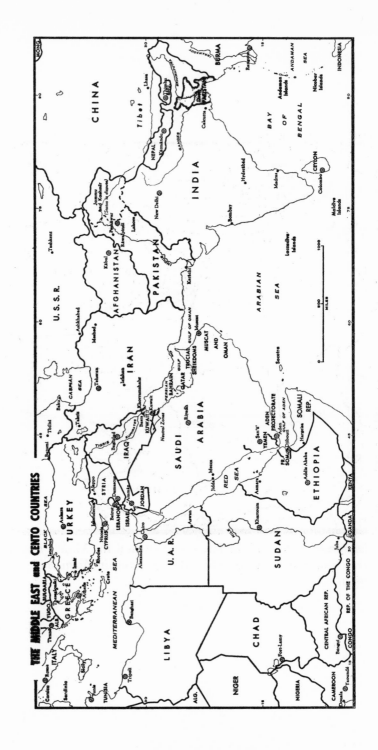

THE MIDDLE EAST and CENTO COUNTRIES

Empire by Treaty

1: THE POSTWAR SETTING

During the interwar years, Britain exercised a preponderant power in the Middle East and there was able to make dispositions generally to her own satisfaction. This Middle East, a classic area of empire and a new theater of direct and extended British interest, was the scene of a short-lived but significant improvisation of British empire, Empire by Mandate or Treaty. The Empire had familiar features: the area was a key center of communications and of access to three continents; it bordered on a powerful state, Russia, and Britain had generally sought to check the growth of Russian influence in it; and it had a raw material, oil, necessary for twentieth-century economy. New features were the growing temper of hostility to empire, the British electorate's unwillingness after 1918 to assume costly imperial burdens, and the Arab character of the aborning nations under French and British control. Empire, then, would have to be maintained by means other than direct control, and, as an issue stemming from other sources as well, Middle Eastern territories did not receive the administrative and political education that for India was the happy legacy of a longer period of imperialism. So, for a new day and a new imperialism, British policy helped to create Middle Eastern states and to provide for them political, military, and administrative tutors. In general, this meant that British ascendancy remained sufficiently assured to gain from Arab rulers the concessions thought essential for a British order.

These concessions involved a tutelary relationship between Britain and the Arab states from which descended like doomed generations a lineage of suspicion, rancor, and frustration. When Arab political leaders sought to gain for their rule the consent even of relatively small Arab groups, they were bound to clamor for their equal status under the Western tradition of international law and to regard tutelage as a flaw outraging the equality that served as a mask for new empire. At best, the imperialist relationship foments an irrational temper in modern subject people that impairs the political education imperialism may afford. For their part, nationalists often create or

1

foster a sense of community by appealing to historical myths. But the joining of anticolonialism with nationalism directs the myth to a scapegoat approach to history and politics that makes calculating and realistic politics very difficult.[1]

When British power declined after the Second World War and, to meet new and common dangers, Britain sought to renew the old dispositions, she met clamorous and adamant refusal. Empire may have involved both consent and power. But when Britain yielded to Indian demands for independence, the nationalist success of India, a bastion of the British position in the Middle East, encouraged an opposition mentality already formidable. The attempted move from disguised inequality to partnership was attended by monumental suspicions, rendering partnership impossible. Equality and independence apparently had to precede partnership. Two considerations, however, had deterred Britain from espousing a course of such simplicity and forthrightness: the vital nature of British positions and concessions in the Middle East; and a mistrust of Arab ability compounded by British commitment to a Jewish homeland in Palestine.

While Britain's power in the Middle East declined, her dependence on the region's oil rapidly increased, and the war that ratified Britain's loss of preponderance saw the emergence of two continental powers with interests and traditions differing from those of Britain. The leaders of the Soviet Union, seeing struggle for power as the ineluctable condition of a divided world, proclaimed hostility to imperialism, including the British Middle Eastern order. Thus, the Soviet Union, having no direct interest in the area's stability, usually favored Arab challenges to British positions. Apprehensions of even more sweeping Soviet ambitions joined Britain and the United States in an alliance that sometimes failed to coordinate their Middle Eastern policies. British and American readings of their Middle Eastern in-

[1] For example: the insistence of the Zionists under the British Mandate that Arab opposition to Zionism was unsubstantial, unworthy, and not popularly supported; the argument of many Indian nationalists that Muslim opposition to an independent, Hindu-dominated India was a mere British invention designed to prolong British rule; the argument of some Egyptian nationalists that nineteenth-century Egypt was a flourishing progressive country with a representative government, and that in 1883 the British deliberately replaced a successful Egyptian general in the Sudan with the incompetent Hicks to insure Egypt's loss of the Sudan so that Britain could be associated with its reconquest. An account of some Egyptian nationalist myths appears in Jafar H. Khesbak, "England and the Nationalist Movement in Egypt, 1918-1924," unpublished Ph.D. thesis, University of Chicago, 1952, p. 25.

terests did not coincide: Britain was concerned with her actual positions and vital oil sources; the United States, though American oil
companies had growing Middle Eastern investment, approached the
region with overriding interest in Cold War strategy, and was inclined
to regard Britain's special advantages as vestiges of a dying colonial
era hopefully allowing to American maneuver a favored future position. Britain, then, faced a formidable enemy and a difficult ally in an
area that presented tortuous problems.

The history of British policy in the Middle East may be paradoxically summarized in the judgment that a succession of misadventures
left essential British interests there largely unimpaired, although they
are no longer protected by the influences and bases Britain once
affirmed to be vital. Although British policy-makers struggled with
some irrepressible contradictions, although they were on occasion
victims of their own miscalculations, and at times lacked foresight,
even in defeat and failure British policy was successful in its major
objective, the maintenance, if not the protection, of essential British
interests. How is this apparent paradox to be explained? Was British
policy a success in spite of itself or was its success the salvaging of
the vital minimum from the reverses of a troubled time of rapid
change?

This story of success, even in retreat, involved a disentangling of
proclaimed vital interests from essential interests. The greatest transformation occurred—though its consequences cannot be accurately
measured—when India, the bastion of the British Middle East, acquired independence. Later, other bases became untenable and client
states or political figures repudiated tutelage. A particular *modus
vivendi* failed to command acceptance. Change engulfed the Middle
East, its neighboring powers, and Britain and her interests as well.
Where in the Far East Britain never aspired to dominance, and where
in Southeast Asia and India Britain's yielding to colonial nationalism
fulfilled the mission of Liberal Imperialism, the Middle East posed
more intractable problems for Britain. There, dominance, much more
recent in origin, and disguised by indirection, grew clumsy with the
British belief, prominent among Conservative imperialists, that Britain
had a special, self-evident mission in the Arab world. The self-evident,
however, sometimes fails to sustain examination and in crisis may
wither in the frustrated gaze of its adherents.

2: BRITAIN'S MIDDLE EASTERN INTERESTS

Three major British interests involving the Middle East commanded the attention of nineteenth-century British statesmen: the European balance of power, the security of India, and unimpaired transit. Turkey's weakness inspired strong and neighboring Russia with designs of dominion over Ottoman realms and those designs Britain felt impelled to oppose. Thus, the maintenance of Europe's power balance and the security of India dictated a policy of maintaining the integrity of the Ottoman Empire. This policy dates back to the end of the eighteenth century, to the younger William Pitt.

As early as the sixteenth century, Russia figured in the plans of those British adventurers who sought trade in Eastern goods. But when British merchants increasingly used the sea route to Eastern markets and later created an East India Company empire, Russia more often appeared as a threat to Levant trade and as an expansionist rival likely to block the approaches to India and even to plunder her riches. Russia and other powerful nations as well were not unvarying factors in British policy, neither eternal friends nor eternal enemies.

Rivalries with other powers prevented Britain from pursuing a single-minded policy towards Russia and Turkey. In early modern times British rivalry with France and the French policy of alliance with Turkey ruled out a consistently pro-Turkish policy. Phil-hellene sentiment prompted Britain to join with France and Russia against Turkey in the course that led to the Turkish defeat at Navarino (1827) and to Greek independence (1832). When, later, Mehmet Ali in Egypt challenged the Sultan's authority, Britain found it expedient again to prevent the disintegration of Ottoman rule. Later, Britain developed a profitable trade in Egyptian cotton, the raw material for high quality Lancashire textiles. The cultivation of this cotton had been notably encouraged by Mehmet Ali.

The Crimean War (1854-1856) saw Britain and France victorious in resisting Russian expansion in the Turkish Empire. For Russia, de-

4

feat meant the Treaty of Paris (1856) which included an agreement not to maintain warships on the Black Sea. Earlier, Russia had been compelled to agree that, when Turkey was at peace, no foreign warships should be admitted to the Straits. In the Franco-Prussian War, however, Russia repudiated the clause concerning the demilitarization of the Black Sea, and this action was regularized in the Convention of London (1871). The Crimean peace settlement also included a Turkish promise to initiate reforms and, in return, a disavowal by the signatory powers of rights of interference in internal Turkish affairs.

Turkey had become weak, and the strength of the European powers was burgeoning. The Ottoman Empire in its weakness had to endure the impact of Western ways, influence, and power and to face the nationalist disaffection of its European subjects, which not only invited intervention but afforded a pretext for it.

This Eastern Question acquired new urgency when Russia imposed on Turkey (1878) the Treaty of San Stefano. In spite of a bitter domestic political controversy initiated by the Liberal statesman, W. E. Gladstone, British policy in the hands of Disraeli was firmly for Turkey. The British opposition to Russian expansionism made possible the Congress of Berlin and another attempt to settle the Eastern Question.[1]

In occupying Cyprus[2] (1878) and Egypt (1882), Britain deviated from the policy of maintaining the territorial integrity of the Otto-

---

[1] As long as British policy aimed to check Russia by protecting Turkey, this aim generally meant the sharing of a major interest with the Hapsburg Empire. Later, European and imperial politics placed Austria-Hungary in alliance with Germany, gaining influence in the Turkish Empire, and Britain in accord with Russia (1907). This entente, in turn, strengthened the Young Turkish Nationalists in their attachment to Germany.

[2] The Berlin Congress (1878), in disposing of some Turkish territory, provided for agreed and partial dismemberment of Turkey. But British negotiators at the Congress also secured an agreement that Turkey would introduce reforms for her Christian and other subjects in Asia. To supervise these reforms British military consuls were sent to Western Asiatic Turkey. Britain also won Turkish agreement to the occupation and administration of Cyprus. This "Key of Western Asia" (Disraeli) presumably gave Britain the position necessary to fulfill a pledge of assistance to Turkey in defending her Asiatic territory against Russian attack. Redemption of the pledge, designed to safeguard British interests in the Suez Canal and the Persian Gulf, was never called for. The later occupation of Egypt provided a more satisfactory base than Cyprus. When in 1954 Britain agreed to evacuate the Canal Zone, the importance of Cyprus to Britain was temporarily reaffirmed. Lord Strang, *Britain in World Affairs* (New York, 1961), pp. 206-207.

man Empire and of relying upon a fleet based in the Western Mediterranean. British policy of succeeding decades entertained less hopefully the possibility of reforms that would significantly enhance Turkey's capacity for self-preservation. But until the Turkish Empire sided with Germany in the First World War, British leaders found too many difficulties in any course other than the maintenance of the Ottoman Empire.

Trade and power interests reached out from the imperial position in India, and British attempts to check piracy and the slave trade also contributed to the creation of special areas of British influence in the Persian Gulf: among them, Bahrain, Kuwait, and Muscat and Oman.[3] Indeed, until 1882, India was the major base from which

[3] Bahrain, a group of islands in the Gulf of Bahrain, where the East India Company established treaty relations in 1820, and in 1880 and 1892 the British government acquired supervisory rights over the islands' foreign relations. When in 1869 the Shah of Persia, which also claims sovereignty over Bahrain, protested against British activities which ignored the Shah's claim, Foreign Secretary Lord Granville replied that the British government had a primary interest in seeing that the Persian Gulf area was policed and that piracy and the slave trade were suppressed. Granville expressed the belief that Persia shared these interests. If Persia effectively assumed discharge of the task, "this country would be relieved of a troublesome and costly duty." J. C. Hurewitz, *Diplomacy in the Near and Middle East* (Princeton, 1956), I, 172-173. Later, for example, on April 5, 1899, Lord Salisbury indicated that the exercise of control or jurisdiction in the Persian Gulf by a European power would be incompatible with British interests.

The exploitation of oil in Bahrain, begun in 1932, is carried on by a Canadian Company, under American management, and by a largely British staff. Bahrain, claimed by Iran since the mid-nineteenth century, has served as a British naval base in the Persian Gulf. Royal Institute of International Affairs, *The Middle East: A Political and an Economic Survey* (2nd ed., New York, 1954), pp. 128-132.

Qatar is a peninsula on the Persian Gulf's west coast. British treaty rights in Qatar go back to 1882 and British oil interests to 1935.

Kuwait, bordering Iraq and Saudi Arabia, was the center of imperial rivalry when the German projectors of the Berlin-Baghdad railway considered making Kuwait a terminus. In 1899, Lord Curzon, British Viceroy in India, made a secret agreement with the Sheikh of Kuwait, who accepted British protection and relinquished to Britain control over his external affairs. But in 1914 the British government conditionally promised to recognize Kuwait as an independent principality under Britain. After the Second World War Kuwait's oil production, controlled by a company jointly owned by British and American firms, expanded enormously. Kuwait's oil revenue provided it with one of the highest per capita national incomes in the world and made it a notable source of capital for the London Stock Exchange.

In Muscat and Oman, a Sultanate commanding the approach to the Persian

Britain approached the Middle East. Thereafter, Egypt and the Suez Canal, which derived its principal importance from British interest in India, and the imperialist rivalries in Africa added new positions for a British approach to the Middle East. Later, in 1903, the British Viceroy in India, Curzon, joined by Sir Arthur Hardinge, British Minister to Persia, made a three weeks' visit to the Persian Gulf area to impress upon its native rulers the paramountcy of British influence there and to deter Russian designs. The journey was made, to use Curzon's words, "in almost swashbuckling style," and saw the confident Curzon uninhibitedly telling the local chiefs: "The peace of these waters must still be maintained; your independence will continue to be upheld; and the influence of the British Government must remain supreme." [4]

These curious, extra-imperial Durbars saw Curzon apparently oblivious to the contradictions he espoused: for example, he talked of independence and, yet, happily described the behavior of the Sultan of Oman as resembling that of a "loyal feudatory of the British Crown." [5] Like Curzon's own official biographer, who, however, noted that a Persian official provided entirely unacceptable conditions for landing at Bushire, Curzon was untroubled by the fact that he himself had dictated arrangements for all the receptions and, probably, the texts of welcoming speeches. [6]

Persia, distinguished from the Arab world by her long history of independence, by her own notable culture and language, and by the prevalence of the Shiite form of Islam, was often the theater of

---

Gulf, British interests go back to the eighteenth century, and the basic British political position, acquired in 1891, was then secured by the government of India. Since the signature of a treaty in 1939, the Sultanate is formally "an independent state in treaty relations with Great Britain." The dispute between Saudi Arabia and the Sultanate over Buraimi oasis has revealed the realities of the British position. See J. B. Kelly, "The Legal and Historical Basis of the British Position in the Persian Gulf," *Middle Eastern Affairs*, No. I (St. Antony's Papers, No. 4; London, 1959).

[4] Earl of Ronaldshay, *The Life of Lord Curzon* (New York, 1928), II, 314, 317.

[5] *Ibid.*, 314-315.

[6] The French *chargé d'affaires* at Saint Petersburg mentioned this point as a malicious guess, which I think is likely enough. *Documents Diplomatiques Francais* (1871-1914), 2nd series, Vol. 4, p. 119. Sir Arthur Hardinge reported to Secretary Lansdowne that Curzon upbraided him for dealing with "mendacious Asiatics" as though they were European statesmen. Lord Newton, *Lord Lansdowne* (London, 1929), p. 243.

rivalry between Russia and Britain. Curzon, arguing that the real "strategic danger to India on the Persian side lies from the direction of the Persian Gulf," [7] had also affirmed that a strong Persia was a British interest. But Persia was not strong, and in 1907 the *entente* of Britain and Russia, seen by Sir Edward Grey as an effort to end conflicts with the aid of Britain's French ally and to emerge from "the old, bad rut" of rivalry with Russia,[8] was followed by what has been called "the strangling of Persia." [9]

British Indian interests in Persia were major and enduring. Until 1860 the government of India contended with the Foreign Office for the control of official relations with Persia. The settlement in favor of the Foreign Office continued to allow a large voice to the government of India.[10]

British Indian interests had dictated the seizure of Aden, which remained under the Indian government until 1937. This ancient entrepot of East-West trade, commanding the southern approaches to the Red Sea, acquired renewed importance with the opening of the Suez Canal. In the age of steam it served as a valuable coaling station and is today a free port and a center of oil-refining. In passing from Indian government control in 1937 it became a Crown Colony, and at that time Britain moved vigorously to impose peace on the adjacent area, the Protectorate of Aden. The Protectorate lands provided the basis for an enduring dispute with Yemen.

[7] *Parliamentary Debates*, Lords, 4th series, CLXXXIII (1908), 1009-1011.

[8] Grey further argued that there was in the Indian frontier area no third party with whom Britain could seek to control the advance of Russia. Viscount Grey of Fallodon, *Twenty-Five Years: 1892-1916* (New York, 1925), I, 147-148.

[9] As a rule, British officials in India and Persia were mistrustful of any deal with Russia. In 1891 Lord Salisbury summarized the problem posed by Persia for British policy: "We have to make Persia as strong as we can by internal developments to resist the supposed aggression; and we have to obtain for ourselves the amount and the kind of influence which will enable us when the crises come to turn the efforts of Persia in the right direction." Salisbury to Lascelles, Salisbury Papers, quoted in Rose Louise Greaves, *Persia and the Defence of India, 1884-1892* (London, 1959), p. 225.

[10] The Indian Political Service staffed British consular posts in southern Persia as well as the British Consulate General in Baghdad. Sir Reader Bullard, *Britain and the Middle East* (London, 1957), p. 40. Lord Curzon, in a famous report on Persia, September 21, 1899, noted: "The political interests of Great Britain in Persia, although they date originally from a period before India had become a British interest at all, were, in their revival a century ago, in the main Indian in inception, and are still largely Indian in character." The report is reprinted in its entirety in Hurewitz, *op. cit.*, I, 219-249.

French initiative in the construction of the Suez Canal transformed the British interest in security of transit in the Middle East. Lord Palmerston, who had opposed the Canal project on the ground that it would open the area to intensified great power rivalry, had memorably expressed the earlier version of this interest: all that should be looked for was security of transit, and some good inns.[11] But in the days of the *Pax Britannica*, security of transit, as in the Persian Gulf, was likely to mean British control, which British official documents would readily and seriously describe as a trust assumed for all nations.

From the Canal's opening (1869), British shipping furnished the bulk of its traffic. In 1875 Prime Minister Disraeli imperially dramatized the British government's purchase of the Khedive of Egypt's shares in the Canal Company. The shares afforded the British government a voice, but not a controlling one, in the management of the Canal, for the Company remained primarily French.[12]

[11] Foreign Secretary Salisbury's instructions to Sir Edward Malet as late as 1879 echo the view: The aim of British policy in Egypt is the maintenance of Egyptian neutrality, by which Salisbury meant that "no great Power shall be more powerful there than England"; continuance of native rule in Egypt "is, for us, the easiest solution of the problem"; and Turkish suzerainty over Egypt provided a means of exercising British control and of changing the governors. Hurewitz, *op. cit.*, I, 191-194, Document 87.

[12] Although the Khedive had provided Egyptian resources and labor for the building of the Canal, de Lesseps had been an astute bargainer and the Egyptian government received no revenue from the Canal's operation until 1936. The Khedive forfeited a major share in the proceeds when he sold his shares to the British government. That transaction turned out to be financially profitable to the British Treasury, even though Disraeli did not secure the controlling voice in management which his account of the imperialist master-stroke implied. In 1880 the Anglo-French controllers of Egyptian finance also disposed of the preference shares. These had entitled the Egyptian government to 15 per cent of the net profits of the Suez Canal Company and, in effect, were Egypt's royalties for the concession. The disposition was a mistake, not only in retrospect, and later in Egyptian eyes associated the Canal with imperialist exploitation. Not until 1936, when the Company as an act of grace, not right, paid Egypt £300,000 a year and permitted the nomination of two Egyptians to the Board of Directors of the Company, was Egyptian interest in the Canal recognized with any substance. Later agreements increased the Egyptianization of the Company and gave the Egyptian government 7 per cent of its net profits. In 1904 the Company requested an extension of its charter from 1968 to 2008 and offered in return £4,000,000 and a share in the profits. The Egyptian General Assembly firmly rejected the offer and the Prime Minister, Butros, who supported the offer, was assassinated. For details of the Concession see Hurewitz, *op. cit.*, I, Document 64. See also, Documents 80-84, 91-93. Also John Marlowe, *A History of Modern Egypt and Anglo-Egyptian Relations, 1800-1953* (New York, 1954) Chaps. III–IV.

In 1888 a Convention of major powers agreed that the Suez Canal
should be open to all nations in time of war as well as in time of
peace. But the Convention was subject to a British reservation that it
was not to go into effect until the British occupation of Egypt, proclaimed as temporary, was ended. When in 1904 the Anglo-French
Entente recognized the British occupation of Egypt, the British government, assuming responsibility for the defense of the Canal and for
freedom of navigation in it, gave effect to the Convention of 1888.[13]

The Canal, however, was under the shadow of growing British
power in Egypt, and its openness to all nations was not maintained
in the First World War, when many of the signatories of the Convention of 1888 were locked in mortal combat. In the war, Britain
proclaimed a protectorate over Egypt and dealt with the Canal as a
waterway under British control.

The establishment of British power in Egypt is a classic example
of Britain's assumption of an unsought imperial burden. Earlier, in
1879, the Khedive Ismail had been deposed and, indeed, as early as
1876, his financial irresponsibility had caused the establishment of
a public debt commission. Thereafter, his successor was subject in
essential matters to English and French Controllers, who were imposed on the country in the interest of Egypt's creditors. Then, there
rose against the Egyptian government a nationalist army movement
under Ahmed Arabi, and this movement's onrush appeared likely to
threaten all European interests in Egypt. Joint action of Britain and
France was contemplated, but the fall of a French government caused
France to withdraw at the last minute from this projected use of force
against Egypt. Thus, in 1882 Britain occupied Egypt, but, as the

---

[13] In a preliminary convention drafted by Britain and France in 1887, British
agreement to the terms was given only "in so far as they should be compatible
with the transitory and exceptional state in which Egypt found itself at the
moment, and that they should in no way restrict the liberty of action of the
British Government during the occupation of Egypt by Her Majesty's Forces."
Manchester Guardian, August 15, 1956, p. 4, "A Century of Suez." Khosrow
Mostofi, "The Suez Dispute: A Case Study of a Treaty," *Western Political
Quarterly*, X (1957), 23-37, ingeniously argued that the British reservations
were not properly made to the 1888 Convention, and that later British action in-
validated the Convention. He quoted (p. 31) from Lord Curzon's statement in
the Commons (July 12, 1898): "The Convention is certainly in existence, but
. . . has not been brought into practical operation. This is owing to the reservations made by the British delegate to the Suez Canal Convention in 1885,
which were renewed by Lord Salisbury and communicated to the powers in
1887."

Liberal W. E. Gladstone was Prime Minister, the occupation was declared to be a temporary measure taken in an emergency.

The temporary, however, became a constant of political geography. Three years later disaster engulfed a British commander in the Sudan, from which Egyptian forces also were withdrawn. As the result of long rivalry with France and Russia, Britain in 1896 began the construction of a major naval base at Alexandria.

By 1897 the British Prime Minister, Lord Salisbury, had also decided that the disintegration of the Ottoman Empire could not be delayed and that to keep Russia from Constantinople was "an antiquated standpoint." [14] Salisbury had begun to revise the earlier policy within five years after the occupation of Egypt. As early as 1887 he had privately indicated his resolve that French diplomacy should not be allowed to push Britain out of Egypt or to force Britain "into a quarrel over Egypt." Salisbury's change of mind meant that the British occupation of Egypt would be prolonged, for, as the future Lord Cromer wrote to him, the Egyptian ruling classes were foreigners in Egypt and utterly lacked the capacity to understand the elements of their country's politics. But the decisive reason for Salisbury's emphasis on Egypt rather than on Turkey was the "African" scramble, the imperialist rivalries over Africa for which Egypt provided Britain with an advantageous base.[15] Britain, thus, would remain in Egypt, though without formal annexation, would reconquer the Sudan for Egypt, and use Alexandria as the major base for opposition to Russia in the Mediterranean and Near East.

With the twentieth century Britain acquired a major interest in Middle Eastern oil. Some of its oil sources had been known for centuries, but not until the later decades of the nineteenth century did the traffic in oil concessions add to the delights and profits of bargaining in Persia, Egypt, and the Ottoman Empire. The tempo of exploitation accelerated markedly with the use of the internal combustion engine and with the use of oil as fuel in warships and other vessels. Before the First World War, oil-well drilling had begun on a considerable scale, the first refinery at Abadan had been completed,

[14] Lord Strang, op. cit., p. 228. Salisbury's judgment of this time is a striking reversal of the British mid-nineteenth century view of the Eastern Question which Harold Temperley summarized: "Constantinople was the first strategic position in the world, and no Great Power could allow another to possess it." England and the Near East: The Crimea (New York, 1936), p. 4.

[15] Lady Gwendolen Cecil, Life of Robert, Marquis of Salisbury (London, 1932), IV, 134-140.

and the Anglo-Persian Oil Company, with the British government a majority stockholder, had been formed. When in the same period imperialist activity involving oil concessions, notably for Germany and Britain, had also increased, Britain providently imposed on the Persian Gulf sheikhs a restriction that they should make oil concessions only with the consent of the British government.[16]

After the First World War, British oil concessions were sought and exploitation undertaken in Iraq and in other areas. Concessions on the whole were secured from weak or client governments. Had the Ottoman Empire survived, it is possible, though not highly probable, that it would have had the strength and administrative skill to command a greater and more useful return from the West. Instead, this single, most lucrative and marketable commodity of the Middle East was disposed of cheaply in a fashion that the world has come to think of as characteristic of imperialism, although in the long history of man's wastefulness the "ism" here appears as but a stand-in for man. In Saudi Arabia the same story was repeated, with native rulers as eager and spendthrift partners of Americans in the use of oil and its revenues. Eventually, important oil finds were made in Kuwait, Bahrain, Qatar, Muscat and Iraq, among the territories where British influence was or is strong.

Oil has come to play an ever-larger role in the domestic, industrial, and transportation economy of Britain and Western Europe. Between 1939 and 1960, oil tripled the percentage of Western Europe's increasing energy requirements it supplied. Nineteen per cent of Western Europe's oil consumption in 1938 came from the Middle East, and the corresponding figure for 1955 was 80 per cent.

Middle Eastern oil, then, was important to Britain as a source of income and as a necessity for her economy in peace and war. During the interwar years British power was so unchallenged by major rivals in the Middle East that the oil resources promised to remain accessible and secure. In Iraq and, notably, Iran, there were nationalist challenges to the oil concessions, but these were storms endured without serious damage. To the British the oil concessions meant points of interest and influence that should be expanded. The order should be a *Pax Britannica*. But, as there can be no peace without arms, which in turn create their problems, the British government was

---

[16] See the valuable account of Stephen H. Longrigg, *Oil in the Middle East*, 2nd ed. (New York, 1961). The details of the early Persian oil story in William Yale, *The Near East* (Ann Arbor, 1958), p. 367, are surprisingly inaccurate.

greatly concerned to secure points where *vis Britannica* could be used to sustain the *Pax Britannica*, and this all the more because the security of transit had increased in importance.

When, for example, the early oil ventures were made in Persia, the central Iranian government was unable to assure security in some local areas. British representatives, as their predecessors had done throughout the nineteenth century, sought influence with local tribes and their chieftains: for example, through British influence with Bakhtiari tribesmen the arbitrary and Russian-oriented Shah, Mohammed Ali, was deposed in 1909 and the Constitution restored.[17] But, as a rule, this British influence was used charily lest Russia use it as the pretext for formidable intervention in her own behalf. In the Second World War, moreover, British policy-makers firmly resolved against working with local tribal leaders and in favor of strengthening the central Iranian government.[18]

Eventually, transit included the long pipelines as well as the security and control of the Suez Canal, which, with the exception of Tapline, were interrupted in the course of the Anglo-French Suez expedition.

For the Arabs the exploitation of oil has meant many things. To the rulers it has meant an opportunity for diplomatic and commercial bargaining as well as a swelling revenue. The revenue, in turn, has helped to transform the power, character, and behavior of sheikhs and rulers. The changing behavior of the rulers affects the ruled as well. Where, at first, the activities of the oil companies were centered in isolated enclaves with little effect on the general way of Iranian or Arab life, later the contact with Western businessmen and technology had a marked effect. Some Arabs acquired the skills of technicians, engineers, and even of managers. Increasingly, with the growth of Arab nationalism, there was a joining of demands for extended Arab participation in the management of the oil operations, with pressure upon Western companies and governments for larger royalties. Later still came demands for nationalization and for the use of the Middle East's most marketable raw material to secure from the West the greatest possible return.

The foundations of the problem, however, were laid when the

[17] Sydney Nettleton Fisher, *The Middle East: A History* (New York, 1959), p. 464; Sir Percy Sykes, *A History of Persia*, 2nd ed. (London, 1921), II, 418-420.

[18] This influence was featured in a British treaty with Persia (1928). For the story of local experience, see Longrigg, *op. cit.*, and Bullard, *The Camels Must Go: An Autobiography* (London, 1961), pp. 232-233.

First World War and its sequel had disintegrated the Ottoman Empire and dispersed Middle Eastern bargaining power. It had done so
by fomenting Arab nationalism and making it a part of high politics.
Thus, as in so many other ways and areas, the First World War
resulted in a new phase of the Eastern Question.

The Ottoman Empire had been preserved in the nineteenth century by the calculations of the European power balance. When the
European powers mobilized their energies against one another for
more than four years, empires toppled and with them ended the
stalemate that maintained the Ottoman Empire. Britain, allied with
France and Russia, faced enemies in Germany, Austria-Hungary, and
Turkey. Early in the war the partition of the Ottoman Empire was
projected. Nevertheless, Constantinople, promised to Tsarist Russia,
ultimately remained with truncated but resolute Turkey, now a nation, that emerged from revolution, war, and postwar fighting. The
new Turkey abandoned the Ottoman past and, with it, appeals to
Islamic unity. The Ottoman Empire was not reformed. A new, secular, and revolutionary Turkey sought reform. The earlier nationalism
of the young Turks had helped to inflame Arab nationalism and by
the latter was also confirmed, for Turkish and Arab nationalism meant
segregation, though in different measure, within the Islamic community.

For Britain the Eastern Question was transformed in two other
respects: the disintegration of the Ottoman Empire was effected to
serve imperial interests and Arab nationalism as well; and the war
not only strained British resources and power but upon its conclusion
inspired a popular, and, hereafter, influential British disinclination to
new and expensive imperial burdens.

Arab nationalism was a new and incalculable force. In the nineteenth century the British government had often favored the nationalism of Western peoples not subject to Britain in Greece, in Italy,
even in the Balkans. But when, for example, a powerful Russia was
likely to be the beneficiary of Balkan nationalism, sympathy for
nationalism yielded in British policy to a concern for the balance of
power. Yet, as Gladstone's attack on the Bulgarian horrors and his
Midlothian campaign bear witness, there was here a powerful current
of British opposition to the enthronement of reasons of state in British
policy. In the Ottoman Empire British policy had vainly looked for
reforms or the regenerating step which would eventually mean the
capacity of the Ottoman Empire to defend itself. Thus, at first the

British government welcomed the Revolt of the Young Turks (1908).

Where the government of India sought wartime security in agreements with Ibn Saud (then ruler of the Nejd, later (1932) King of Saudi Arabia) and forceful action in Mesopotamia, the British Foreign Office, recognizing the difficulties for Britain in exercising an imperium over Muslim people and in fighting the Caliph in Constantinople, sought to find among the Arabs a new Muslim center. Fatefully, Britain then abetted a revolt in the Hejaz against the Turks. Its leaders, some of them former Ottoman officers, proclaimed themselves to be the leaders of the Arab national movement, and Hussain the Hashemite Sharif of Mecca, whose sons initiated the revolt, on one occasion took the title, "King of the Arab people."

The Arab world extended across many natural obstacles, historical traditions, and religious and racial minorities, for the Arabist sea swept many shores. The firm charting of this sea, the marking of its boundaries, and the political regulation of its tides were tasks to tax the energies of a single-minded imperial power. But there was no single-mindedness. Given the diversity of Arab lands and people, it is not surprising that the Arab Revolt issued in fragmentation rather than unity.[19] But, though it was insignificant in numbers and unspectacular in military achievement against the background of the Western and Eastern fronts in Europe, the Arab Revolt was a national awakening, portentous in its contribution to nationalist myth and in its political consequences.

But the Muslim or Arab center was not found, and the role has remained unfulfilled, for the candidates tend to cancel one another. And the revolt itself ended in further frustration: new imperial holdings of Britain and France meant new masters to learn from, profit from, and eject, and in 1917 the Balfour Declaration committed the British government to support the establishment of a homeland for the Jewish people in Palestine, that is, Arab populated territory. The

[19] The social background of this fragmentation is well presented in Morroe Berger, *The Arabs* (New York, 1962). Ernest Manheim in reviewing Hamady's *Temperament and Character of the Arabs*, succinctly remarked: "There were rulers but no states, judges but no courts, settlements of families and tradesmen but no city corporations. Public institutions as seats of a code of behavior outside the kinship group did not have a hold over the individual. Sensitivity to the opinion of others and the fear of shame helped to enforce conformity to law and custom. Loyalty to one's relatives took precedence over the requirements of the job or the norms of the public interest." *Middle Eastern Affairs* (May 1962), 147-148.

consequences of the First World War appear in the division of the Middle East, where Britain had made extensive commitments, some of them contradictory. Middle Eastern oil had meanwhile acquired commanding importance. The British dilemma in the Middle East was that Britain had supported Arab nationalism and contributed to its frustration, and had assumed new imperial burdens at a time when a portion of the British public had become less assured of Britain's imperial mission and certainly reluctant to carry its burdens of taxation and military responsibilities.

In Britain's impact on the Middle East we may see the meeting of a Western and an Eastern culture. The earlier phases of the encounter took place on terms of some equality. The recognition of the religious and cultural differences gave rise to the regime of capitulations, which in the Ottoman Empire, Egypt, and Iran removed foreign nationals from the native courts based on Islamic law and, often enough, from taxation. As Western technological, administrative, and financial superiority became manifest, the capitulations served the interests of Western imperialist dominance. Ironically, the movement against them was a triumph of Western influence, the influence of the conception of the secularized state. Turkey and Iran abolished them on their own initiative. They were nullified in the mandatory regimes. But in Egypt, where foreign interests were large and where there was neither mandate nor revolution, the formal end of capitulations extended from 1937 to 1949.

The fate of capitulations may serve as a key to the impact of the West and the British on the Middle East. The special temptation of the later Western imperialist period is that the West at the height of its technical and organizing power encountered other cultures which were not then flourishing and under Western impact entered upon a time of crisis. The Western response was often an arrogant one: a confirmation of the sense of superiority of Western civilization and progress. Happily, that does not exhaust the story. British adventurers and scholars became great Orientalists and Arabists, revealing the glories of their own past to the Eastern and Arab people.

The British imperial mission in the Middle East, however, remains blurred in ambiguity. Not transformation but security of transit was the paramount interest. Later, the security of the region and the oil supplies against invaders and the Arabs themselves was a major objective. For a long period the Arabs themselves did not take kindly to technical and manual training. Arab Army officers were sometimes trained in British Army schools, but few Arabs, compared to Indians, went to British universities. Egyptians and other Arabs either attended Egyptian universities, the American University of Beirut, or the universities of Britain's ally and Middle Eastern rival, France.

Nevertheless, the British presence in the Middle East was a source of cultural change and a stimulus to Arab nationalism. Though the British did not always will these changes, they inspired them. The ambivalence and agonized frustration of T. E. Lawrence, a British leader of the Arab Revolt, involve a British reaction, highly personal to him and yet typical. Lawrence rejoiced in the discomforts of bedouin life and admired the bedouin Arab. At times he professed regret at his part in misleading the Arabs. Without question he was troubled by his role in nation-making and lamented the propulsion of the Arabs into the modern world. His affection for the Arabs was shared by some of the most devoted British servants in the Arab world. John Bagot Glubb loved the Arabs, that is, the bedouin, and for a long time served with them in Jordan. Henry Philby worked in Saudi Arabia. To cite those figures is to underline an irony in the later American prominence in Saudi Arabia, for that patriarchal, bedouin kingdom should have delighted the many British imperialists who rejoiced to serve the bedouin but found the Arab of the modern world less manageable and engaging. But, to speak a truism, all places are becoming modern. In propelling that simultaneous contemporaneity, the British have played at certain times the most prominent role.

3: THE INTERWAR YEARS

Britain's legacy from the war in the Middle East consisted of new imperial gains and contradictory commitments. But the readiness of British public opinion to bear the burdens accompanying the gains, and even to rejoice in the gains, had become questionable. True, only a small portion of public opinion doubted the very right of Empire. There persisted a widespread self-assurance about British ability to serve as mentor to backward peoples. This assurance was supported by advocates of the League of Nations who argued that Britain's acceptance of mandatory responsibility would serve the cause of the League. Strong demands for economic retrenchment, however, worked to reduce the resources of strength necessary to maintain the Empire. During the war the self-governing members of the Empire had grown notably in self-assertion and self-confidence. These future dominions were separately represented at the Paris Peace Conference, and Canada, Australia, New Zealand, and South Africa each signed the peace treaties on its own behalf. The Easter Week rising in 1916 proclaimed the challenge of an Irish Republic to the Empire. During the war's final year the American President, Woodrow Wilson, in eloquently espousing national self-determination, evoked a response with global echoes.

The prospect, then, was that any further extension of empire would be challenged. Asiatic and colonial nationalism, indeed, meant that colonial and Asian resistance to imperialism developed and, on occasion—in Afghanistan, India, Iran, Egypt, and among the Arabs—became formidable.

At the end of 1918 British politicians did not generally see their country's positions in terms of such prospects. Lord Curzon, destined to discredit the imperialist position by his failure to keep in touch with the changing colonial scene and by allowing love of office to flaw the discharge of duty as counsellor, told the House of Lords in 1918 that the war's end saw the British Empire at its peak of unity and strength and with its voice at the weightiest in determining the future of mankind.[1] Indeed, Lord Curzon, looking on the Middle East with the eyes of a man obsessed with India and Persia, saw the postwar situation as permitting the completion of a work of righteousness, the imperial dream of "creating a chain of vassal states stretching from the Mediterranean to the Pamirs and protecting not the Indian frontiers merely, but our communication with our further Empire." [2]

The collapse of Tsarist Russia further transformed the Eastern Question. Apart from the support of Turkish and Persian nationalism in 1919-1921, a critical period, the Soviet Union exercised little direct influence in the Middle East. Turkey also provided a notable change. The Sultan's government signed the Treaty of Sèvres (1920), ending the First World War for Turkey and providing for the renunciation of Turkey's Arab lands as well as for the cession of Eastern Thrace and Smyrna to Greece. The latter, supported by the French, American, and British fleets, had already occupied Smyrna, but the subsequent fighting strengthened the Turkish Nationalists under Mustafa Kemal, who compelled both the Greeks and the Allies to the negotiation of new treaties. British interests in Turkey were reduced, for under the dictatorship of Kemal the Turkish nationalist republic swept away the privileges of foreigners. The new government agreed to the demilitarization of the Straits and to an international guarantee of free navigation through them. In the long run, after a reversal of a British policy hostile to Turkey (1919-1922), British relations with Turkey, where French cultural influence had been weakened, were friendly. Indeed, in Turkey it was believed that the testament of Kemal Ataturk advised the Turks to seek neutrality in a future general war and then, at its end, to enter the war on the side of Britain, which would surely be on the winning side.

In the First World War neutral Persia had served as the scene of

---

[1] Harold Nicolson, *Curzon: The Last Phase, 1919-1925* (London, 1934), p. 2. Nicolson's judgment (p. 5) is worth repeating: Curzon possessed intelligence, ideals, energy, unequalled knowledge and experience; in the postwar years his judgment was correct, yet under him British policy fell from "the very summit of authority to a level of impotence such as, since the Restoration, it has seldom reached." Nicolson in explaining Curzon's failure to appreciate the secular and Western character of Turkey's nationalism under Kemal, noted that Curzon was not an empiricist. He suffered the fate of many ageing statesmen in that he based his opinion on what he already knew, and what he knew had ceased to be a reality (p. 102).

[2] *Ibid.*, p. 121.

a complex tug-of-war. There German commercial interests had been large, and Germany was the beneficiary of Persian antipathy to the dominant influences of Britain and Russia. German guerrilla forces operated in Persia, and Turkish and Russian forces had fought in Northwest Persia. Britain and Russia had organized and made use of Persian armed forces in Persia. On the Persian coast British agents had even assumed responsibility for navigation lights. The triumphant Bolsheviks in 1921[3] made a treaty with Persia whereby they renounced the extra-territorial and other unequal rights claimed by Tsarist Russia, although the Treaty's Article VI, little noticed then, permitted the Soviet Union to send troops into Persia, if the latter served as the base for forces aimed against the Soviet Union.[4]

From 1919 onwards Britain, which in the eyes of British officials such as Lord Curzon was the principal element of stability in Persia, appeared to Persians as the embodiment of the threats associated with an exclusive position of dominance. Thus Soviet hostility to imperialism met with considerable success, and the British government encountered increased mistrust. By the summer of 1919 Britain had negotiated a treaty with Persia and in it solemnly repeated undertakings with respect to the independence and integrity of Persia's Empire which, among other matters, agreed to take British advisors for her Treasury, British officers for her Army, a British loan, and

[3] Until the 1907 entente with Russia, Britain usually had the advantage of appealing to liberal and some nationalist forces in Persia. After the First World War the British position declined in the measure that the Soviet Union had been removed from Persia and had even disavowed any special claim in the country. Hereafter, as T. Cuyler Young has noted, Britain took the Russian place on Satan's throne in the Persian Hell. "Britain's reputation in Persia is fabulous for ubiquitous and subtle intrigues, the British getting credit for most of history's coincidences and untoward accidents." "The National and International Relations of Iran," p. 193 in Young, editor, Near Eastern Culture and Society (Princeton, 1951).

[4] Subsequently, the Soviet representative in Teheran, Theodore A. Rothstein, replied (December 12, 1921) to some guileful, though entirely legitimate, Iranian questions concerning Soviet interpretation of the meaning of certain articles in the Treaty (February 26, 1921). In replying for propaganda effect, Rothstein considerably minimized the concessions secured by the Soviet Union. But Article VI was reaffirmed in an Iranian Soviet Treaty ratified on January 31, 1928. The texts are in J. C. Hurewitz, Diplomacy in the Near and Middle East (Princeton, 1956), II, 90-94, and (excerpts) 154-156. See, also, Nasrollah Fatemi, Diplomatic History of Persia: 1917-1923 (New York, 1952), Chap. XVI; G. Lenczowski, Russia and the West in Iran (Ithaca, 1949), Chap. 3; M. Beloff, The Foreign Policy of Soviet Russia (New York, 1949), II, Chap. 9.

British assistance in constructing Persian railways. The treaty, which Lord Curzon saw as the result of a free decision of the Persian government, met with bitter and successful opposition in Persia and abroad.[5] Iranians blamed Britain for the Peace Conference decision not to hear the case of Persia, a nonbelligerent. The case was a stern and exaggerated indictment of imperial powers in Persia, a portent of later British experiences there,[6] as well as a demand for territory reaching to the rivers Oxus and Euphrates.

The restoration of order and stability in Persia was achieved by Reza Pahlevi, who assumed the royal title upon the deposition of the former Shah and the extinction of the Qajar dynasty (1925). In abolishing capitulations and asserting the authority of the central government, this nationalist ruler moved resolutely against the special privileges of foreigners in his country. In 1931, when the world depression reduced government revenues from oil, the Shah precipitated a long diplomatic struggle with Britain when he canceled the Anglo-Persian Oil Company's concession. The British position rested on the inviolability of contracts. Later, in 1933, the Company negotiated an agreement which by 1938 reduced the area of the Company's concession to 100,000 square miles and arranged for intensified training of Persians in the oil business, as well as for a complex schedule of payments to assure Persia a minimum revenue protected against the uncertainties of sales and devaluation of the pound.

During the war Britain had in the Sykes-Picot Agreement (1916) recognized French interest in Syria, which indeed she had acknowledged in 1912. Now, at the very least, this disposition of Arab territory

[5] When Prime Minister Seyyid Zia-ed-Din moved to end Iranian consideration of the Anglo-Persian Agreement, a dispatch from Teheran reported that Europeans and, especially, the British in Persia believed that neither the Majlis nor any Persian Cabinet would accept the agreement which was merely a hindrance to good relations (*The Times*, March 3, 1921). The ultimate failure of the Treaty may also be ascribed to the failure of Britain to maintain such strength and intervention in Persia as would enable Britain to provide for the security of Persia against the Soviet Union. Hence, some Iranians attacked Britain for pursuing the Curzon policy, and then when Britain sought retrenchment and withdrawal, further attacked the Curzon policy because it would not be effective.

[6] An Iranian scholar, Nasrollah Fatemi, in his *Diplomatic History of Persia*, p. 1, described the Anglo-Persian Treaty as a masterpiece of British astuteness. Negotiations, he charged, were initiated in Teheran when Persian nationalists were in Paris and the Persian government, emasculated of its patriots, was staffed by pro-British ministers. This charge rests upon some juggling of dates as well as placing actions in unusual perspectives.

ran counter to the expectations of Arab nationalists. As a consequence, British association with the Arab nationalist cause, of which T. E. Lawrence was a spokesman at the Paris Peace Conference, roused ready French suspicions.[7] French troops also had to deal with a small force of Hussain's son, Faisal, who had been proclaimed by the Syrian National Congress as King of Syria (including Palestine). Meanwhile, at the San Remo Conference (1920) the rival Western allies had agreed that Iraq and Palestine should be mandated to Britain under the League of Nations, and Syria (and Lebanon) should similarly go to France. The mandate system abolished capitulations and pretended to replace exclusive control of one state over German colonies and former Turkish lands by rendering the mandatory accountable to the League for his administration, and for hastening the mandated territory's preparation for self-government. The system was ill-received in Arab lands, where nationalists with some exaggeration described it as the old imperialism and a humiliating frustration of nationalism.

The San Remo Conference dealt also with oil concessions and the problem of distributing German shares in the Turkish Petroleum Company. American oil companies already on the Middle Eastern scene, and urged by Herbert Hoover, protested their exclusion from mandated territories where equality of treatment was to prevail. While agreement in principle to an American share had long been provided for, the final allotment of 23.75 per cent in the Iraq Petroleum Company to American interests was not completed until, after the great Kirkuk finds of 1927, the famous Red Line Agreement (1928) was concluded.

In the Fertile Crescent area, stretching from Mesopotamia to the Mediterranean, the peace settlement after the First World War saw not unity but fragmentation. Iraq and Palestine (including the later

[7] The French government was irritated by British insistence upon the necessity of respecting obligations to the Arabs and, on occasion, countered by supporting Iranian opposition to Britain. Lawrence, mistrusting the French and regarding them as interlopers in the Arab world, proposed the line of policy that French suspicions took for British policy. As the Arab lands would be divided among Arab, French, and British centers, Lawrence believed that the Arabs would seek maximum concessions by playing one foreign power against the other. But Britain, he suggested, could remain ahead in this game by always anticipating the necessity of making concessions: "Our remedy and safeguard will be to trend continually 'left.'" *Documents on British Foreign Policy*, edited by E. L. Woodward and Rohan Butler, 1st series, IV, No. 296, 422-424, September 25, 1919.

Transjordan) were mandated to Britain and were politically launched in different directions. Syria and Lebanon were mandatory territories of France. But in a major part of the Arabian peninsula unity was achieved under native auspices and without serious foreign intervention. There, by 1930, the conquests of Ibn Saud, notably at the expense of the Hashemites who had been driven from the Hejaz but under British auspices had also been established in Transjordan (1923) and Iraq (1921), had created the Kingdom of Saudi Arabia. The successes of Ibn Saud also transformed his earlier relations with Britain. In 1915 he had agreed to submit his external relations to British control and in return received a subsidy from the government of India. The payments stopped in 1924, and by the Treaty of Jedda (1927) Britain recognized Saudi Arabia's complete independence.[8]

A basic conflict of interest embittered Britain's relations with the Yemen. The Imam Yahya (1904-1948), the suitably anachronistic ruler of an archaic principality, had favored the Ottoman Empire in the First World War. And the British government had assisted Ahmed bin Idris, the Amir of Sabya, north of Yemen, who fought the Turks and challenged the Imam. The defeat of Turkey freed the Imam of Turkish suzerainty (1918). But the British position in Aden and its adjoining areas evoked the Imam's claims to parts of the area where tribes alleged to be under his suzerainty moved. The Imam and his successor sought assistance from Britain's enemies: Fascist Italy, with which Yemen made a secret agreement in 1927; and, after the Second World War, from Egypt, Saudi Arabia, the Soviet Union, and China.[9]

The British dilemma in governing the newly-won Arab lands appears starkly in the dispositions made for the government of Iraq. There, at first, the British administration was greatly influenced by officials with Indian experience.[10] But other British representatives,

---

[8] Hurewitz, op. cit., II, 149-150; Hurewitz, "Unity and Disunity in the Middle East," International Conciliation, No. 481 (1952), pp. 199-260; H. St. John B. Philby, Arabia (New York, 1930).

[9] An Anglo-Yemen treaty (1934), to last for forty years, pledged a halt to violations of the existing frontier without, however, proposing more than a temporary maintenance of it. Text in Hurewitz, op. cit., pp. 196-197.

[10] The former Liberal Prime Minister, Asquith, speaking in opposition to the government, said that in Mesopotamia the British authorities had tried and repudiated three different policies: government on the Indian model; exploitation; and considering it as a strategic link in Empire defenses. Report of Commons Debate in The Times, March 10, 1922, p. 6.

especially after an Iraqi rising in 1920, felt that Indian administration, involving greater control of the Arab people than Britain should aim to wield, provided a model of government too ambitious and too taut for the Middle East.[11] In this judgment, which prevailed in policy, three considerations played the most prominent role—the first emphasized the differences between the Arab lands and India; the second took account of British promises to the Arabs and the temper of the Arab world expressed, for example, by the General Syrian Congress on July 2, 1919: ". . . we protest against Article 22 of the Covenant of the League of Nations, placing us among the nations in their middle stage of development which stand in need of a mandatory power"; the third took account of the heavy pressure on the British government to reduce expenditures and overseas commitments.

If Britain was to refrain from exercising direct control and assuming corresponding responsibility, and if account were to be taken of local nationalism and mandatory responsibility, then the Arab states would have to be placed on the road to sovereignty. Under such an arrangement British influence would have to be secured by treaty arrangements. The necessity of a treaty was a lesson enjoined, though without happy auspices, by Britain's Egyptian experience. In 1919 the British government had appointed a commission under the chairmanship of the "civil servant of the British Empire," as Lord Milner thought of himself, to inquire into the causes of Egyptian disorders and to recommend a constitutional disposition of Egypt under the Protectorate. Against the Commission the Nationalists attempted, with substantial initial success, to maintain a boycott. The Milner report, signed in 1920, noted that at first sight Britain's choice appeared to be "either to abandon our position in Egypt altogether, or to maintain it by sheer force." As the Egyptians did not think of themselves as part of the British Empire, they would not appreciate even "Dominion Home Rule." The mission, then, favored the independence of Egypt and an Anglo-Egyptian treaty.

> All safeguards, as it seemed to us, could be provided in the terms of a Treaty of Alliance by which Egypt, in return for Great Britain's undertaking to defend her integrity and independence, would agree

[11] Captain W. Ormsby Gore, "The Organization of British Responsibilities in the Middle East," *Journal of the Royal Central Asian Society*, 6-8 (1919-1921), 93; Stephen H. Longrigg, *Iraq, 1900 to 1950* (New York, 1953), pp. 92-123.

to be guided by Great Britain in her foreign relations and would at the same time confer upon Great Britain certain definite rights in Egyptian territory.[12]

The settlement for Iraq and Transjordan was worked out in 1921 at a conference of British Middle Eastern experts in Cairo. The initiative was taken by Winston Churchill, then Secretary of State for the Colonies.[13] The conference approved the bestowal of the Crown

[12] *Report of the Special Commission to Egypt* (London, HMSO, 1921), Cmd. 1131, pp. 16, 18, 19. The Report concluded by arguing that the moment was favorable for a treaty which would place British-Egyptian relations on a satisfactory and enduring basis. For Britain the advantage would mean that her interests would be "carefully defined and placed beyond challenge in a Treaty accepted by the Egyptians." But the revolutionary character of the situation appears in the remark of the Wafdist leader, Saad Zaghlul: "I am not on the side of the extremists, but I have no doubt that they are my reserve of strength —today and tomorrow." Quoted in Jafar H. Khesbak, "England and the Nationalist Movement in Egypt, 1918-1924," unpublished Ph.D. thesis, University of Chicago, 1952, p. 75. T. E. Lawrence wrote of Iraq to *The Times* in 1920: "I shall be told that the idea of Brown Dominions in the British Empire is grotesque. Yet the Montagu scheme [a measure of self-government in India] and the Milner scheme are approaches to it, and the only alternative seems to be conquest, which the ordinary Englishman does not want and cannot afford." Quoted in John Evelyn Wrench, *Alfred Lord Milner, 1905-1925* (London, 1958), p. 358.

[13] Churchill in February, 1921, was given unified control over British Middle Eastern matters. This disposition supplanted the earlier arrangement with responsibility divided among the India, War, and Foreign Offices. Churchill was authorized to arrange for the establishment of stable governments and to reduce spending and garrisons. *Parliamentary Debates*, Commons, 5th series, CXXXVIII, cols. 539-542, June 14, 1921.

Some of the British calculations at the time of the Cairo Conference, calculations which formed interwar British policy, were expressed in Winston Churchill's letter to Sir George Ritchie, President of the Dundee Liberal Association: As Britain could not continue spending large sums in Mesopotamia, British forces there would have to be drastically reduced. Earlier reductions still left Britain with financial charges in Mesopotamia that could more profitably be devoted to British territories in West and East Africa, which offered better opportunities "for imperial development as compared with the Middle East." Failing a satisfactory arrangement, Britain would have to withdraw completely. This, however, would mean the disgrace of relinquishing the mandate to anarchy after having "ignominiously scuttled for the coast." Churchill's hope was that "by means of Arab government, supported by a moderate military force, we may be able to discharge our duties without imposing unjustifiable expense on the British Exchequer. The fact that we should be calling into being an Arab administration in Baghdad made it indispensable that we should treat the Arabian

of Iraq on Faisal, and it was agreed that Iraq should as quickly as possible be treated as an independent state. British mandatory responsibilities were provided for in several treaties negotiated between Britain and Iraq. In the face of severe Iraqi nationalist criticism, Britain finally yielded and in 1932 persuaded a skeptical League of Nations to accept Iraq as a member. The misgivings of the League about terminating the Iraqi mandate were in part met by a declaration of the British High Commissioner in Iraq that if Iraq proved unworthy of the confidence placed in her, the British government would assume moral responsibility.[14]

In preparing to end the Iraqi mandate, Britain in 1930 negotiated a new Iraqi treaty which was to last for twenty-five years after Iraq's admission to the League. The treaty of alliance and accompanying notes called for full consultation of both parties in foreign policy matters of common interest, mutual assistance in war, the provision by Iraq of communications and rights of transport to British troops, and the leasing of sites for British air bases and troop stations.[15] The emphasis on air bases arose from concern not only with defense but

---

question as a whole so far as it concerns the British interests." *The Times*, March 4, 1921.

Later, Churchill said that Britain was not so much holding Mesopotamia as allowing the country to hold itself. The great reductions of garrison "had been obtained by policy, by air power, and by local forces." *The Times*, March 10, 1922.

A leader in *The Times*, which under Lord Northcliffe was engaged in an antigovernment campaign, was severely critical of Churchill's concentration on military rather than on civil aviation, for example in the Canal Zone. "Five stations to protect a narrow belt less than 100 miles in length!" This policy meant a pouring of the taxpayer's money "into the absorbing desert sands." *The Times*, March 8, 1921, p. 13.

[14] The odd, constitutional role of the British government is revealed in a statement of the High Commissioner to the Iraqi government concerning conscription: conscription required some popular appreciation of its necessity; if there were such popular support, then the forces commanded by the Iraqi government would be sufficient for the application of conscription. "If, however, the project did not enjoy popular support, it would be fatal to attempt to dragoon the Iraq people by foreign troops into accepting it, and it would thereby only become more unpopular." Great Britain, Colonial Office, *Report by His Brittanic Majesty's Government to the Council of the League of Nations on the Administration of Iraq* (1928), pp. 15-16. The advice itself was well warranted, for conscription would then have been opposed by the Kurds and the Shiites in the south. Thus, Britain might have had to intervene or face the disintegration of Iraq.

[15] Text in Hurewitz, *op. cit.*, pp. 178-181. Article 5 declared that the presence of British forces "shall not in any manner constitute an occupation."

with the maintenance of order in the Middle East. As a result of the Cairo Conference the latter function was assigned to the British Air Ministry. Considerations of economy played a determining role in this arrangement. Air power and armored cars were to be the thrifty replacements of the old imperial army.[16] But, as was often pointed out later, air power was almost unusable against heavy centers of population in Palestine and Baghdad where later Britain had to face serious challenges.

Some Arab territory (eventually, Syria and Lebanon) was marked for France. Under Britain's mandatory authority in Palestine, the Emirate of Transjordan, later to be the Kingdom of Jordan, was established. This all but unviable state, placed under a ruler already on the spot, Abdullah—who in T. E. Lawrence's eyes was not "the armed prophet," not a man for revolutions and setting the desert on fire[17]— long provided Britain with a *point d'appui* in the Middle East. In this bedouin state British officers helped to form and train the Arab Legion, long considered the best of Arab armies and a monument to the affection of some Britons for the bedouin.[18]

In the interwar years, the survival of these arrangements and the security of British access to Middle Eastern oil may be explained by the powerful position of Britain in the Middle East. First of all, Britain ruled in India, and the Indian army was available in case of emergency. British naval, aerial, and military forces had the use of bases in Egypt, Transjordan, Palestine, Iraq, the Persian Gulf, and Aden.

The British position was not challenged by formidable rivals. The Soviet Union had little impact on the Middle East and could not then seriously implement its designs on the region. The United States had not developed a major interest there. Although those years saw British relations with France often threaded with mutual suspicion,

[16] Captain Ormsby Gore, *op. cit.*, 96, argued that "modern developments of the arts of war" would have the most telling effect . . . "a small striking force" . . . "a few aeroplanes, and a few light armored cars, and you won't want garrisons of 50,000 or 60,000 infantry."

[17] T. E. Lawrence, *The Seven Pillars of Wisdom* (Garden City, 1937), p. 67. He found Abdullah intelligent, politically wise and judicious, eager for Arab independence, but determined that the Arab states would remain under the Hashemite family. Lawrence reproached Abdullah with playing "to the British gallery." "His value would come perhaps in the peace after success."

For Syria and a fuller account of the diplomacy of the Arab cause, see Zeine N. Zeine, *The Struggle for Arab Independence* (Beirut, 1960).

[18] Alec Kirkbride, *A Crackle of Thorns* (London, 1956).

especially somber-hued in the Middle East, no major conflict issued
from their Middle Eastern interests. The major revisionist powers,
Italy and, later, Nazi Germany, sought to appeal to Arab discontent
with some success. But Italian designs on Ethiopia also permitted
Britain to establish her position in the Egyptian Canal Zone on a
treaty basis.

In 1882 Britain had occupied Egypt as a temporary and emergency
measure. The temporary became a constant of political geography.
When Britain faced the Ottoman Empire as a belligerent in 1914,
the British government formally separated Egypt from the Turkish
Empire and proclaimed a British protectorate over the country.

Initially, the British occupation of Egypt had frustrated the nationalist movement of Arabi. Thereafter, the removal of British presence
and power became an Egyptian national cause. The British authorities, on their part, did not aspire either to exercise full control of
Egypt or greatly to transform Egyptian education, society, and state.
European interests, especially the French, also were vigilantly suspicious of any British initiative, and their watchfulness too impeded
and discouraged British activity. British intervention also maintained
the Khedive, generally unpopular with the Egyptian nationalists, although Abbas II (1892-1904) encouraged them, and Egyptian politics
from 1919 to 1952 revolved around the three centers of the Palace, the
nationalist Wafd party, and the British.

The impact of the First World War on Britain and Egypt involved
the growth of the great nationalist movement for Egyptian independence which the Wafd party embodied; a recognition by the
British government of the strategic importance of its position in
Egypt; and a popular disinclination to extend old burdens, especially
for empire, to which British policy had to be accommodated.

Fatefully, Egypt remained in anomalous relationship with Britain.
Kitchener, who was British Agent and Consul-General in Egypt, 1911-
1914, described his position as "incomprehensible." As an instinctive
strong man, Kitchener, preferring serious government to comic opera,
had hoped to compel the deposition of the Khedive and the establishment of a formal British Vice-Royalty over Egypt and the Sudan.[19]
While Britain proclaimed a protectorate in 1914, she failed to in-
corporate Egypt in the British Empire or place the country under

[19] Sir Philip Magnus, *Kitchener: Portrait of an Imperialist* (New York, 1959),
pp. 270, 272-274.

full British control when the war was won. Meanwhile, the Egyptian nationalist movement, the Wafd-al-misri, the Egyptian delegation, was denied a hearing at the Paris Peace Conference. Subsequently, Lord Curzon thought of British policy in Egypt as excluding other powers from responsibility for imperial affairs and providing assurance for imperial interests in the Sudan and communications with India.[20] When disorders erupted in Egypt, the British dilemma was sharply etched. The dilemma was formulated in the terms of reference of the Milner Commission, sent out in 1919 to inquire into the disorders as well as into the form of government, under the Protectorate, which was best designed to promote peace and prosperity in Egypt. On December 29, 1919, the Commission described its purpose: ". . . to reconcile the aspirations of the Egyptian people with the special interests which Great Britain has in Egypt." [21] In spite of Milner's and Curzon's serious exertions, the Egyptian response was quite hostile. For some weeks in December 1921 and January 1922 no Egyptian Prime Minister willing to take over responsibility for the Egyptian government was forthcoming.

To conciliate the nationalists, to assure the British position, and to allow for the British aversion to new burdens, Britain in 1922 recognized Egyptian sovereignty. This was a unilateral action, an attempt made in despair of further negotiations with Egypt, to grant the British concession and to assert before the world the primacy of the British position. But Britain still reserved to herself disposition of matters affecting imperial communications, foreign minorities and interests, defense against foreign aggression, and the Sudan. Now this was precisely the difficulty. Egypt was in turmoil and the British presence proved to be an irritation compounding a frustration. In retrospect, the British High Commissioner in Egypt (1925-1929), Lord Lloyd, condemning Britain's refusal to be imperially forthright, argued that the presence of British power in Egypt meant responsibility, and that it was useless to say Britain would not use her power. "However tempting such a course might be in theory, in practice it was quite impossible—Egypt herself at this stage would not allow us —to retire to our tents and take no part in her political struggles." [22]

What, then, was the sanction of the position required by Britain?

[20] Nicolson, *op. cit.*, pp. 171-172.
[21] *Ibid.*, p. 174.
[22] Lord Lloyd, *Egypt Since Cromer* (London, 1934), II, 156.

Only power, supported by arguments about the key position of Egypt and, sometimes, about the incapacity of Egyptians.[23]

Lord Cromer, the guiding spirit of the early occupation, had clear-sightedly emphasized Britain's dilemma. With the Egyptians she could only have "such artificial bonds" of union as those created by British sympathy and beneficent government. Britain could never command in Egypt the loyalty "felt by a self-governing people for" beneficent indigenous rulers. "Neither by the display of sympathy, nor by good government, can we forge bonds which will be other than brittle." [24]

Cromer claimed that British intervention in Egypt had ended the use of the whiplash, and had lessened corruption and the burdens of *corvée*. He believed that, though Egypt had made considerable progress under British tutelage, the distance separating Egypt from the capacity of governing herself with due regard for international obligations and decency was so great that in planning occupation policy the British government should envisage British presence in Egypt as a long-term affair. Indeed, benevolent as Cromer's policy was in some respects, it was primarily a policy of unobtrusive autocracy without hope of legitimate succession. Thus arose the self-perpetuating justification of the British position in Egypt. British representatives would not undertake major reforms in Egypt, first because the occupation was a temporary affair, and later, because Egypt was sovereign. But Britain was unable to relinquish her presence because Egypt was clearly in need of regeneration and thus unable to govern herself.[25]

The control of Egypt and of the nexus of communications there

[23] "The one thing that, until 1920, we refused to contend or to admit, even to ourselves, was that we occupied Egypt by force." Nicolson, *op. cit.*, p. 162.

[24] Cromer, *Modern Egypt* (New York, 1908), II, 569-570. Cromer recognized that ingratitude to the alien rulers was a dictate of human nature itself. But the recognition of this difficulty did not deter him from the conclusion: "In any case, whatever be the moral harvest we may reap, we must continue to do our duty, and our duty has been indicated by the Apostle St. Paul. We must not be 'weary in well-doing.'" *Ibid.*, p. 571.

When Cromer left Egypt in 1907, few Egyptians expressed any sense of gratitude for his services. On the last day of his stay in Egypt, Cromer drove through deserted streets, "mournful testimony to the strength of popular hatred of the British occupation." Lt. Col. P. G. Elgood, *Egypt and the Army* (London, 1924), pp. 24-25.

[25] John Marlowe, *A History of Modern Egypt and Anglo-Egyptian Relations, 1800-1953* (New York, 1954), p. 253.

appeared to be all the more necessary in view of such lively candidates for the divided patrimony of the Ottoman Empire as France. But Britain, also, was prepared to yield much to Egyptian national aspirations and to slough off the burden of transforming Egypt. The result of this compromise between strategic considerations and imperialism-without-burdens was a policy of indirect or limited empire that sought, as in Iraq, to maintain a privileged position without maintaining the burden of imposing an imperial order and peace.[26]

After 1922 Britain, having recognized Egyptian sovereignty, found the Egyptian government unwilling to make a treaty arrangement to regularize Britain's concern with the defense of Egypt, the Canal Zone, and the Sudan. The Italian attack on Ethiopia (1935), however, by confronting Egypt with the threat of a pincers movement from Libya and Ethiopia, induced the Egyptian government to seek protection in the Anglo-Egyptian Treaty (1936), providing for the evacuation of British troops from the Delta and Upper Egypt, permitting Britain to garrison the Suez Canal Zone for twenty years, and establishing an alliance without terminal date.

Thus, with Egypt and with Iraq, with which Britain in 1930 concluded an "unequal treaty" permitting a number of British airbases in Iraq, Britain was successful in maintaining a special position based on treaty partnership. There was an element of diplomatic charade in this—in Iran, notably in Iraq, less so in Egypt—and there was more than a trace of officials under British influence negotiating with the British government.[27]

[26] *Ibid.*, pp. 254-255; also Albert Hourani, "The Anglo-Egyptian Agreement: Some Causes and Implications," *The Middle East Journal*, IX (1955), 242-247.

[27] "We persuaded an Anglophile Government of our own creation that we would defend its northern frontier, and with the help of a personal bribe of £130,000, stolen from the British taxpayer, 'to popularize the Anglo-Persian Agreement' (Englishmen do not know about this sum which the Foreign Office paid over in 1919, but Islam does), the Anglo-Persian Agreement was signed." The partisan *Times* correspondent here does not explain the bribe, which may be the subsidy the British government had paid to the Persian government in the war years. *The Times*, July 10, 1922.

Albert Hourani has persuasively argued that a sense of unreality about politics and pervasive suspicions go back in the Middle East to the time of the declining Ottoman Empire, when the rivalries of the technically superior European powers were often expressed in the rivalries of the Middle Easterners. "The parties and movements of the Middle East lost the sense of their own reality, and looked on each other as puppets whose strings were pulled by forces they could not understand; hence the belief in the omnipresence of the Great Powers, in the hidden

The prevailing situation may be revealed in the following incident. In the summer of 1934 the British diplomatic staff in Egypt was greatly reduced by illness and absences when King Fuad's illness raised fears about his death. British representatives were worried about a rumor that Fuad had named a regency council, including a wealthy pasha likely to be very unpopular and to arouse criticism of the British. Shortly afterwards, Egypt's Prime Minister Abdul Fettah Yehia consulted the Acting High Commissioner, Maurice Peterson, about possible steps to be taken in anticipation of the crisis likely to attend the King's death. Peterson urged a reform of the Egyptian Cabinet and proposed names. The advice was not taken at first. But eventually Peterson's persistence resulted in the accession of a new Prime Minister, Tewfik Nessim. And during the crisis Peterson publicly inspected the Cairo police, for he had learned from Lord Lloyd that, in the Roman manner, Britain had the duty of maintaining Egyptian public order. It was "incumbent upon us, without wanton interference, to prevent misgovernment of that nature and degree which without our presence would inevitably invite the disorders we were bound to suppress." [28]

hand, in the ubiquitous secret agent." "The Middle East and the Crisis of 1956," St. Antony's Papers, No. IV (London, 1958), 15.

The considerable power and the then publicly unacknowledged limits of the power of British representatives in Egypt are well revealed in Sir Geoffrey Thompson, Front Line Diplomat (London, 1959), pp. 86-90. George Kirk has recalled that the gains of Arab nationalism in World War I were achieved largely by foreign arms and that there has been an enduring Arab tradition of looking for a great-power ally to work for them, Britain, Germany, and later the Soviet Union. The Egyptian nationalist Mustafa Kamil told his followers about 1900 that the liberation of the fatherland would not require much exertion from them. "The loyal Egyptian has no other duty than to spread the truth about his nation and fatherland in Europe and request its help." George Kirk, "The Middle Eastern Scene" in The Year Book of World Affairs, 1960 (London, 1960), p. 155.

Among the Iranians the webs of suspicion reached baroque complexity and often served to obscure any personal sense of responsibility for their own government. Some Iranians believed that the first Reza Shah Pahlevi was a British agent, and that not only the coup d'etat of 1921 but the Shah's cancellation of the Anglo-Iranian Oil Company's contract and his subsequent struggle against British interests in the League of Nations were British-inspired masks to disguise the fact of British control. Sir Reader Bullard, The Camels Must Go: An Autobiography (London, 1961), p. 229. Bullard emphasized the hard bargaining that took place in making the agreement as did Longrigg in Oil in the Middle East (New York, 1961), p. 59.

[28] Sir Maurice Peterson, Both Sides of the Curtain (London, 1950), pp. 99-102, 106, 109, 110.

In the interwar years Egypt was not notable for her Arabic character or consciousness. But even in Egypt, there was no readiness to
entertain any interpretation of the Balfour Declaration acceptable to
the Zionists. Elsewhere, in the Arab world, opposition to Zionism was
almost universal. Indeed, if, as H. A. R. Gibb observed, Arabism
originally involved a borrowing of the European concept of linguistic
nationalism and the creation of an Arab nation by an act of will,
then the imperialist powers, Britain and France, and Zionism, by giving a common, if negative, aim to Arabism, are among the abettors
of Arabism's growth.[29] Neither Zionist nor Arab, apart from a few
individuals, seriously sought accommodation or communication. Perhaps only in the confusion of the interwar years, when contradictions
in policy and politics were sometimes lightly entertained, could the
Arab-Zionist conflict have been allowed to gather explosive force.

While the San Remo Conference assigned Palestine to the British
government, the latter's mandatory authority to establish a national
home for the Jewish people, to develop self-governing institutions in
Palestine, and to safeguard the rights of the local population and
minorities, derived from the Council of the League of Nations. The
responsibility was a hopeless one. The Zionists interpreted a national
home as a Jewish state, and Arab opposition only appeared to confirm
and justify the Zionist position.[30] The Arabs refused to see the Balfour Declaration as binding and, at first, even refused to recognize the
mandate. Arab armed resistance broke out several times, but meanwhile the Zionist organization established in the Jewish Agency a
state within a state, a development made possible by the British
government's desire to reduce its military establishment.

In successive White Papers (1922 and 1930) the British government pointed out the anomalies of its responsibility in creating "a
binational but unitary state." [31] Indeed, by 1930, the Arabs, fearful
of the increasing Jewish immigration, were calling for self-government.[32]

[29] Elie Kedourie, "Panarabism and British Policy," *Political Quarterly*, XXVIII
(1957), 137-148; H. A. R. Gibb in Philip Ireland, *The Near East* (Chicago,
1942), p. 70.
[30] Churchill as Colonial Secretary, on July 1, 1922, said that the British government had no such aim in view as a wholly Jewish state in Palestine or the imposition of Jewish nationality upon the people of Palestine. Great Britain, *Parliamentary Papers*, 1922, Cmd. 1700, pp. 17-18.
[31] Paul Hanna, *British Policy in Palestine* (Washington, 1942), p. 69.
[32] Captain W. Ormsby Gore, M.P., formerly of the Arab Bureau, which had

The initial dilemma was of Britain's own making in espousing the Balfour Declaration as well as Arab nationalism and compensation for France. Many motives—humanitarian, idealistic, desire to win the war, and considerations of international strategy—gathered into a force that prompted the British government to issue the Balfour Declaration. The Zionist leader, Chaim Weizmann, had early in the war called attention to the strategic value for Britain that might be provided by a Jewish community in Palestine on the approaches to Suez. But Britain's Arab policy after 1921 sought Arab good will. Palestine, as a safeguard against Arab hostility, was too expensive a proposition, for support of Zionism fomented Arab hostility to Britain.

Nevertheless, Britain sought to administer the contradictory Mandate on terms that would assure the Zionists a minimum position. Three developments in the 1930's drove the British government to the much-criticized proposal for partitioning Palestine and, with its failure, to the policy of curtailing Jewish immigration into Palestine. These were: the beginnings of Hitler's persecution of the Jews which added the impetus of growing fanaticism and of the desperation attendant upon a search for an asylum to the demand for a Jewish state; the necessity of making dispositions to deal with the growing likelihood of German and Italian challenges to Britain; an overt Arab rebellion in Palestine, lasting from 1936 to 1939.

The Arab rebellion was initially notable for its popular, peasant character, which meant, here and elsewhere, that the Arab nationalist movement was beginning to pass from the leadership of land-owning sheikhs who had an interest in accommodation with Britain to groups less amenable to Western calculations and interests.[33] After considering this rebellion, the Peel Commission (1937) concluded that the Mandate could be implemented only if Arab and Jewish national antagonisms could be composed. But, the *Report* continued, the Mandate inspired the antagonism, based, as it was, on conflicting national aspirations concerning Palestine. After a masterful and lucid

---

fostered the Arab Revolt, said on February 18, 1920: "Palestine, above all the countries of the world, is the one where at present self-determination means anarchy." See Gore, *op. cit.*, 90. In the Commons Churchill explained: There is a conflict between the promise of a national home in Palestine and the British policy of consulting the wishes of the people in mandated territories. Representative institutions would be used "to veto any further Jewish immigration." *Parliamentary Debates*, Commons 5th series, CXLIII, col. 265.

[33] John Marlowe, *The Seat of Pilate: An Account of the Palestine Mandate* (London, 1959), pp. 137-138.

account of Palestine complexities, the *Report* concluded that "Partition seems to offer at least a chance of ultimate peace. We can see none in any other plan." [34]

Thus, to meet, after a fashion, the demand for self-government and to allay fears arising from Jewish immigration, and, in general, to halt the deterioration of a bad situation, the Peel Commission recommended the partition of Palestine and the creation of Arab and Jewish states. The Zionists, critical of the proposal and the small area allotted to them, were at any rate interested in discussing partition. In the face of general and adamant Arab opposition, which in the eyes of the British government would have made force necessary for the imposition of partition, the partition proposal was abandoned as unworkable. Finally, the White Paper of 1939 restricted Jewish immigration. For the years 1939 to 1944, ten thousand immigrants a year would be permitted as well as an additional number of 25,000 Jewish refugees in all. After 1944 Jewish immigration would continue only if the Palestinian Arabs approved. The Mandates Commission of the League decided that the new White Paper did not accord with the terms of the Mandate, but the outbreak of war prevented the Council of the League from acting on the Commission's judgments.

Thus, by 1939 the Arabs had learned that Britain's resources were limited and that British will might be swayed by violence. Britain, regarded by many Arabs as the enemy, was at war with Nazi Germany, allied with Italy. Few Arabs publicly wished Britain well. The Zionists, looking on Germany as a mortal enemy, were prepared to aid Britain against the Axis. But they also learned that they had come to the end of the road with Britain as a mandatory power. Every instinct prompted them to oppose the restriction on Jewish immigration. A Jewish state appeared to be the one necessity for them. To secure a Jewish state, they were prepared to use all the opportunities that the war and Britain's necessities gave them.

[34] *Palestine Royal Commission Report*, Cmd. 5479 (London, 1937), p. 376.

4: BRITAIN AND THE MIDDLE EAST
IN THE SECOND WORLD WAR

The interwar years saw the Middle East as an area where Britain held a blurred quasi-imperial predominance, while the Arab and Persian world stirred in an ill-defined struggle for equality and the Arab world protested against the Arab irridenta-to-be in Palestine. And the Second World War, in underscoring Thucydides' conclusion that war fomented revolution, set changes in process that helped to mould the features of the contemporary Middle East.[1]

As the area of the struggle against the Axis extended to embrace the approaches of the Middle East, Britain by mighty efforts achieved there an astonishing dominance that in the war's aftermath began to erode from the force of other currents issuing from the war. The mortal contest strained British resources and strength, and the strain left its mark on British-held positions in the Middle East. Those which had served in weathering, if not quite mastering, the storm appeared to be indispensable props of any future order.

As Nazi control reached out over the European continent, British military and financial aid went to Greece and Turkey on a generous scale that argued desperate heroism, even though the aid was inadequate for Greece. And in these measures Britain made commitments to the two powers that readily put Britain in the line of Soviet expansionism at war's end. The Nazi attack on the Soviet Union made the Turkish position more precarious, and the early Soviet retreats unveiled fearsome prospects of German advances to Iraq. Once again, with Britain and Russia in accord, Persia felt herself strangled.

Nazi mastery of the European continent and its power in the Northern Mediterranean gave a special importance to British Middle Eastern bases as the staging areas for military operations. Supplies were brought around Africa to the Suez base. From here, with the

[1] For the war years there is a valuable account of the area in George Kirk, *The Middle East in the War* (New York, 1952), a part of the history of the war years of the *Survey of International Affairs*. In the British History of the Second World War, see T. S. O. Playfair, *The Mediterranean and Middle East*, Vols. I-III (London, 1954, 1956, 1960).

American landings in Algeria and Morocco, North Africa and the bases from which to cross into Europe were secured. Thus, the war appeared to ratify the wisdom of the British policy of having bases and treaty privileges in Iraq, Jordan, and the Suez Canal Zone.

In the war years the bases meant British control of the area and on occasion overt British intervention. In turn, British control and intervention fomented nationalist resentment. As a rule, British privileges and control had won acquiescence in the Middle East, primarily when the British position appeared as a protection against an activist imperialism such as that of Fascist Italy.

It was certain that Arab nationalism, kept under British control in wartime, would later emerge with special vigor as British pressure was relaxed. More than that, in 1945 Britain had felt impelled to help in the ejection of France from Syria and Lebanon. This left Britain as the sole imperialist Middle Eastern power and, therefore, the target of Arab nationalism.

Britain perhaps could have fostered a continuing common bond with the Arabs by joining them in resistance to Zionism and to any fulfillment of the Palestine mandate. But the British commitment here was honorably maintained, at any rate on a minimum basis; and, to underscore the creditability of the British effort, it should be recalled that the Zionists had already turned against the British mandatory power on the grounds that the Zionists had little of advantage to expect from Britain.

By mid-1945, then, Britain's paramountcy in the Middle East had increased, and was increasing, but a multitude of other developments, detailed in this and the next chapter, conspired to effect its diminution.

The war began after Britain had already lost advantages and valuable positions. Egypt and Iraq followed the British lead only to the point of breaking off diplomatic relations with Germany. When France fell and Italy entered the fighting, the Arab world drew the lessons of respect for the Axis powers that fear, as well as grievances against an imperial master, could impart.

After the Nazi-Soviet Non-Aggression Pact and the war's beginning, Turkey both proclaimed her neutrality and signed a treaty (October 1939) with Britain and France. In it the latter powers promised to aid Turkey against an attack, while Turkey promised to aid them if the war involved the Mediterranean. But Turkey, arguing that the fall of France had in effect abrogated the treaty pledge, re-

fused to sway from non-belligerency when Italy entered the war. At
that time, British military and civilian leaders found Turkish neutrality the most acceptable course for their own country. When the
Nazi attack on Yugoslavia and Greece was imminent, Churchill and
the British military leaders vainly sought Turkish participation in the
war. Neutrality did not prevent close cooperation between the many
British agents in Turkey and the authorities of the country, for Turkey
feared a German as well as a Soviet victory. To assure Turkish neutrality, Britain and, later, the United States preemptively contracted
for primary Turkish goods.

As the defeat of Germany appeared more likely in 1943, Winston
Churchill exerted persuasion and pressure to get Turkey in the war
and so to open an Allied approach to the heart of the European continent. The Turkish refusal was unshakeable; but, meanwhile, Britain
had assumed a vast economic burden for the support of the Turkish
economy plagued by shortages, inflationary pressures, and the heavy
costs of defense preparations.

The fall of France meant ready Nazi access to the Mediterranean
and the possibility that French territories in the Middle East, Syria
and Lebanon, would be used for the support of Nazi designs in the
Arab world.[2] On June 17, 1940, the British government promised to
defend French colonial territories against Germany and sought French
cooperation. General de Gaulle's Free French, however, did not readily secure control of Syria and Lebanon. De Gaulle's agent, General
Catroux, then decided that the Petainist forces in those countries
could be supplanted only if the Arab people, supported by British
and Free French forces, acted together. To gain Arab support, the
Free French, with British approval, proclaimed (June 8, 1941) the
independence of the Syrian and Lebanese people. From this military
action in Syria, June-July 1941, there stemmed progressively bitter
French suspicions that Britain was using the Arabs against French
interests in the Middle East. British representatives there were inclined to see the French attributing their unpopularity with the Arabs
to Britain. Where the British representatives thought that de Gaulle
was struggling against fulfilling his pledge of Syrian-Lebanese inde-

---

[2] A British government statement (July 1, 1940) indicated that Britain would
not tolerate Nazi occupation or use of Middle Eastern territory or a drift to internal disorder in the Middle East. E. L. Woodward, *British Foreign Policy in the
Second World War* (London, 1962), p. 108.

pendence, the French saw from another angle the growth of British influence as Syria and Lebanon became part of the sterling area.[3]

The United States and the Soviet Union recognized the independence of Syria and Lebanon. These two Arab states became founding members of the United Nations. At about the same time, fighting ensued between the Syrian and the Free French authorities. When the latter shelled Damascus (May 1945), Churchill demanded that de Gaulle's forces withdraw to their barracks. By 1946 the French were effectively out of Syria and Lebanon.

This incident inflated French suspicions, already strongly directed to such British officials in Syria as General Spears and Stirling.[4] During the war Syria and Lebanon became part of the sterling area and the extension of British influence through the Middle East Supply Center added some fuel to suspicions. De Gaulle and many French representatives could not take seriously Britain's concern with keeping general Arab opinion friendly. De Gaulle charged the British leader with making France the scapegoat for Britain's unpopularity. His final and prophetic remark: we today, but you tomorrow.

Mussolini's entry into the war was inspired by the belief that France had been despatched, as well as by a fear that further delay in joining in the kill of France would perhaps find Germany as the protector of France against Italian demands. In the Mediterranean Mussolini hoped to get Tunis, Malta, Cyprus, and a protectorate over Egypt, Syria, and Iraq.[5] On its part, the British government indicated (June 19) that it had assumed freedom of action with respect to Italian-occupied territories and agreements with Italy concerning the Middle East. Initially, however, this was not a formidable threat, for until

[3] The British government provided monthly sums of over £500,000 to pay for the French administration and troops in Syria-Lebanon. Woodward, op. cit., p. 122. The depth of Franco-British suspicion may be sensed in Mary Borden, Journey Down a Blind Alley (New York, 1946); Edwin Spears [her husband], Assignment to Catastrophe, 2 vols. (London, 1954); General Catroux, Dans la bataille de la Mediterraneé (Paris, 1949); and The War Memoirs of Charles de Gaulle, 3 vols. (New York, 1954-1959). In 1941 Churchill urged on de Gaulle the necessity of meeting "Arab aspirations" in Syria and Lebanon: The Grand Alliance, Vol. III of The Second World War (Boston, 1950), 328.

[4] The latter, of bash-the-French views, in the manner of T. E. Lawrence, is the author of Safety Last.

[5] These demands, as revealed to Fascist Party leaders on May 16, 1940, were reported by the British Ambassador, Sir Percy Loraine. See Woodward, op. cit., p. 57, n. 1.

the summer of 1940 British forces in the Middle East were on a scale designed primarily to provide internal security in the region rather than to counter the moves of the Axis.[6] Nevertheless, after Dunkirk, Prime Minister Churchill emphasized the importance of the Middle East to Britain by sending equipment and men, believed to be sorely needed at home, to reinforce General Wavell in the Middle East.

The Mediterranean, then, became a theater of war waged on the sea and its islands, on the peninsulas projecting from southern Europe, and in North Africa. Egypt remained the principal British base, for, to the Western powers, Suez was the strategic center of access to Africa, the Red Sea, and beyond. From Libya, where Italian forces had been numerically and technically superior to British forces in Egypt, the Italian attack was launched and faltered. In 1941-1942 the North African war turned against the Italians, who were supplanted by their Nazi ally in the Balkans and Greece, in North Africa, and, finally, in Italy as well.

Britain, in facing German forces in North Africa and Greece, found her resources at the snapping point. Greece and Crete were lost (1941) long before the British halted the advance of Rommel's *Afrika Korps* into Egypt, and preparations were made for the renewed British drive at El-Alamein roughly coinciding with the American-British landings in French North Africa (1942).

To the Middle East Britain sent forces at the expense of home defenses and positions in Malaya. Japan's entry into the war caused a diversion of forces from the Middle East. The ensuing weaknesses were enhanced by the temporary dwindling of American supplies to the Middle East after the Japanese attack on Pearl Harbor brought the United States into the war.

For most of the war, that is, from 1940 until well into 1943, supplies had to be brought not through the Mediterranean but around the Cape, and yet for several years a Western offensive against Hitler could be mounted only in the Mediterranean. Indeed, the supply problem and the multiplicity of British Middle Eastern ventures prompted two major British decisions concerning the Middle East.

First of all, on June 29, 1941, Oliver Lyttelton was appointed as British Minister of State Resident in the Middle East.[7] This new

---

[6] Sir John Kennedy, *The Business of War* (New York, 1958), pp. 194, 201.

[7] The Minister Resident was of cabinet rank and in an emergency could act in the name of the War Cabinet. Lyttelton negotiated with de Gaulle the agreements concerning Syria and Lebanon (May, 1942). Similar offices were established

post of War Cabinet rank was created to relieve the Commander of forces in the Middle East of extraneous responsibilities as well as to provide him with political guidance and to coordinate diplomatic activity. The Minister's main work of coordination, as things turned out, was in the fields of administration where the growing activity of many government departments demanded direction. In the Middle East the Resident also had to guide the government of occupied enemy territory.

The second decision was to establish the Middle East Supply Center (1941), which developed out of several attempts to cope with supplying to the Allied Armies the tools of war and to the civilian population of the Middle East, its basic necessities. But to do the latter required the extension of control over Middle Eastern economy and far-reaching adjustments within any single country. In Africa, British forces embarked upon the conquest of the Italian colonial empire, Eritrea, Somaliland, and Ethiopia. Libya, too, appeared to be an easy prey until German forces formed into the *Afrika Korps* took the initiative. Through 1941 and the first nine months of 1942 German momentum in Europe appeared overwhelming. Yugoslavia, Greece, and Crete were subjected to Nazi rule. Nazi columns swept into Russia and seemed likely to threaten the Caucasus. Thus, in 1942, most of the producing wells at Kirkuk and two other places in Iraq were plugged by Royal Engineers to prevent their use by Nazi forces.[8]

The heavy commitment of British forces in the Mediterranean reveals Churchill's estimate of the importance of the Middle East to Britain. In strictly strategic thinking Singapore may have been rated higher than the Middle East, but Churchill was not prepared to act rigidly on that calculation. The Middle East was "an area that was ours," [9] and the urgent sense of its importance, on occasion, led British leaders to plan against more formidable Nazi designs in the Middle East than Hitler seriously contemplated. Nevertheless, available British forces were inadequate in numbers and equipment to the demands prompted by immediate necessity and the fears of foresight. The Commander-in-Chief of British Middle Eastern forces, General

---

for the Far East very late in the war, and in 1942 Harold Macmillan was named Minister Resident in Northwest Africa. The latter's authority extended to Italy and Greece. Woodward, *op. cit.*, p. xxiii.

[8] Stephen H. Longrigg, *Oil in the Middle East* (New York, 1961), p. 121.

[9] See Kennedy, *op. cit.*, p. 41.

Wavell, repeatedly emphasized in 1941 that his forces were gravely overstretched and that for some matters, as in Iraq, a political rather than a military solution should be attempted. As disaster became the familiar camp-follower of British armies in Greece and Crete, though not in East Africa, the political uncertainty of the Arab and Iranian world heightened.

A political solution, the necessary basis for the deployment of British forces, meant the confirmation or renewal of Britain's working arrangement with the "moderate" Middle Eastern nationalists, expressed in such treaties as those with Iraq and Egypt.

Of those years Freya Stark, who worked for the British government in attempting to rally democratic forces in the Middle East, has written concerning Egypt: ". . . if we took to leaning against anything it would be a fifth column." [10] Indeed, in the war years, Britain made three memorable interventions in the Middle East, apart from two interventions in Syria and Lebanon.

First of all, British and Soviet forces (August 1941) occupied Iran, which had proclaimed its neutrality on the outbreak of the war. German commercial interests had multiplied, and the autocratic Shah refused to respond satisfactorily to British concern about the presence of Axis agents in his country. Some three weeks after the entry of British and Russian troops, the Shah abdicated in favor of his son, Mohammed Reza Pahlevi, the present ruler of Iran. As the two invading powers professed that they did not intend an occupation of Iran, they negotiated a Tripartite Treaty (January 28, 1942), expressing their determination to respect Iranian independence and territorial integrity. Thus, they agreed to withdraw their forces within six months after the end of hostilities against Germany and her partners and to attempt to protect the livelihood of Iran against the shortages and interruptions caused by the war. In return, the Iranian government promised cooperation with the British and Soviet governments and forces and to make every necessary provision for their communications and transportation requirements. In supplying the Soviet Union with Lend-Lease material, the United States associated itself with the two powers in Iran. Roosevelt also joined Churchill and Stalin in the Teheran Declaration (December 1, 1943), which repeated the previous pledge to aid the Iranian economy and to respect the country's sovereignty.

The presence of the Americans prompted the Iranians to use them,

[10] Freya Stark, *Dust in the Lion's Paw: An Autobiography* (London, 1961).

in the war and later, against Britain and Russia, who early in the century had divided Iran into spheres of influence and in the Second World War had occupied their country. In 1943-1944, as Iranian oil production increased, British and American representatives sought new Persian oil concessions. Then, in September 1944 a Soviet Vice-Commissar for Foreign Affairs arrived in Teheran to seek a five-year agreement for Soviet oil exploration in Northern Iran. All parties were then informed that the Iranian Cabinet had decided against making any oil concessions during the war. Communist forces, including Iranian communists and Soviet troops, were marshalled to press the government. As a result the Iranian Prime Minister resigned, but in December 1944 the Iranian Majlis adopted a law sponsored by the nationalist, Dr. Mohammed Mossadegh. The law sternly forbade any further negotiations on oil concession unless the Majlis specifically authorized them.[11]

In 1941 the British treaty position in Iraq was challenged by a *coup d'état* staged by Rashid Ali al-Gailani and nationalist army officers. When the new government sought to reduce the British forces in Iraq and their rights of passage, British forces reinforced by Transjordan's Arab Legion moved into action. The Rashid Ali government, which had received military aid from Germany, broke up and fled. The Regent, who had been rescued from the revolutionaries by the American Minister, returned.

For the remainder of the war Britain worked with Iraqi leaders, who realistically accepted the temporary British predominance and worked on the basis of interest shared with Britain in oil development and revenues as well as in projects for the economic development of Iraq and for Arab unity. Nationalist discontent simmered in the pervasive presence of the British.

Sir Geoffrey Thompson, who served in Iraq from 1942 to the end of the war, recalled that "we seemed to have a finger in every pie in the country, from the administration of the Port of Basra to Iraqi relations with the Kurds." In his post as Counsellor to the British Embassy in Baghdad he had become acquainted with people "such as the British advisers to the Ministries of Interior and Justice, the British head of the C.I.D., the British Director-General of the Iraqi State Railways." Thompson himself wrote editorials several times weekly for the *Iraq Times*. Another revealing note concerns General Sir Henry Maitland Wilson, who "understood better than most of his

[11] Longrigg, *op. cit.*, pp. 130-131.

personal staff that our troops were in Iraq not as an army of occupation, but in accordance with our rights under the existing Anglo-Iraqi
Treaty." [12]

In Egypt the experience of the war years pointed to the treaty of
1936 as an instrument of British dominance. As adequate facilities
had not been built in the Canal Zone, and indeed in 1939 the British
government felt impelled to pay half the costs of building the proposed barracks, British troops remained in Cairo and the Delta.
Shortly before Italy joined the fighting in 1940, the Egyptian government wavered briefly. But Egypt was transformed as a war base for
the fighting in North Africa, and for the war years the British Ambassador there, Sir Miles Lampson, inevitably exercised more influence than even the British High Commissioner had. The Wafd Party
under the ascendancy of Nahas, who had ceased to be the incor-
ruptible of earlier years and had become dictatorial, favored the anti-
Axis cause. The young King Farouk was impressed by German victories and, in part as the result of his feud with the Wafd, was inclined to select advisors ultimately mistrusted by the British. On
February 4, 1942, the British Ambassador, supported by military
forces including tanks, delivered an ultimatum to Farouk at Abdin
Palace. Farouk yielded and the Wafd leader, Nahas, became Prime
Minister.[13]

For the next two years the Wafd government provided satisfactory
support to the British war effort. As the fighting ebbed away to remove Egypt from the danger zone, the public temper in Egypt began
to change. The war economy fostered a plague of inflation to inten-
sify Egyptian poverty, an experience that readily inspired attacks on
the British as its authors. The Wafd itself, a nationalist party that
had waged anti-British campaigns before the war, was bound to return to demanding the fulfillment of Egypt's nationalist aspirations
as a matter of right and as a reward for wartime cooperation. When
Farouk dismissed the Wafd in October 1944, Nahas and his party in
opposition were free to press remorselessly the cause of Egyptian nationalism. And they did so all the more clamorously to obliterate the
memory of their wartime cooperation with the national enemy.

[12] *Front Line Diplomat* (London, 1959), pp. 175, 177, 178, 181.
[13] General de Gaulle ironically described the display of tanks as in support of
the "warm recommendation" of the British Ambassador, Sir Miles Lampson. In
1941 Nahas remarked to de Gaulle: "You and I have one characteristic in common. In our countries we have the majority, not the power." *The War Memoirs
of Charles de Gaulle*, Vol. II, *Unity: 1942-1944* (New York, 1959), 15.

Eventually the British government, in accord with a decision taken at Yalta, approved Egypt's declaration of war on the Axis by which Egypt qualified for the United Nations and for a voice in shaping the postwar world. The Egyptian Prime Minister who undertook this step was assassinated. In June 1945 the Egyptian government indicated that it would not seek the implementation of the Anglo-Egyptian treaty of 1936; instead, it called for the total withdrawal of British forces from Egypt.

Meanwhile, pan-Arabism had entered upon a more vigorous life and in unexpected forms. Pan-Arabism, which appeals for the unity of the Arabic peoples, draws sustenance from a common religious tradition, a common language, and memories of Arab empire and glory. British officials had abetted Arab nationalism in the First World War, but Arab weakness and divisions and Britain's interests had ended in the fragmentation of the Middle East. In the interwar years the absence of any serious challenger of British power confirmed a traditional and grossly maligned British preference for dealing with divided rather than unified forces. Then, the proponents of Arab unity were Arabs, and particularly Iraqis and Syrians. The Fertile Crescent had no traditional boundaries and the union of Iraq and Syria, and possibly Jordan, made economic sense as well as providing more effective means of resisting Zionism. Such a proposal was the Fertile Crescent scheme presented (December 1942) by Nuri es-Said of Iraq to the Australian, R. Casey, British Minister of State.

Meanwhile, many British officials believed that the war had confirmed the necessity of the Palestine White Paper of 1939. Placing a limit on Zionist immigration meant a rough appeasement decision in favor of the Arabs. It became a British commonplace to argue that the White Paper had helped to hold that Arab world for British interests. For the future the obvious course required a continued search for Arab good will. As early as 1941, Foreign Minister Anthony Eden speaking at the Mansion House in London expressed official British favor to the cause of Arab unity, and he reiterated the policy statement in 1943. This emphasis on Arab unity, running counter to the understandable British preference for division among rival negotiators, was initially made to counter the adverse effects of British intervention against Rashid Ali, and German statements in support of pan-Arab independence.

The work of the Middle East Supply Center provided economic arguments for the necessity of Arab cooperation. For some eighteen months in 1943 and 1944 the initiative of the Center resulted in a series of economic conferences in Cairo.[14] In these meetings the physical and economic bases of Arab Union were discussed.

But a somewhat unexpected Arab leader, Egypt, appeared. Now, the Arab world outside of Saudi Arabia included many minority groups. Egypt—in particular, Egyptian cities—had an extremely heterogeneous character and in the past had been particularly concerned with her own identity and independence. There were many wealthy foreigners long resident in Egypt, and to a considerable extent Arabism in Egypt lent itself to reformism. Egypt, however, had other real incentives to stress her Arab aspects, for to have allowed others to lead the pan-Arab cause would have meant the reduction of her stature and influence. At any rate, the political promise of the cause is evident in that King Farouk earlier had espoused phases of it, and Nahas and the Wafd favored it as did the Wafd's successors in office. Nahas carried on further preliminary work in 1944, and an Arab Conference meeting in Alexandria (September 25 to October 8, 1944) drafted in a Protocol the aims of an Arab League and the lines of a proposed constitution.[15]

The Pact of the Arab League was signed on March 22, 1945. The organization of the League, with its permanent seat in Cairo, included a Council and Secretary-General, a political committee, and various functional committees. But behind the Arab rhetoric of unity the League was an uneasy balance of rivalries and mistrust. Tiny Lebanon was a strikingly plural society, and the Lebanese Christians were not minded to merge their interests in a Muslim world. Syria was both attracted by prospects of union with Iraq and even more fearful of the union. Iraq, with the expectation of increasing oil revenues, was unwilling to share that wealth with other neighbors. Saudi Arabia saw the Hashemites of Iraq and Jordan as the likely bearers of a feud against the House of Ibn Saud. Egypt and Iraq seeking dominance mistrusted each other. In short, pan-Arabism strikingly embodied the conflicting interests of all pan-movements.

What is surprising is the fact that a pan-Arab sentiment was created and, on occasion, exercised genuine influence. But, at first, pan-Arabism was primarily negative, directed against Zionism and the imperial powers ruling Arab people. In two appendices to the Arab

[14] *The Economist* (CXLVII), Oct. 14, 1944, 507.
[15] See the large documentary collection in M. Khalil (ed.), *The Arab States and the Arab League: A Documentary Record* (Beirut, 1963), 2 vols.

League constitution the *de jure* independence of Palestine, as an Arab country, was asserted, and the League's Council was charged to aid Arab people under non-Arab control in their aspirations to independence.[16] Thus, the Arab League, which the British government approved, aligned itself with the revolutionary forces that were to surge in the postwar Middle East.

But the very sharpness of the conflict between Zionist and Arab demands strengthened British pragmatism. The British government did not look for over-all policies and solutions in the Middle East. It had a policy for the Arabs and another for Palestine. Each policy took some account of the other but there was no attempt to look for an architectonic unity in policy designed to deal with such painful contradictions. Jews in Palestine were inescapably anti-Nazi, and the Cold War has multiplied instances of disregard and ingratitude for the committed and generosity to the doubtful and wavering. Some Zionists were permitted to volunteer for service with British forces. But the British government was reluctant to provide arms to the Jewish population of Palestine, although, as in the past, it did so in emergencies. The wartime coalition government was resolved to seek the good will of the Arabs and leaned to a partition of Palestine that would have meant a small state for the Zionists. The cabinet, however, did not go beyond favoring the principle of partition. The rationale was that "while neither race can be permitted to dominate the whole of Palestine, there is no reason why each race should not rule part of it." The British Foreign Office, however, generally objected on the grounds that partition was unfair to the Arabs, would embitter British relations with the Arab states, and would rouse Arab fears of unlimited Jewish immigration. The Prime Minister, who regarded the White Paper of 1939 as a British breach of faith with the Jews, sought to preserve capacity for maneuver by refraining from any public announcement of a British plan.[17]

With the prospect of Nazi defeat, the Zionists, thus, found British usefulness at an end. Hitler's extermination policies added a desperate urgency to Zionist determination to open Palestine's door to the Jewish refugees from Europe. In 1942 the World Zionist movement

[16] The President of the World Zionist movement and of the Jewish Agency in Palestine, in a tactical move—for Zionist plans for a Jewish state had been formulated three years earlier—protested (March 27, 1945) to Foreign Minister Anthony Eden against the Arab League's derogation of Britain's mandatory authority.

[17] Woodward, *op. cit.*, pp. 392-395.

adopted the Biltmore Program calling for the establishment of a
Jewish state in the whole of the Palestine mandate. Shortly after the
European fighting had ended, the Jewish Agency made similar de-
mands of the British government. The days of the Zionist activist,
David Ben-Gurion, had replaced the era of the liberal Zionist, Chaim
Weizmann.

The prospect in Palestine was tortuous and foreboding. The Zionists were prepared to use all the weapons at their disposal, especially
their influence in the United States. American officials were to find
the Arab-Zionist dispute particularly unyielding. As the Cold War
developed, it became a cliché of State Department and Pentagon
circles to talk of the necessity of looking at the "harsh realities" of
this or that situation. The harsh reality of Palestine was less instructive
as an introduction than it might have been, for it had helped to tame
even that willful optimist, Franklin D. Roosevelt, before his death.

Before the fighting ended in Europe the first engagement of the
Cold War had taken place in Greece. The occasion was an attempt to
seize power made by Greek communist forces in the course of the
liberation of Greece. The British army resisted and there began the
unrolling of the long Greek Civil War. In the initial fighting, Stalin
appears to have behaved with formal correctness. Earlier, in 1944,
Churchill, believing that the progress of Soviet armies was effectively
deciding the political fate of Eastern Europe, made a temporary agreement with Stalin regarding the relative amount of control which
Britain and the Soviet Union should possess in Hungary, Rumania,
Bulgaria, Yugoslavia, and Greece, the last of which should be wholly
under provisional British authority. In spite of American objections,
Churchill followed this course because his proposal for a Balkan invasion had been turned down. The American position, which was
certainly naive, called for postponing political decisions until the peace
conference. In the meantime, this position amounted to an attack on
any expressed desire for spheres of influence as a survival of imperialism and a betrayal of the international world of law that was coming
into being. Thus, by the end of the war Britain was not only providing
large-scale support to Turkey against renewed Soviet pressure but was
committed to the support of the Greek government against what developed into a communist-inspired civil war.

5: THE FIRST POSTWAR YEARS

From late 1942 to the summer of 1945 Britain controlled a large part of the Middle East. British control, with which the Soviet Union was associated in Iran and the United States even more closely associated in the Middle East Supply Center and in Iran, had a pervasiveness that appeared to justify the repetition of Lord Curzon's rejoicing after the First World War. The war years had seen Britain's power triumphant in the area. In the Far East and Southern Asia, Japanese forces had driven Britain from imperial positions in Hong Kong, Borneo, Malaya, and Burma. Under pressure she had offered complete self-government to India, though on terms which the Indian Congress Party had rejected. In the Middle East, however, British power had garnered victories and extended influence.

But challenges had appeared before the end of the Japanese war. Indeed, a recession of British power was inevitable and the retreat of power is always difficult. The surprising feature is the succession of British reverses that made of the postwar years a time of troubles for Britain.

First of all, the misnamed nation of shopkeepers had sustained a war effort against the Axis that in making victory possible had strained British economic resources. On occasion Winston Churchill had somewhat incredulously said that, when the war ended with an impoverished Britain, the electorate would throw him out of office. Britain imperatively had to turn to economic reconstruction, to importing, manufacturing, exporting, and investing overseas. She could not continue to maintain the over-stretched power achieved in the war. During the war years the Coalition government agreed on a considerable program of social security and education. The social welfare program acquired electoral impetus when the Labour Party won an impressive majority in the elections held in June 1945. Thus, Britain faced the task of economic reconstruction under a government pledged to planning and social welfare.

But the Labour victory had its international impact as well. While its principal leaders, Prime Minister Clement Attlee, Foreign Secretary Ernest Bevin, and others, had been prominent in the wartime Coalition government, an important section of the Labour Party had the opposition mentality of a party that hitherto had not held power with majority support. They had high hopes that they could really "make it new" in the sphere of politics at home and abroad. The Labour Party had professed confidence that it could get along with the Soviet Union, that Left understands Left, and it was on voluminous record in its expressions of sympathy with the political aspirations of colonial people as well as with Zionism. With its victory, the expectations aroused by its past contributed to the seething clamor for independence that assailed the British government.

Its history also predisposed the Labour Party to warm support of international organization. Thus, the Labour government espoused the United Nations, which, with its universal membership, proved to be increasingly hostile to the survival of imperialism of Western origin. But the United Nations soon appeared to be of limited effectiveness, for it assumed the cooperation of Britain and the two superpowers, as they were then called, the Soviet Union and the United States. And, although Churchill had sometimes advocated courses of action based on misgivings about Soviet cooperation, the alternative to Big Three cooperation seemed to be too dismal a prospect on which to base future policy. Even in the Middle East, at any rate until May 1946, the British policy of seeking Arab good will assumed either the continuation of cooperation or, at any rate, that British espousal of Arabism might deny the Soviet Union the likely advantages of a Soviet encouragement of pan-Arabism.

The Soviet Union, which had played so small a role in the Middle East in the interwar years, displayed a growing interest during the war, when it established diplomatic relations with a number of the Arab states. The Soviet Union had three advantages in dealing with the Arab world, that is, the Middle East excluding Turkey and Iran. While caution enjoined it to consider the possibility of Islamic nationalism among its own people, it had played no role among the Arabs and thus started with the blamelessness that Arab ignorance of it permitted; it professed anti-imperialism and was, therefore, prepared to support Arab nationalists against the British, who not only bore the burden of an imperialist past but had to act in the Middle East in order to secure vital interests; the Soviet Union, having no primary interest in the stability of the Middle East, had a large measure of freedom of action and propaganda. But these formidable advantages were not skillfully used until 1955.

The explanation of Soviet failure to make progress in the Arab world before the Egyptian-Communist arms deal is not an obvious one. First of all, Stalin seems to have concentrated on the extension of Soviet power from bases which he surely controlled. This caution prompted him to devote himself to consolidating his new satellite empire and to pressure on adjacent Greece, Turkey, and Iran. Stalin also may have been a traditional Russian expansionist for whom the Straits and the Persian Gulf were the proper goals. Molotov, it is true, also asked for a trusteeship over Tripolitania. But, apart from Greece and Turkey, the Soviet retreat in the face of diplomatic resistance is the striking feature. Stalin's Iranian policy and even that of his successors in 1953 were marked by caution and a fear that Soviet intrusion upon vital Western interests might mean war.[1]

Soviet policy not only failed to exploit Middle Eastern opportunities but it contributed to bringing the United States into the Middle East more quickly and fully than might have been expected. American interest in Middle Eastern oil had been increasing. In Saudi Arabia, the United States had even built an air base at Dhahran, to serve for transport in the war against Japan. In view of Britain's dependence on American aid, the British government was eager to associate the United States with its own dominance in the Middle East and especially to gain American participation in a responsible appraisal of the Palestine problem. With the major exception of Palestine, the British effort succeeded in part and, to the degree that it did, the American association with Britain in the Middle East may have obscured the decline of British power there from the British government itself. Until 1951, or perhaps 1953, the American government recognized Britain's primary responsibility in the Middle East. In doing so, however, the United States became party to a dwindling truth and a growing fiction, and American recognition was tempered by another judgment that Britain's position in the Middle East was a legacy of imperialism.

Neither the United States nor Britain formulated a Middle Eastern policy that embraced the range of interests and realities of the area.

[1] Guy Wint in reviewing Walter Z. Laqueur, *The Soviet Union and the Middle East* (London, 1959), wrote: "Stalin nearly always believed his opponents more resolute than in fact they were." *The Observer*, September 27, 1959.

Where American policy-makers had earlier been blindly critical of British imperialism, that is, policies issuing from concern with strategic and power-political arrangements in Southern Europe, their opposition to imperialism also made them for a time more sensitively open to the forces of the future in the Middle East. These rival approaches rendered cooperation fitful and hampered by suspicion; for the United States, in essaying the diverse roles of Britain's ally, critic, and successor, widely evoked British doubts about the first role and in imperialist circles anger about the third role, an anger also voiced by some left-wing critics who either opposed a new imperialism or used it to defend a pro-Soviet course.

The United States dramatically entered the Middle East on a large scale in opposition to Soviet threats. Impressive naval demonstrations in the Mediterranean had revealed a will to resist which had also been expressed in protests against the Soviet position in Iran in 1946. But the major American entry in the Middle East came on its periphery, when the Truman Doctrine was proclaimed. In February 1947, in the course of a severe winter, the burdens on the British economy—to which the terms of the American loan of 1946 added—caused the British government to inform the United States that it would have to discontinue supporting Greece and Turkey against communist pressure. Here Britain's financial stringency provided the occasion for recognizing that the policy of Big Three cooperation was approaching the stoniest dead end. The United States took over the British policy and in the Truman Doctrine gave it a characteristically American formulation. The Doctrine was an elaboration of the containment policy designed to restrain Soviet expansion and ultimately to transform Soviet policy by the vigilant interposition of counter-forces to Soviet probes. The containment policy, originally designed with Europe in mind, acquired a universal formulation in the Truman Doctrine, which spoke of aiding countries prepared to resist communist aggression.

The reaction of Secretary of State George Marshall to the British withdrawal, expressed to Secretary Forrestal, was, perhaps, of equal significance: ". . . this dumped in our lap another most serious problem—that it was tantamount to British abdication from the Middle East with obvious implications as to their successor." [2]

[2] Walter Millis (ed.), *The Forrestal Diaries* (New York, 1957), p. 245. The very wording, free as it is of any trace of exultation, reveals reluctance to recognize the responsibilities that greatness of power thrust upon the United States.

The British government, then, with reduced resources and a divided will, faced a Middle East where other great powers were also in a position to acquire major influence. There appeared to be no divided will in Labour's Foreign Secretary, Ernest Bevin. A long-time trade unionist, whose wartime tenure of the Ministry of Manpower, a ministry almost designed to blight reputations, had enhanced his stature, Bevin brought to diplomacy a trade-unionist's belief in negotiation and a reputation for bluntness and tenacity. The bluntness, in part, had been cultivated and skillfully exploited, but it also expressed the dogged self-righteousness of a mind that reposed in massive and simple certainties. In his foreign policy Bevin hoped to make possible the elevation of the standard of living of Asian and African people. He was equally insistent that the livelihood of British workers was dependent on the security of British Middle Eastern interests. And to head off an avalanche of demands upon the new Foreign Secretary, he uttered expressive, though ineffective, warnings that there should be no queue-jumping concerning grievances. After a year of un-Hamlet-like confrontation of a sea of troubles, Bevin described his work: "All the world is in trouble and I have to deal with all the troubles at once." An Egyptian nationalist, however, expressed a sentiment widely prevalent among the Arabs: the number of Britain's difficulties would not deter them from pressing Britain.

Though Bevin could appear adamant, he knew the difficulties of Britain's position. His Cabinet colleagues were preoccupied with the many problems of a new government which takes over in the transition from war to peace and is dedicated to a far-ranging program of social reform and the nationalization of a number of economic activities. Some of his Party colleagues early began to blame him for the harsh temper of the postwar world. When the Labour government turned to India and in 1947 indicated its willingness to grant India full and unqualified self-government, the abdication from Empire in India, so generally acclaimed, incited other people to press for the same treatment all the more clamorously because the decision clearly signified a diminished willingness to use power. Bevin insisted that British interests would be protected, but his colleagues were divided on the measures necessary to do so. The divisions of mind and will appeared in the Cabinet and in Prime Minister Attlee himself. The recognition of this divided mind prompted some Middle Eastern leaders, in Palestine, Egypt, and Iran, to press their challenges to British authority to nearly self-destructive extremes. In the elections

of 1951 the Conservative leader, Churchill, boasted that he would
not have been so naive as to allow Middle Eastern leaders to read
his mind: the Iranian Premier, Dr. Mossadegh, he charged, had "pene-
trated and measured accurately the will power of the men he had to
deal with in Whitehall." [3]

The independence of India, which had once provided the impetus
for British establishment in the Middle East, deprived Britain of a
major base and the manpower for control of the Middle East. The
utility of that base was demonstrated for the last time in the summer
of 1946, when the communist-dominated Tudeh Party was in the
Iranian government and a formidable strike occurred in the Anglo-
Iranian oil fields. Ships and troops were sent from India to the Iraqi
port of Basra adjacent to Iran. The incident and later events revealed
that the venerable imperialist adage that British supremacy in India
was bound up with British control in the Persian Gulf was equally
true when turned about to state that British effectiveness in the
Persian Gulf rested upon British power in India. [4]

The loss of India meant a precarious British position in the Middle
East. Deliberate dismantling of authority and power is always difficult, and more difficult in Britain's case, for Britain did not have
great resources of power but had gained and exercised influence
through that complex network of imperial relationships that may be
compared to an ingenious holding company. The Labour government
was heir to a multitude of British arrangements and commitments.
These could not all be scrutinized at once. Even if they had been, the
new British leaders could not make general new arrangements at once.
One commitment may involve several others and they in turn en-
tangle relationships with still more. Renunciation of one great possession, India, was in itself an extraordinary gesture. But what the imperial master thought of as principled highmindedness and realistic
accommodation, colonial nationalists with equal realism saw as weakness full of the promise of concessions.

Bevin's initial formulation of British Middle Eastern policy was
studiedly practical in approach. To be practical meant the maintenance of continuity of policy in respect to commitments and expectations fostered by Britain. There was nothing doctrinaire in maintaining continuity, for he recognized that innovation would be necessary

[3] *The Manchester Guardian Weekly*, October 4, 1951.
[4] Lovat Fraser, *India Under Lord Curzon and After* (London, 1911), p. 112.
"If we lose control of the Gulf, we shall not rule long in India."

to meet new conditions. He consulted with the permanent officials of the Foreign Office and gave them a respectful attention which won their marked loyalty. For Bevin the objective of foreign policy was the protection of British interests. A reading of the speeches of Labour's back-benchers will reveal that the obviousness of that remark was not acceptable to all members of parliament. Bevin had no liking for the left-wing Labourites who could understand and excuse all Soviet self-seeking, and who placed an exaggerated value on British gestures of renunciation. He was vehement against those who proposed to initiate a new era by internationalizing British interests, yet would permit other powers to hold on to their own.[5] British interests were Britain's special responsibility, but they were to be expressed in relation to the interests of others. The more completely Britain was able to relate her interests to the interests of other states and people, the more secure British interests would be.

The British economy and the wages of British workingmen were dependent on Middle Eastern oil, British enterprises in the Middle East, and security of transit through the Suez Canal. To an International Conference of Agricultural Producers, Bevin (May 20, 1946) defined an objective of diplomacy as fulfilling the aspirations of the masses of the world's people to a higher standard of living.[6] To that end the British government, late in 1945, replaced the Middle East Supply Center, which the American government was averse to maintaining, with the Middle East Office. Thereby, the Center's valuable work of providing technical assistance to the area's states could be continued. The Office, provided with a staff of technical experts who knew the Middle East well, played a valuable but limited role, although Egypt made no use of it. The other Arab states, for their part, remembering the days of control, wanted experts under their own management.[7]

Lord Altrincham, who had been Minister Resident in the Middle East (1944-1945), formulated the British position in the Middle East in terms that echoed the views which Bevin approvingly heard from his advisors. The Arabs, the major population of the Middle East,

[5] *Report of the 46th Annual Conference of the Labour Party* (London, 1947), p. 176.

[6] Quoted in Elizabeth Monroe, "Mr. Bevin's Arab Policy," *St. Antony Papers*, No. 11 (London, 1961), p. 20. Bevin was often as plain and blunt a man as he pretended to be, but on occasion, as here, his language could also be that of a tortuous, blunt man.

[7] *Ibid.*, p. 21.

had been Britain's steadfast friends in both World Wars. After initial disillusionment, they were heartened by the Anglo-Iraqi Treaty (1932) and the Anglo-Egyptian Treaty (1936). Their loyalty in the Second World War confirmed the wise necessity of Britain's Arab policy. This approach was in harmony with the needs of the age. The shreds of tutelage must yield to an approach stressing a mutually beneficent partnership. The days of power politics and spheres of influence were at an end. On the other hand, nations do have special interests in certain areas as, for example, Russia has in her immediate neighbors.[8]

This gently politic embracing of contradiction provides a clue to the dilemmas of British policy. But the most notable feature is that Lord Altrincham was prescribing the mixture as before, that is, the policy of the interwar years freshened with a dash of United Nations rhetoric. Arab nationalists had not been happy either about the Iraqi or Egyptian treaties. At the time of their negotiation, the British position had been accepted because British power was predominant and could serve the interests of ruling Arab groups. After 1945 these conditions had changed. The accumulation of sterling balances in the war years meant that Britain had become a debtor to such states as Egypt and Iraq. British power was in retreat. In India, Burma, and Ceylon, Britain came to terms with Asian nationalism, but in the Middle East Britain could not establish a similar relationship with Arab nationalism. Indeed, from 1948 to 1954, Arab nationalism provided few inducements even for British negotiations, especially after the ejection of France from the Levant and the Arab failure in Palestine made Britain the immediate and available enemy. The Arab governments were readily vulnerable to nationalist agitation and the special positions that Britain sought ran counter to Arab nationalist demands.

There was then a psychological contradiction involved in the British cultivation of Arab good will and the lessons the British drew from wartime experience. The latter confirmed the value of Britain's Middle Eastern alliances, bases, and privileges, the heritage of indirect empire. The contradiction was intensified by the cumulative burden of two conflicts in British Middle Eastern interests too great to resolve. The first involved Britain's mandatory responsibility in Palestine and the starkly divergent views of the Zionists and Arabs. The second was between Britain's expectations of the Arabs and the consequence of the British and Western impact on the Arabs.

[8] Address to the Royal Empire Society, *The Times*, November 15, 1945.

With the bedouin Arabs Britain could establish relations that involved Arab dependence. To the bedouin, British agents could offer some services and military training. For the ruler of Transjordan, Britain could train a well-equipped and disciplined army and provide devoted administrative talent. But the British and Western impact on the Middle East was destroying bedouin life and proliferating banks, bureaucracy, trained military officers with political aspirations, oil fields, refineries, Arab technicians, as well as the transitional figures, partly Arab, partly Western-educated, often disappointed in their quest for preferment, who form so large a part of the nationalist intelligentsia.

The content of their nationalism ranged from Islamic revivalism to European secular nationalism. In religious and cultural reaction against the West, Arabic nationalism often expressed the ambivalence —a ready support of neutralism—of a new nationalism. On the one hand, there is a desire for modernization and Western resources of power and wealth and, on the other hand, the assertion of Arab superiority to the West. Unfortunately, Arab nationalism had no common focus but only common enemies—its former imperial masters, France and Britain, and Zionism. Arab nationalism did not support boundaries and state structures. It sought to wipe out boundaries and merge states in a greater unity. Meanwhile, the existing Arab states, weak and ineffective as they were for the new task of guiding social change, were in their own right assertive enough to prevent the achievement of Arab unity, although Arabism, in turn, weakened the state.

Bevin understood that past British relations with the Arabs had been on a limited basis.[9] The fostering of pan-Arabism might now serve to direct this nationalism. To British officials, and more to those in the Middle East than to ministers, Labour or Conservative, some of whom were well-disposed to the minimum Zionist cause, Arab unity did not signify so shoreless and limitless a thing as Arab nationalism. It meant Arab cooperation in development programs, an Arab version of the Middle East Supply Center, and, in politics, a kind of substitute for Ottoman centralization to maintain the security of the Middle East. Above all, it meant working with an emotion already in existence, held under control by Britain's wartime supremacy but certain to course strongly at the end of the war. Such an approach, it

---

[9] Expressed in reference to Egypt (May 24, 1946), *Weekly Hansard*, Commons, No. 18, cols. 787-789.

was hoped, would persuade the Arabs to think regionally and to look on the special positions sought by Britain not as outraging nationalist sentiment but as contributions of the Arab people to a cooperative venture which also involved defense.

The fostering of Arab unity was probably also intended to make Arab opposition to the Zionists more formidable and, yet, more tractable. But Arab unity soon meant Arab nationalism; and, indeed, the Arab League, originally encouraged by British officials, ultimately served as an Egyptian tool against Britain. The fostering of Arab unity foundered in the Arab-Israeli War. The policy in its beginnings harked back to the days of assured British predominance. Reduced British power, the presence of other powers, and the prospect of being engulfed in great power rivalries meant that there were few Arab leaders willing to come to terms acceptable to Britain, for after 1945 Britain had little to offer the Arabs that could impress the imaginations of nationalist leaders and their mobile followers.

A. PALESTINE, THE ARAB-ISRAELI WAR, AND ISRAEL

Palestine presented Britain with the legacy of the ambiguous Balfour Declaration and of the vague promises to Arab nationalism. Ambiguity is often justly praised as the conscious or even unconscious mark of a statesman who does not insist on fixed moulds for the future. Ambiguity may also mean that a problem is not settled, that time and growth, instead of reducing or obscuring a problem, nourish mightily the conflicting interests and demands that made the problem. The largely unintended ambiguity of the Balfour Declaration is, then, the apparently well-meaning but light-headed ancestor of the present Arab-Israeli problem.

The experience of the Second World War had made the British position in Palestine almost impossible. The attitude of the Arabs both in opposition to Britain and in cooperation with her underscored for most British officials in the Middle East the necessity of maintaining a policy acceptable to the Arabs. A recognition of this reinforced the reluctance of Arab representatives to compromise. The Zionists drew different lessons. The wholesale extermination of European Jewry inspired an intense hope for a Jewish asylum that the Zionists were determined to exploit. In doing so, they effected one of the most extraordinary accomplishments of nationalism, Israel, a

nation-state created by the immigration of a Diaspora and by conquest, sustained in part by the American branch of the Diaspora. In
the war's final period the Zionist leader, Ben-Gurion, fought single-
mindedly to that end. The Zionists, moreover, were no mean realists
about their own capacity or about their ability to use American and
Soviet pressure on Britain for their own ends.

For the new Labour government there was the additional difficulty
that the Labour Party had Jewish pro-Zionist members and had
usually supported the Zionist case, all the more as the prominence
of socialism in Palestine also made the Zionist rather than the Arab
cause more congenial to Labour. In 1939 the Labour Party Conference had called for rescinding the newly issued White Paper policy.
The Labour Party Conference late in 1944 revealed overwhelming
support for a resolution to allow all of Palestine to become a Jewish
homeland. Indeed, the Party called for examining the possibility of
extending the boundaries of Palestine. In 1945 Foreign Secretary
Bevin soon faced the problem and was convinced of its difficulty by
his expert advisors. The gulf between Zionist and Arab demands was
unbridgeable to the ingenuity of British negotiators. The temper of
the Zionists and official American support for their cause ruled out a
solution imposed at the expense of Zionism. The advisors' virtual
unanimity, as well as the vital importance of the Middle East to
British economy, swayed Bevin (and Attlee, who was also Minister of
Defense and had the advice of the War Office), and the remaining
members of the Cabinet were too busy with other matters to provide
effective opposition.

The forces playing upon Britain from the Arabs, the Zionists, and
the friends of the Zionists were such that the problem could not be
solved in terms that would take account of British interests. Theo-
retically, there were three possible solutions: the maintenance of the
Mandate by the British government, but such a course was made increasingly difficult by Zionist challenges, as well as by terrorism, and
ran counter to the government's desire to reduce expenses and military
manpower; the imposition of a solution, a unitary state or a parti-
tioned Palestine, with the help of the United States—which would
not be forthcoming—and so to this course there were the insuperable
objections of Britain's war weariness, and the need for economizing
as well as for maintaining Britain's Arab interests; to give up the
Mandate and return the problem to the United Nations, which, how-

ever, did not then have the will or competence to solve it.[10] A solution involved at the least a very difficult decision and a willingness to
support it with force. As this willingness was excluded on grounds of
British foreign interest as well as on domestic grounds, the British
government eventually excluded the second solution and, less am-
biguously, the first. The third and remaining course was not a peaceful solution. Within limits placed by foreign intervention and United
Nations mediation, it simply allowed the play of local armed forces
to stake out the lines of an armistice.

Zionists had proclaimed that V-E Day would be their D-Day. Even
the moderate Zionists rejected the British White Paper of 1939 as im-
moral and illegal. From this it was, then, necessary to proceed against
British efforts to maintain the White Paper policy. But British officials
agreed that the limitation of immigration into Palestine was the
necessary minimum for peaceful conditions in the Arab world. To
this the Zionist rejoinder was a categorical denial. First, they alleged
that the restriction was a betrayal of the Mandate and the Zionists
asked for their right whatever the cost. They further argued against
pan-Arabism, that the Arab states, except as members of the United
Nations, should have no special voice in a Palestine solution. Finally,
some Zionist apologists urged that Arab opposition was at most the
unworthy voice of the backward Arab elite, fearful of the intrusion of
any progressive force in the Middle East.

Foreign Secretary Bevin was occasionally even audible in his misery
on confronting the Palestine problem, which fell under the jurisdiction of the Colonial Office but profoundly affected Middle Eastern
policy. He readily thought that the Labour Party had been made the
victim of a Zionist confidence game. A Cabinet sub-Committee apparently rejected an earlier Coalition government decision to partition
Palestine, for partition, it was pointed out, would require the use of
force. Soon the rigorous demands of the Zionists and the strong opposition of the Arab leaders assailed Bevin. President Truman wrote
(August 31, 1945) to Attlee asking that 100,000 Jewish refugees from

[10] In mid-1946 Churchill told the Commons that, if the Conservative government had been returned in 1945, he had intended to ask for full American participation in dealing with the Palestine problem. If that were not forthcoming, he
had resolved to hand over the Mandate to the United Nations, for the Zionists'
postwar demands put an unfair and intolerable burden on Britain. *Weekly Hansard, Commons,* August 1, 1946. His statement is confirmed by other indications
of the British wartime position and it points to the steps taken by the Labour
government.

Europe be permitted to enter Palestine. The Colonial Office talked of allowing about 1,500 immigrants a month to Palestine, but the Jewish Agency refused to accept a gesture that only palliated the White Paper restriction on immigration, so hateful to the Zionists.[11]

On November 13, 1945, Bevin announced the results of his early thinking, consultation, and negotiations: a new Inquiry into the Palestine problem to examine conditions in Palestine relevant to Jewish immigration and settlement as well as to consider the condition and the desires of refugee Jews in Europe, and to consult experts and representatives of Arabs and Jews. This, of course, was not a policy but a means of delay. True, the British government needed better information about the temper of Zionist and Arab nationalism. The Inquiry, however, arose not out of awareness of ignorance or thirst for learning, but out of a desire to instruct the American government and people and out of a hope to delay the pangs of decision-making. The important aspect of the Commission of Inquiry is that it was Anglo-American. The association of the United States with the Palestine problem represented, to Bevin, a promising beginning. Bevin, indeed, was so pleased that he rashly added to a questioner: "I will stake my political future on solving this problem, but not in the limited sphere presented to me now." [12]

The Commission had another advantage, apart from that of postponing the immediate pressure for a policy decision. Bevin hoped that the participation of the Americans in the Commission would, also, mean the use by the United States of its influence with the Zionists in favor of practical courses. If a Jewish state could only be established and maintained by force of arms, its success might drive the Arabs to seek assistance from the Soviet Union. Bevin then favored keeping Palestine a unitary state composed of Arab and Jewish parts. Such an arrangement might compel the conflicting parties to cooperate and would make for a more viable Palestine defense organiza-

---

[11] Before mid-October the campaign against the White Paper policy had resulted in intensified illegal immigration and overt raids on a British detention camp. Soon afterwards, Zionist resistance forces were coordinated in attacks on British naval vessels engaged against illegal immigrants and on a railway station as well as oil refineries at Haifa. The objective was to "demonstrate that an anti-Zionist policy, too, will be difficult to apply, and that it will involve a higher cost even than a pro-Zionist policy." The Jerusalem correspondent of the *Zionist Review* quoted by George Kirk in *The Middle East, 1945-1950*, the Royal Institute of International Affairs (New York, 1954), p. 198.

[12] *Parliamentary Debates*, Commons, 5th series, November 13, 1945.

tion as well as for the continued stationing of British forces in Palestine. Bevin looked to a great Arab-Zionist compromise as the solution for Palestine. The expectation was belied at the cost of the dangers foreseen by Bevin and many Middle Eastern diplomats. As Bevin added to the Foreign Office's faith in negotiation the trade unionist's faith in rough but rational bargaining, it may be said that both faiths were found wanting in Palestine.

The creation of the Commission of Inquiry and Bevin's announcement of it to the Commons evoked astonishingly different reactions. Chaim Weizmann saw in it the Labour government's repudiation of its earlier attacks on the White Paper. Churchill's friendliness to Zionism had failed the Jews, and the Labour Party proved even more undependable. Harry Sacher concluded that Bevin was thinking of a Palestine solution without Zionism. Richard Crossman, who served on the Commission, thought then that Bevin, in view of American support for Zionism, must have an open mind on Palestine and must be prepared to deviate from past British policy and in favor of the Zionists.[13]

The Commissioners made a unanimous report in favor of a unitary state (April 30-May 1, 1946) when Bevin was busy with many other matters. At the time, the British government had offered to get out of Egypt. Thus Palestine might have to continue as a base, and in Bevin's mind the Arabs and Zionists would have to recognize that they would have better terms under Britain than under any other arrangement.[14] President Truman, moreover, upset the Inquiry's elaborate compromise by publicly endorsing only its pro-Zionist sec-

[13] Chaim Weizmann, *Trial and Error* (New York, 1949), p. 439; Harry Sacher, *Israel: The Establishment of a State* (London, 1952), p. 51; Richard Crossman, *Palestine Mission* (New York, 1947), p. 14. Elizabeth Monroe, "Mr. Bevin's Arab Policy," *St. Antony Papers*, No. 11 (London, 1961), pp. 9-48, is a valuable account of a story that usually suffers from partisanship in the telling. Her discussion of the charge of anti-Semitism against Bevin is particularly good. Zionist apologists, she argues, have too readily made Bevin's concern with British interests an occasion for charging him with anti-Semitism. When he was made Foreign Secretary, he came to believe that the Zionists had earlier misled the Labour Party. Later he was embittered by the inflexibility of the Zionists who not only compounded his difficulties but were killing British soldiers.

[14] The Commission sought to dispel the Arab-Jewish conflict by recommending as a statement of principle that "Palestine shall be neither a Jewish state nor an Arab state," and that neither community in Palestine shall dominate the other. Further to mitigate the conflict, the Commission recommended that no prospect of immediate self-government should be entertained and that the Mandate should be maintained until the execution of a new trusteeship agreement under the

tions for immediate implementation, for example, the recommendation that 100,000 Jewish refugees be admitted to Palestine. Indeed, as events developed, the Palestine issue was, perhaps, the worst of all possible issues for the British government to use in attempting to associate the United States with Britain in the exploitation of and responsibility for the Middle East.

In spite of Bevin's pledge to implement a unanimous report, Prime Minister Attlee and Secretary Bevin, after submitting the report to their civilian and military advisors, indicated that the report would not be implemented until violence ceased, the Jewish and Arab groups gave up their arms, and the United States was willing to participate in imposing the solution. Richard Crossman, a Labour M.P. who served on the Commission and for a unanimous report had yielded his preference for partition, concluded that the British government should have implemented the Commission's recommendations. Instead, he argued, the government abandoned principle for expediency under the pretense that it had to consider repercussions in the Arab world. In a very pro-Zionist book Harry Sacher expressed the belief that a wholehearted and fair-minded imposition of the Commission's report would have removed the dynamism from the extremist Jewish groups.[15]

Later, the British government briefly had the prospect of association with the United States in considering a version of a wartime project to provide for extensive local autonomy to Jewish and Arab provinces in Palestine (the Morrison-Grady plan). This project was considered as a means of implementing the Anglo-American Commission's Report. But the prospect, made possible by the State and Defense Departments' influence, soon vanished in the fall Congressional electioneering. By this time the palpable delaying tactics of the Labour government, faced as it was by Soviet influence in Iran and difficulties in Egypt, had encountered Zionist terrorism and, at home, bitter criticism from the Conservative opposition. Thus, the Labour gov-

United Nations. An abbreviated version of the "Report of the Anglo-American Committee of Inquiry," is in *Decade of American Foreign Policy, 1941-1949,* Senate Document 123, 81st Congress, 1st Session (Washington, 1950), p. 813.

In the immediately succeeding months the British government did not act vigorously in the matter of Palestine. There was, here, an element of overconfidence to which Miss Monroe refers in connection with Egypt. "The effect of British over-confidence in British powers in May 1946 was to allow initiative to pass to those who knew their minds. From then on, all other British proposals were doomed." Monroe, *op. cit.,* p. 29.

[15] Sacher, *Israel: The Establishment of a State,* p. 189.

ernment felt impelled to impose severe countermeasures in Palestine.

As the difficult winter of 1946-1947 added to Britain's economic difficulties and compounded foreign policy problems, Secretary Bevin moved from a grimly studied optimism about the international scene to an urgent, almost desperate, firmness. On Palestine (February 7, 1947) he made a final offer to Arabs and Jews alike. Britain's authority should be used for the preparation of Palestine for self-government. In the meantime Arab and Jewish areas were to have an increasing share of local government, and a serious concession was made in respect to Jewish immigration. But Arab and Jewish representatives concurred in rejecting the proposal.

Harassed by Zionist terrorism in Palestine—which could only have been checked by repressive policies that probably would have been distasteful to the British electorate and would have alienated the United States—the British government announced (February 14, 1947) its decision to consult the United Nations about the Mandate. On September 26, 1947, the British Colonial Secretary informed the United Nations that if no settlement commanding Jewish and Arab agreement was forthcoming, British forces would withdraw from the Mandate. In its first decision the British government apparently expected that there might be another delay and possibly an invitation to prolong its stay in Palestine, with renewed authority. The United Nations appointed its own commission, which made its solemn recommendations about partition. But the United Nations evoked neither the willingness nor the force to impose its solution, and this had been the crux of the matter from the beginning. The Soviet Union supported any measure including partition that would mean the British departure from Palestine. The United States government also favored partition, though with expressions of regret about the unwillingness of the British government to use its forces to prevent an experiment in anarchy. Britain had resolved to leave Palestine, and, indeed, at that time in 1947, the British Middle Eastern base would be the Suez Canal Zone with a port in Kenya serving as a storage point. By late January 1948, the American State and Defense Departments were arguing that partition was unworkable—in the light of American interests in the Middle East.[16] To cite a final example of wavering,

[16] Walter Millis (ed.), *The Forrestal Diaries*, pp. 360, 411. The British arguments in the United Nations are presented in *The Yearbook of the United Nations, 1947-1948* (Lake Success, 1949), pp. 231-232, 239, 404, 409, 421-422, 425, 446, 449-450.

American Senator Warren Austin proposed (March 19, 1948) to the Security Council a temporary trusteeship over Palestine and upon its rejection by Zionist authorities called for the arrangement of a Palestine truce by the Security Council as well as for a session of the General Assembly. The final British withdrawal from the Mandate had been preceded by overt British military action against Jewish forces,[17] avowedly to permit their own withdrawal unscathed. The departure was followed by the proclamation of the State of Israel (May 14, 1948), which was instantly recognized by the United States and followed by the Arab attack on Israel. The United Nations, which had been unable to solve the issue, succeeded in halting the fighting only after months of intermittent fighting and Arab defeat. It was able to effect an armistice only after the combatants had tested each other's strength and a refugee problem of monumental proportions had been created.

British policy, until the decision to withdraw, had sought to discharge the Mandate by seeking the agreement of the immediately interested parties, by recognizing the Mandatory's international responsibilities, and, thus, the desirability of consulting other powers and the United Nations as the successor to the League. To serve British interests, in the light of Britain's own difficulties over Palestine and the Middle East, Britain also sought to associate the United States with her position in the Middle East. Anglo-American divergence was sharp after the decision to abrogate the Mandate was taken. The policy of the United States supported Israel without taking account of the wider regional picture. Britain, more mindful of this, based its policy on the expectation of an Arab victory. And this expectation looked to a victory of general Arab forces. Thus, the British government did not expect that Abdullah of Transjordan would be the major victor.

The establishment of Israel fomented a major tension in the Middle East. Its establishment was the result of the terms in which Britain saw her Middle Eastern position. These terms involved a number of miscalculations: about the temper of postwar Zionism; about the temper of the Arabs who, in effect, were encouraged in a wholly unconstructive opposition by British unwillingness to antagonize them; and about the destructive interplay of American and Soviet influence.

[17] Netanel Lorch, *The Edge of the Sword: Israel's War of Independence, 1947-1949* (New York, 1961), p. 110.

But the British departed with astonishing steadiness, still not realizing
Arab weakness. In admitting new waves of immigrants, the new state
roused Arab fears of further Zionist expansion. The Arab refugees,
supported by Western contributions to the United Nations, were
meanwhile neglected by their Arab brothers so that they could remain as testimony of the wrongs suffered by the Arabs. The failure
of the Arab military effort against the Zionists was a real failure of
pan-Arabism, for the lack of military coordination and the rash pre-
cipitating of unprepared or ill-equipped armies into battle were only
too expressive of Arabism's weakness, a weakness that took the form
of quick enthusiasm for grandiose projects, unsupported by the cold
appraisal of realism. Eventually, Britain and, more justly, the United
States were blamed for the Zionist victory in Palestine. Between 1948
and 1952 Britain found difficulty in attempts to conduct serious negotiations with the representatives of Middle Eastern states, who,
with good reason, feared that the expression of willingness to negotiate
might be the signal for assassination.

The Arab criticism of Britain is noteworthy because there had been
sharp American criticism of British aid to the Arabs, including arms
deliveries and the presence of British officers in Jordan's Arab Legion
that had occupied the land assigned to the Arabs by the United
Nations Partition decision and had laid siege to Jerusalem. In Britain,
there was a growing resentment of American opposition to Britain's
course in the Middle East. The failure of Anglo-American coordination in Palestine sparked the beginnings of crisis between the two
countries. But Anglo-American amity was soon restored by a greater
common danger, the critical situation created by the Soviet blockade
of Berlin.

For British policy in the Middle East the establishment of Israel
meant two things. The first, partly expressed in the Arab charge of
British responsibility for Israel, was that Arab opposition to Britain
was intensified either because the charge was believed or because the
British government had not been powerful or decisive enough to
effect a solution favorable to the Arabs. True, the establishment of
Israel was interpreted by the Arabs as the creation of a permanent
threat to themselves, and their apprehension made them on occasion
willing to look for British aid against Israel. But, and this is the
second consequence, Britain no longer could hope for anything from
the pan-Arab movement. For the future Britain was no longer con-

cerned to promote Arab unity, although the cause received verbal
obeisance in projects for regional defense. At best, British interests
had to be pursued entirely in diplomatic relations with individual
Arab states.

Foreign Secretary Bevin signalized a turn of British policy after the
Israelis (January 1949) shot down four British Spitfires from the
Canal Zone on reconnaissance over the Egyptian-Israeli battlefield.
The British government's attempts to support Egypt against renewed
attack in the period after the rupture of the Second Truce and to
compel Israel to accept a cease-fire and an armistice had led the government to a clumsy position. It had threatened invoking the Anglo-
Egyptian treaty of 1936 against Israel. Earlier, however, the Egyptian
government had argued before the Security Council that the Treaty
was invalid. British aid under the Treaty was among the last things
Egypt wanted. Britain recognized Israel *de facto* on January 29, 1949.

After the signing of the armistice, the Security Council (August 4,
1949) ruled that an embargo on arms to Middle Eastern states was
no longer justified. Nevertheless, American voices joined Israeli criticism of the prospect of the Arab states receiving British arms under
the terms of their treaties with Britain. Finally, on May 25, 1950, the
United States, France, and Britain published a new statement of
Middle Eastern policy. It represented an ingenious and apparently
cheap means of jointly promoting their somewhat diverse interests in
the Middle East. The three powers declared against a Middle Eastern
arms race and expressed their determination to consider any Middle
Eastern requests for arms in terms of each country's requirements for
defense and, echoing the standard British position, the defense needs
of the whole region. The signatories, in professing their concern with
the area's stability, also declared their readiness to take measures both
within and outside the United Nations against Middle Eastern states
that violated frontiers or armistice lines.

This policy represented an attempt to maintain the *status quo* created by that much mediated arbitrament of arms, the Arab-Israeli
War, all the more as it appeared likely that for a long time only
armistices, not treaties, would at best mark the end of that war. The
effectiveness of the policy depended on two conditions that turned
out to be decidedly impermanent: the determination of the three
powers to work closely together and Western retention of a monopoly
as arms supplier to the Middle East.

B. JORDAN

In the Palestine fighting, Transjordan's performance appeared to justify Britain's Jordanian policy. But the success of the Arab Legion in gaining the West Bank (Arab Palestine) eventually helped to destroy the Jordanian base of British power. Thereafter, Britain found that the country served only as an increasingly uneasy *point d'appui* in the Middle East.

The establishment of Transjordan, which Arabs and especially Zionists often described as a masterpiece of British calculation and planning, was a work of improvisation. Hussain's son, Abdullah, had been acclaimed King of Iraq by a number of Arab leaders. The British government, however, was more concerned about Abdullah's brother, Faisal, whom the French had ejected from Syria. Abdullah headed north from the Hejaz with a force proclaimed to be directed against the French in Syria. On his march, January 1921, he entered the Transjordanian city of Amman where he was greeted with light-hearted realism by the British representative.[18] Meanwhile, the Cairo Conference faced this new development in the light of the British government's desire to reduce expenses and commitments. The British officials at Cairo did not want to see any advance of French troops to Amman and were unwilling to dispatch British forces against Abdullah. So, Abdullah's *fait accompli* was accepted on condition that he refrain from menacing Syria. Abdullah was to rule in the territory east of the Jordan River, and the Palestine Mandate was drafted to exempt Transjordan from some of the provisions that were to apply to Palestine west of the Jordan. Though Abdullah was promised eventual independence even in the agreement of 1928, which regulated British relations with Transjordan until 1946, the administration of the area was supervised by British officials and its foreign relations were carried on through the British Resident, as indeed the responsibilities of the Mandate required. The annual budget law of Transjordan had to be submitted to the advice of the British government, which also was permitted to station and raise troops in the country. On its part the British government provided an annual grant-in-aid, which rose rapidly from £84,000 (Palestine pounds) in 1930-1931 to £404,005 (Palestine pounds) in 1938-1939.[19]

[18] Sir Alec Kirkbride, *A Crackle of Thorns* (London, 1956); Benjamin Shwadran, *Jordan: A State of Tension* (New York, 1959), pp. 129-144.
[19] Shwadran, *Jordan: A State of Tension*, pp. 164, 188.

Until the Second World War, then, Transjordan provided the British government with bases in the Middle East and with a point of leverage to be used against the Zionists in Palestine as well as —more as a consequence than a purpose—to add to the division of Arab ranks. While Transjordan played a small role in the war, it aspired to a large role in postwar plans. Abdullah remained an apt pupil of his British advisors in opting for realistic policies. But he, too, had a dream of Arab unity, the Greater Syria Plan. Abdullah looked to the establishment of himself in Syria and the addition of Lebanon, Palestine, and eventually Iraq to this base. When, during the war years, Britain fostered the policy of Arab unity, Abdullah pressed hard for Transjordanian independence as well as for the fulfillment of the Greater Syria Plan.[20]

Wider British interests prevented the British government from supporting his plan, and Abdullah's land actually remained under the mandatory supervision until 1946. Inevitably, the Arab League was formed on lines determined by the larger and independent Arab states.

On March 22, 1946, Britain and Transjordan signed a treaty which recognized Abdullah as an independent sovereign. The treaty and its annex—in line with Britain's policy of securing her former positions by such arrangements—provided for cooperation in mutual defense against armed attack or the likelihood of hostilities as well as for the stationing of British troops in Transjordan with the privilege of extraterritoriality and the placing of British officers for training Abdullah's British-subsidized army.[21] These provisions provided Egyptian political leaders with a ready pretext for questioning the reality of Transjordanian independence. Their attacks were also repeated by Soviet spokesmen in the United Nations, to which Jordan was not admitted at the time. On March 15, 1948, as part of the British design of negotiating treaties with most of the Arab states as a provision in

[20] Abdullah, in effect, sought to take over *the succession* in Syria, the position held by his brother Faisal before the French ejected him. But the union of the Syrian area around a Hashemite ruler had no attraction for modern Arab nationalists who had little interest in patriarchal rulers, and the project was attacked with equal vigor by the rulers of rival Arab states, notably Egypt and Saudi Arabia. John Marlowe, *The Seat of Pilate* (London, 1959), pp. 220-223. See *Memoirs of King Abdullah of Transjordan* (New York, 1950), pp. 254-259, 262-269; for the limits on the usefulness of this work caused by the translator's deletions see H. W. Glidden's review in *The Middle East Journal*, V (1951), 251-252.

[21] The British subsidy rose to £2,000,000, then to £9,000,000 and beyond.

behalf of regional defense, a new treaty[22] was negotiated. Its phrasing allowed more for the susceptibilities of independent Transjordanians and of world opinion but preserved the special British position.[23]

Abdullah's mistrust of the willingness of Arabs to support their rhetorical ambitions was amply justified by his experience of joint Arab efforts to prepare resistance against Israel. Earlier, the influence of the Mufti of Jerusalem was opposed to Abdullah as, in some measure, was the Palestine Arab Higher Committee. The Council of the Arab League, on behalf of its members, resolved (February 9, 1948) to oppose the establishment of a Jewish state. In a kind of travesty of the American government's attitude towards political decisions taken during the European fighting in 1944-1945, the League called upon its members to send their armies to Palestine to forestall Zionism and at the same time to refrain from claiming territory occupied by their forces.[24]

Here Abdullah had a number of advantages. First of all, his territory adjoined Palestine, his Arab Legion had had some fighting experience and, indeed, had been engaged in patrols in Palestine itself. Secondly, as a long-term critic of Arab unrealism and irresponsibility, he had learned to moderate and limit his ambitions, though not his tongue and pen. His moderation won for him the enmity of many Arab leaders, the Zionists' offer of negotiations and bargains, and finally British support as the chief Arab beneficiary of the imminent *de facto* partition of Palestine. The Arab Legion and Iraqi troops oc-

[22] United Kingdom, Treaty Series No. 26 (1948), Cmd. 7404.

[23] For example an annex provided that as long as world security required such measures, Abdullah would invite Britain to place air force units at Amman and Mafrak. British forces were not to enjoy extra-territoriality and there was no provision for stationing British troops in Transjordan during times of peace. British diplomats called the treaty the "New Look Treaty." *The Economist*, Vol. 154, March 28, 1948, 449. The clause dealing with mutual defense proved to be embarrassing during the Palestine War and in 1956: "In the event of either High Contracting Party becoming engaged in war or the menace of hostilities each High Contracting Party will invite the other to bring . . . to territory controlled by him the necessary forces of all arms."

[24] In a meeting at Aley in Lebanon, October 1947, the Arab League resolved to have its members invade Palestine if the United Nations approved a proposal to partition Palestine. The Egyptian Prime Minister, Al-Nokrashy, was very dubious of the prospects of Arab victory and saw that at best only Abdullah, to whom Egypt was hostile, would be the beneficiary. Marlowe, *The Seat of Pilate*, pp. 234-235. In a personal note George Kirk has indicated that Nokrashy's views as reported smack of hindsight. If he held such views, why then did Nokrashy hold on to office until his murder in December 1948?

cupied West Bank Jordan, a move which had the full support of Bevin and the British government, and Egyptian troops occupied Southern Palestine. After the failure of Brigadier Clayton of the Middle East Office to secure a unified approach at the Cairo Arab League meeting, the British government sought in Abdullah some hope of calculation and realism in a war that was less a "proof of Arab unity than an attempt to manufacture it." [25]

The West Bank of Jordan was his to administer and Abdullah took it. Although it may be conceded that his annexation of Arab Palestine made desirable the extension of Transjordanian citizenship to all Palestinian Arabs, Abdullah, nevertheless, was the only Arab leader to show hospitality and generosity to the Arab refugees. Arab nationalists elsewhere continued to pillory Abdullah for his realism, which they equated with treachery, for his association with Britain and for his annexation of Palestine. Later, Abdullah appointed a successor to the Mufti who in characteristic fashion continued to attack the annexation of the West Bank as the equivalent of the partition of Palestine between Arabs and Jews. In 1949 Britain officially recognized King Abdullah's state under its new name of the Hashemite Kingdom of Jordan, which Abdullah had actually adopted after the 1946 treaty. The enlargement was soon marked by new elections and governmental rearrangements to strengthen the constitutionalism of the new state. The Jordanian legislature, April 24, 1950, decided in favor of the unification of the West Bank and Jordan. This had been preceded by Jordanian negotiations with Israel, which had no formal result. Jordan yielded to Arab League criticism to the point of proclaiming opposition to a separate peace with Israel, but on May 15, 1950, the Political Committee of the League found that Jordan's annexation of the West Bank violated the League's resolution of April 12, 1950, against a separate peace with Israel, though no sanctions were ultimately imposed. For its part the British government on April 27, 1950, accorded *de jure* recognition to newly aggrandized Jordan and significantly indicated that the mutual defense treaty of 1948 applied to it.[26]

But, in so expanding, Abdullah had, fatally for himself, transformed his kingdom. Earlier, his subjects had mainly been an illiterate or

[25] Esmond Wright, "Abdullah's Jordan: 1947-1951," *Middle East Journal*, V (1951), 447.

[26] *Parliamentary Debates*, Commons, 5th series, Vol. 474, cols. 1137-1139, April 27, 1950.

backward people over whom he ruled sometimes quite arbitrarily and often against British recommendations. The doubling of the number of his subjects by incorporating the Arab people of Palestine, of whom the urban element was educated, strongly anti-British, aggressively political, zealous, even fanatical against Israel, added skills and economic promise to his kingdom at the cost of political instability. The new subjects were of uncertain loyalty at best, and the newly liberalized kingdom soon faced the ordeal of press censorship, bitter criticism of the connection with Britain, and a struggle over the budget. On July 20, 1951, Abdullah was assassinated by an agent of the ex-Mufti of Jerusalem while on a prayer visit to Al-Aqsa mosque in Jerusalem, the third most sacred shrine of Sunni Islam. His death removed Britain's most promising Arab pupil and left the unstable realm to a successor of unstable mind. At one time this weakness might have been reassuring to Britain, for it would have meant that the rulers of Jordan could not seriously challenge her. Jordan's weakness, however, was to make her vulnerable to many Arab pressures, and in responding to them the Jordanian king, Hussain, was to discover that his principal basis of survival was the fear entertained by his self-appointed heirs and others, a fear of the struggle that would follow the death of his realm.

C. IRAQ

The weakness and backwardness of Jordan made the connection with Britain advantageous. The benefit to Jordan appeared also in the annexation of the Jordan West Bank, which, however, enormously increased the sources of turbulence and opposition to the government. Iraq presented a different experience. There, the advantages of the British connection were recognized by some leading politicians. These leading political figures were often able to command the influence and pressure of the government to secure a majority in the legislature or, at any rate, to permit their continuance in power. Usually outside their ranks were the leaders of political parties, engaged primarily in a struggle for power and inevitably conducting it with the irresponsibility of outsiders. Both the leading political figures and their rivals formed a small body which attempted to use Iraqi nationalism to secure concessions from Britain, to win the support of town populations, and to turn the latter against their rivals. In attempting to

render the British position in Iraq more acceptable to Iraqi nationalism, the British government made many concessions. When the effort
appeared to be on the rim of success, rioting in Baghdad destroyed the
fruit of long negotiations.

Censorship and strict regulation of political activities were only
slowly relaxed after the war. The reaction against Britain's wartime
influence and the shortages and inflation imputed to Britain's responsibility added strength to the nationalist demand that Iraq be accorded full sovereignty and equality. Now this very demand, vague
enough in positive significance but with a versatile range of negations,
ran counter to the interests which Britain sought to protect.

The interests were: the oil fields and pipelines of the Iraq Petroleum
Company; the security provided for them by the special predominance of British advisors in Iraq; the security provided for the oil
and for Iraq and regional defense by the bases and military privileges
held by Britain under the Treaty of 1930. As the Cold War developed,
the British position in Iraq afforded the possibility of conveying British help to Turkey against the Soviet Union. The nationalist temper,
for its part, recognized the Cold War not as a threat but as an opportunity for Iraq. To be independent, Iraq had to be free of the special
relationship with Britain, all the more because that relationship might
mean involvement in rivalry with the Soviet Union. Independence
encompassed more than politics. It could also mean the reduction of
Britain's control of Iraqi oil. A basic difficulty with this attitude is
that it readily rejected concessions that involved substantial practical
gains.

When limited political activity was permitted in Iraq, political controversy became quite bitter. The bitterness derived in some measure
from the permanent split after 1941 between the Regent's supporters
and those of Rashid Ali. After 1945 the latter groups were prepared
to make common cause with the communists. Further, the decision
to withdraw from the Palestine Mandate exacerbated Iraqi opinion
against a Britain unable to fulfill the implications of her professed
friendship with the Arabs.

Nevertheless, Foreign Secretary Bevin pursued his policy of seeking
Arab friendship.[27] In the postwar years oil royalties were increased

[27] The Middle Eastern articles of a number of pro-Zionist journalists have the
objective of emphasizing Arab perfidy and ingratitude in order to raise questions
about the usefulness of the British policy of seeking Arab friendship. Jon Kimche's
writings, 1948-1952, which I have found useful, are a good example.

and, compared to Egypt, Iraq was treated very generously in the release of sterling balances.

Late in 1947 negotiations were begun to revise the Treaty of 1930, so that it would appear as an agreement between equals.[28] As completed, it provided for an alliance of Britain and Iraq which pledged both parties not to follow a foreign policy inconsistent with the alliance.[29] As in the 1948 treaty with Jordan and an offer made to Egypt in 1946, defense matters were to be the concern not of a dominant Britain but of a joint Anglo-Iraqi Defense Board. Here, as in the other cases, Britain sought to promote a mutual participation of Britain and Iraq in the regional defense of the Arab world. The pretense was delicate, even generous, but inefficacious. The military power of Britain, after all, made the Treaty unequal, even though Iraq defied the power—but to achieve equality in this sense all states may have to be rendered small. Iraq permitted the Royal Air Force to maintain two bases in operational readiness and was prepared to invite British forces for joint efforts against an impending threat. In the treaty Britain waived her extra-territorial privileges and yielded her share in the control of Iraqi railways and of the Port of Basra.

The Treaty, signed at Portsmouth on January 15, 1948, was regarded by Bevin as a model for other arrangements in the Middle East. *The Economist* described it as "a first step to putting Britain's Middle East relationships on a postwar footing," and found particular satisfaction in that the Treaty was the product of Iraqi initiative.[30] The Treaty was based on calculations of mutual interest. For

[28] On postwar Iraq and the Iraqi-British negotiations see Stephen H. Longrigg, *Iraq: 1900 to 1950* (New York, 1953), pp. 334-351; Majid Khadduri, *Independent Iraq: 1932-1958* (2nd ed., New York, 1960), pp. 259-278.

[29] The members of the Arab League increasingly regarded the special relationship of Britain and Iraq as inconsistent with the pan-Arabism of the League. The conception of independence, as held by former colonial people, has had a dynamic that has finally given to independence the meaning of excluding special privileges for the former colonial power. Recently this view was strikingly expressed by President Modibo Keita of Mali. In a discussion following his speech at Chatham House (June 7, 1961), his views were summarized: "The Republic of Mali demanded the evacuation of French bases on her territory not as an unfriendly act but as a logical consequence of her independent status, since such bases could have been allowed between equal Powers but not between an ex-colony and a colonial Power." "The Foreign Policy of Mali," *International Affairs*, XXXVII (October 1961), 438-439.

[30] *The Economist*, Vol. 154, January 17, 1948, 89, added the observation that revealed the dilemma of the British position. Mutual good will and interest are more important than documents, even treaties. "British relations with the Middle

twenty years Iraq would receive British protection against a possible Soviet threat in the Middle East; continued military assistance and training; British technical assistance; and, in addition, oil revenues and the economic development that the oil royalties made possible, for example, in expanding irrigation facilities. In return, the vital British interests in Iraqi oil and friendly association with the Arab states seemed to be assured. Unfortunately, the pro-Treaty Iraqi politicians and the British advisors on Arab affairs either failed to assess the temper of Iraq or thought that the proposed Treaty would have magic effects. The criticisms of Iraqi Nationalists presented pictures of British controls and cunning in dealing with Iraqi puppet politicians that are in striking contrast with the actual intentions and, for that matter, the ability of British representatives. But the British government's advisors appear to have believed that the Iraqi government could command the acceptance of the Treaty by the Iraqi public.

Similar misreadings, appearing in connection with Iran and Egypt, suggest that the many preoccupations of the British Foreign Secretary prevented him from a searching consideration of Middle Eastern problems and left him content with the advice of a small group who maintained but limited contact with a small circle of the Arab world. Bevin was munificent with what he could offer and, admittedly, to do something seemed imperative. But, as the conditions were not propitious, his generous offer was, in effect, wasted. Secretary Bevin could not be master in determining the timing of his gestures, but he had some latitude and had earlier shown a keen appreciation of the importance of timing.

The signing of the Treaty was followed by rioting in Baghdad. Even before the Iraqi Premier, Salih Jahr, returned to his country, the pro-British Regent, who had previously supported the Treaty, bowed before the storm of nationalist and communist opposition. In session with Cabinet members, political leaders, and legislators, he and they decided that as the Treaty did not fulfill Iraq's national

---

East have just so much stability as the regimes which sustain them." Nationalist criticism of the arrangement had already appeared and was natural enough, as Britain was the paramount power. It need cause no alarm—and here the confidence is very puzzling—"provided the fact is kept constantly in view that Britain has direct responsibility for the security, social advancement, and prosperity of the peoples of the Middle East." This is to be reassured by the very heart of the problem. Perhaps the pretence of omniscience, the special temptation of writers for weekly journals—here I do not mean to repine at the nature of things—inspired this statement of a problem as a source of reassurance.

aspirations, it should not be ratified. The very unpopular Premier was at fault in that he failed to explain the Treaty and arrange for its defense. In itself, this should have warned British officials, for the Premier in effect left matters to unofficial reports and creative rumors. The Palestine situation was sharpening Arab nationalism against Britain. The city mobs had a special grievance in that a failure of the wheat crop had resulted in serious bread shortages. Against continued rioting there was little hope of using the army, in which nationalism was strong. Political leaders found it more profitable not to support the police but to use the violence to seek political advancement. In this incident appears a dilemma of Iraq and of some other Middle Eastern states: opportunists and communists can bring down a moderate government but can not form a stable government.[31]

The nationalist victory in causing the Treaty to be scrapped has its instructive side. As the new arrangement had not been ratified, the Treaty of 1930 prevailed. In turn, this was even less acceptable, but it had been ratified and was to last until 1957. The Israeli triumph contributed to moderating Iraqi turmoil for a time. Nuri-es-Said, Premier of Iraq fourteen times, became Premier and pursued his policy of promoting British-Iraqi cooperation. Of the First World War generation, like King Abdullah, Nuri believed that Iraqi security and prosperity required the alliance with Britain. Cooperation would, in time, he believed, mean the realization of the Iraqi nationalist cause. His deftness in barring rivals (including young rivals) from power won him enemies who joined the chorus that proclaimed his favor to the West as a betrayal of Arabism to imperialism.

D. IRAN

The Repulse of the First Soviet Challenge

The presence of American, Soviet, and British forces in Iran and the immediate aftermath of the war strengthened the desire of Iranian politicians to seek untrammeled independence and to fulfill their national causes by exploiting the rivalries of the great powers. In the war years Britain had looked on Southern Iran as a sphere of special interest and responsibility. The Soviet Union with forces in Northern Iran sought to extend its influence there in what appeared to be a resumption of the Russian drive to the Persian Gulf.

Before the war's end the Soviet Union had unsuccessfully bid for

[31] Khadduri, *op. cit.*

oil concessions. Afterwards, it sought to use popular dissatisfaction with the repressiveness of the central government, Kurdish nationalism (in Mahadabad), and Azerbaijani Turkish and Turcoman localism to create local governments under Soviet control and the protection of the Soviet Army. Soviet representatives had rebuffed British and American suggestions for the evacuation of foreign troops from Iran prior to the date provided in the Teheran agreement. Then the Soviet forces failed to evacuate Iran in March 1946, as they had pledged. At first, the Soviet intention was apparently limited to using local positions to create a more favorable national government. Later, however, the Soviet policy effectively meant the disruption of Iran. Thus, though the Soviet Union had appealed to those interested in local autonomy and social change, it had also left itself open to charges of creating a threat to peace. These charges were laid before the first general meeting of the United Nations Security Council and Assembly.

The early withdrawal of American forces from Iran had, perhaps, invited the Soviet action and, at any rate, left the British solitary and exposed. Foreign Secretary Bevin, feeling a little like Noah in the later days of the Flood, faced this Soviet challenge with repressed anger. He recognized that the British position in Iran had to be maintained and that the Soviet expansionist attempt had to be checked. The consequences of determined resistance seemed to be almost as dangerous as failure to check the Soviet effort would have been disastrous. By various proposals he essayed delay but in spite of his misgivings and those of the American Secretary of State, James Byrnes, the Soviet action in Iran was placed before the first session of the United Nations Security Council.

The ball, then, was taken by the new Iranian Premier, the aged and wily Qavam-es-Sultanah. Using American and United Nations' pressure for all they were worth, he secured a bargain with the Soviet Union. Under its terms the Soviet troops were evacuated and Azerbaijan was recognized by the Soviet Union as an internal affair of Iran which, in turn, pledged benevolence to the province. The issue to which the Soviet Union subordinated other interests was the agreement that a proposal for a joint but Russian-dominated oil company and concession in Northern Iran would soon be submitted to the Majlis. In this Soviet withdrawal American opposition in the United Nations to Soviet policy and American support of the Iranian government had played a significant, perhaps, a decisive part.

Later, in August 1946, three members of the Tudeh Party (the masses), in which communist direction had by late 1944 become paramount, were included in Qavam's government. The same summer saw the play of the other aspect of Soviet Iranian policy: support of attempts to weaken the British position there and an effort to secure a friendly Iranian government. After securing the promise of an Iranian oil concession, communists were prominent in a bitter strike in the Anglo-Iranian oil fields. The British government was so disturbed that it dispatched troops from India to Basra in Iraq, from where they could readily go into action in the area around Abadan. In September, an anti-Tudeh tribal revolt in Southern Iran demanded a change in the Iranian government.[32]

Qavam yielded to the demands. In this turning against the Soviet Union, the new American Ambassador in Teheran, George V. Allen, added notably to the stiffening of Iranian resistance and, indeed, was a portent of the later vigor of American policy elsewhere. In the last months of 1946 Persian government forces entered Azerbaijan and inflicted heavy punishment on those who had lent themselves to the Soviet attempt to dismember Iran.

American support also encouraged the Iranian Majlis to reject the Soviet-Iranian oil concession (October 22, 1947).[33] The British government showed some hesitation about the utter exclusion of the Soviet Union from the further exploitation of Iranian oil.[34] The hesitation was grounded in the fear that Britain would be left as the sole target of Iranian nationalism, which might then seek to use the United States against the British position, a course sure to have communist support. The fear appeared to be confirmed in the jubilant

[32] Sir Reader Bullard, as previously mentioned, has stated that the British government, in its desire to see the Iranian government strengthened, had resolved to refrain from using the tribes against the government. In view of the seriousness of the situation in the oil fields, the British government was as unlikely to be doctrinaire about this new policy as the United States was concerning Soviet missiles in Cuba. The tribes regularly received a subsidy from the Anglo-Iranian Oil Company. George Lenczowski, Russia and the West in Iran, 1918-1948 (Ithaca, 1949), pp. 304-306, implied that he believed the tribal rebellion was British-supported.

[33] Ambassador Allen had publicly expressed support for the project of sending Iranian troops to Azerbaijan to supervise elections there. On September 11, 1947, he indicated that an Iranian refusal to ratify the Soviet oil concession would meet with American understanding and support.

[34] Note presented by the British Ambassador in Teheran to the Iranian Premier as reported in The Times, September 15, 1947.

terms of the law of the Majlis (October 22, 1947) which nullified the Soviet concession. Its final paragraph, following earlier ones that claimed Iranian oil for Iranian exploitation and forbade oil grants to foreigners, required the Iranian government to enter negotiations to regain the nation's rights where—as in the south—they had been impaired and to inform the Majlis of the result.[35]

THE BACKGROUND OF THE NATIONALIZATION DISPUTE

In formulating a policy for Iran, the British and, later, the American governments responded ineffectively, though in different ways, to the difficulties presented by the Iranian government and society. The society was primarily agricultural and traditionalist. The cultivator of the soil rarely owned the land which, indeed, was mainly held by large landlords who were the dominant forces in local politics and the national legislature. The tension that would in any case have characterized the relationship between landlord and cultivator was greatly heightened by the belief growing among the peasants that a change in their condition was possible and by the corresponding fears of the landowners. Soviet agents sought to exploit this tension; and the Shah himself, seeking to follow a reformist constitutional policy, urged agrarian reform and, on his own estates, later attempted to give a model of such reform. In his early reformism, however, he was not vigorous and in Iranian fashion was not taken very seriously.

The Iranian government, moreover, was not a satisfactory instrument of reform. Dominated as it was by landowners and officials on the make, it suffered from serious inefficiency as well as from the ineffectiveness resulting from the opposition of its agents to reform or even administration for national ends, or from their disbelief in such means and ends. The civil service was overgrown and in eighteenth-century fashion provided sinecures and a form of welfare state for the families of politicians. Two qualities distinguished it: inertness and a capacity to absorb money. Thus corruption flourished on a scale that ranged from the discouraging to the epic.

In the government of such a society the cities played an unusually

[35] The text is in Benjamin Shwadran, *The Middle East, Oil and the Great Powers* (New York, 1955), pp. 80-81. For the postwar events in Iran see John Marlowe, *The Persian Gulf in the Twentieth Century* (New York, 1962), pp. 141-152; Lenczowski, *Russia and the West in Iran*, pp. 284-315; George Kirk, *The Middle East, 1945-1950*, Royal Institute of International Affairs, Survey of International Affairs (New York, 1954), pp. 56-93.

prominent role, for they contained the levers of power and administration that not infrequently supported the frailty of authority. The
cities were the sites of universities and schools, of military establishments, and the scenes of work of professional people. But they were
also the centers of a beginning industry, including a number of state
enterprises, the heritage of the nationalist economy of the Shah's father.[36] The cities' complex life embraced traditional industries, markets, and handicrafts. It also included relationships of worker and
employer and trade unions that lent themselves to the Marxist slogans
of class struggle.

Nationalism, partly Western but resting on a consciousness of a
long and distinct Persian history, had stirred all groups, notably those
in the cities. As a phenomenon of the elite in the cities and country,
it was directed against the most prominent influence, the British,
which included the Imperial Bank of Iran, and the oil fields, so re-
mote from Teheran that politicians knew very little about them. But
aware of their own ineffectiveness and weakness, the politicians of
Iranian nationalism looked to use the rivalries of foreign powers for
the fulfillment of their ends.[37] The Soviet challenge to Iran had not
fostered united Iranian resistance. In part, this may be explained by
the accord between Iranian leftist extremism and Soviet agents.[38]

[36] Amin Banani, *The Modernization of Iran* (Stanford, 1961).

[37] Many Middle Easterners had looked to a German victory in the Second World
War, and with them the German defeat tended to increase the stock of the Soviet
Union. An Iranian Cabinet minister once asked a newspaper proprietor in Iran
why the latter did not attack the Russians as harshly as he did the British.
"What?" said the Persian, "attack the Russians? Why, they kidnap people." In
such circumstances an attack may be considered as an unhelpful compliment. See
Bullard, *op. cit.*, p. 229. Bullard, *op. cit.*, p. 222, considered Iranian patience with
the dangerously strong Hitler, for example, as "a wish fulfillment of a people who
for a very long time had been weak and helpless."

[38] Parties did not exist in the time of the Shah's father. When parties were
formed during the war and later, they were more significant as nationalist organizations or the personal following of leaders than as political parties prominent
in the legislature. The accession of the British Labour government to power
caused some confusion; on the right there was fear of an Anglo-Soviet accord in
socialism at Iran's expense. But communist agents sharply attacked the British
Labour government as reactionary. The inability of the British Labour government, in its early days, to make any striking declaration or proposal for Iran gave
plausibility to the Soviet criticism.

The Tudeh gained its greatest influence as the champion of reform by nationalist agitation against Western imperialism. After overreaching itself in 1946-1947,
it resumed its old course in support of Dr. Mossadegh and the National Front.

In the past Iranian politics had not been characterized by moderation, though its extremism had been tempered by a capacity for subtle
maneuver and the skillful treading of a dangerous course. The tyranny
of the Shah's father, the reaction to foreign control, and postwar inflation contributed to the growth of extremist parties of the left and
right. This extremism was further promoted by the Iranian recognition that after the war they were not restricted to the use of one
foreign power against another but had the greater latitude afforded
by the presence of three interested powers.

In facing postwar Iran, the British government responded firmly
and with traditional moderation to the Soviet threat. Thereafter, however, the British government followed what can at best be described
as the unimaginative course of holding to its own interests, with some
modifications favorable to Iran.

The American government had opposed the Soviet challenge to
Iran and encouraged the Iranian government in the rejections of Soviet demands. Here American policy had supported Iranian nationalism and had been effective. The experience helped to confirm American policy-makers in their willingness to look to Iranian nationalism
as a source of strength against Soviet expansionism. Nevertheless, the
confirmation was at best unsteady and did not take proper account
of the possible irrationality of Iranian nationalism. Direct and tangible American interest in Iran was slight, even though at the end of
1946 American interest in Middle Eastern oil supplies found another
fulfillment in the agreement of the Anglo-Iranian Company to provide about 20 per cent of its output to American companies distributing oil in Asia and Africa. American policy early appeared to encourage a formidable Iranian economic development program. But
then doubts about Iran's capacity to use the aid intervened, and it
was not forthcoming.

Iranian hopes of Allied economic assistance rested on their interpretation of such Allied wartime engagements as the Teheran Decla-

L. P. Elwell-Sutton, "Political Parties in Iran: 1941-1948," *The Middle East
Journal*, III (1949), 45-62. The party was outlawed after the attempted assassination of the Shah (February 4, 1949) and went underground to emerge effectively
in the oil crisis. At that time the government linked the assailant both to the
Tudeh party of the left and the rightist and nationalist Mullah, Kashani. The
allegation may have been correct. At any rate, it certainly revealed that the government recognized the possibility of the joining of the efforts of left and right
that occurred in the nationalization controversy. Mohammed Reza Shah Pahlevi,
Mission for My Country (New York, 1961), p. 57.

ration (1943). Franklin D. Roosevelt himself may have encouraged
such hopes, for shortly after the Teheran Conference he referred to
Iran as a most suitable country to be economically developed and
technically modernized by the Western powers and to stand as a
refutation of charges of imperialism.[39]

Qavam's government, having assembled an astonishingly numerous
and uncoordinated group of projects for a plan estimated to cost
about $1,840,000,000, unsuccessfully sought a loan of $250,000,000
from the International Bank for Reconstruction and Development.
The Bank's refusal, well-grounded in the criticisms even of economists
who had been friendly to Iran, such as Arthur Millspaugh, was seen
by many Iranians as the responsibility of the United States. As the
Bank had asked pointed questions about the Iranian Plan, some
"rethinking" took place and the drafting (1947-1948) of a Plan was
entrusted to an American firm, Overseas Consultants Incorporated.
The results of their six-months labor was the Seven Years' Plan projected in 1947, to cost $650,000,000, of which $390,000,000 would be
provided in Iranian currency while foreign currency, including a loan,
would amount to $260,000,000.[40]

Such a costly enterprise would require increased revenue from the
oil company and large American loans, but no serious American aid
for development was forthcoming. The reason for this is that American policy to Iran first turned to a buildup of Iranian military
strength. On June 20, 1947, an American credit of $25,000,000 for
military aid was granted and on October 6, 1947, an agreement providing for an American military training mission was signed. This
military assistance was an enterprise not simply dictated by Iranian
necessities. It was an extension of the aid to Turkey provided under

[39] Roosevelt told the Shah that after the war he would like to return to Iran
to help in the reafforestation of the country. Mohammed Reza Shah Pahlevi,
op. cit., p. 80.

[40] The Seven Years' Plan was notable in that it represented Iranian initiative.
But there was a wide gulf between the Iranian search for advice in the construction of a plan and the implementation of the Plan. The first Iranian Chairmen
of the Plan were better known as stand-patters. The Plan did not begin moving,
for no serious foreign aid appeared and even the Shah's visit to Washington to
plead for aid (November 17, 1949) brought no tangible results. The years 1949-
1950 were times of grave economic difficulty in Iran. Finally, the Plan foundered
in the course of the troubles attendant upon the nationalization of the oil industry.
For early accounts of the Plan, see S. Rezazadeh Shafaq, "The Iranian Seven
Year Development Plan: Background and Organization" and J. D. Lutz (Overseas Consultants, Inc.), "Problems and Proposals," The Middle East Journal, IV
(1950), 100-105.

the Truman Doctrine, for if Turkey was to be strengthened against the Soviet Union, the security of possible Soviet approaches to Turkey also required attention.[41] In the period, 1947-1948, the American government was committing large sums elsewhere and was not ready to add Iranian burdens to engagements already heavy. Successive American Ambassadors, John Wiley and Henry Grady (appointed in June 1950), recognized that Iran needed and demanded a large capital loan. But the collapse of the Kuomintang in China also served to warn against the futility of granting money to states unprepared to use the grants effectively, a point vividly impressed on the Shah when he visited the United States in 1949.[42] For the moment the United States administration had become skeptical of the value of aid to underdeveloped countries. With respect to Iran, economists had sternly warned that without administrative and tax reforms, aid to Iran might be politically and economically pointless.

In early 1950 the Shah himself espoused a reform and anti-corruption drive, and it is not merely coincidental that his reformist effort was headed off by the oil nationalization campaign. American military assistance elicited sharp Soviet attacks on Iran, echoed in the latter nation by some nationalist assaults on American military influence. Meanwhile, as inflation continued and no progress in economic development occurred, the nationalist drive increasingly became an agitation against the British Imperial Bank in Iran and the Anglo-Iranian Oil Concession.

IRAN NATIONALIZES THE OIL INDUSTRY AND EJECTS BRITAIN

In 1949 the Anglo-Iranian Oil Company responded to the government's request for a new agreement. This supplementary agreement

[41] The organization of NATO roused fears in Turkey and Iran that American attention had been diverted to Western Europe. Thus, the Iranian government on occasion drew American attention to Soviet menaces and Stalin's government helped the Iranians in this matter.

[42] Mohammed Reza Shah Pahlevi, op. cit., p. 89.

In The United States in the World Arena (New York, 1960), pp. 243-246, 250-258, W. W. Rostow develops the thesis that the first response of the United States to the Soviet challenge was a military one and was succeeded by a recognition that in many countries stability was first to be fostered by promoting economic growth. Then, the Korean War, which turned the United States to a renewed military emphasis for a long time and away from the thinking that inspired the Point Four Program, convinced the Soviet Union that the military approach in foreign policy would have to yield to a more diverse and flexible one. But this pattern does not fit American policy in Iran and the Middle East.

proved to be both technical and complex. Earlier, the Iranian government's revenue from the Concession had been straitened because
the Company's payments to Iran were partly determined by dividend
payments in the United Kingdom. British companies generally had
limited such payments at the request of the British Chancellor of the
Exchequer.[43] The new agreement, which provided for retroactive payments as well as a stable and substantial minimum revenue, presented political difficulties to the Iranian government which had initiated the agreement. In late 1949 the proponents of nationalizing the
oil industry had filibustered to prevent action on the agreement until
after elections took place.[44] Later, the Iranian Premier, Ali Razmara,
delayed presenting the agreement to the Majlis. Meanwhile Aramco's
negotiations of a simpler 50/50 sharing arrangement made this Anglo-
Iranian Supplementary Agreement appear to be ungenerously out-of-
step with the terms prevailing in the oil industry.

Simplicity of terms would have afforded the Company a propaganda advantage. But the Company management, aware of the complex matters involved in the contract, seems to have believed that the
public relations question should be left to the Iranian government.
Indeed, the Company and, it appears, the representatives of the
British government adopted the no-cause-for-alarm stance considered
appropriate for the level-headed weathering of a crisis. But level-
headedness requires more than a fixed position.

The Company's public relations difficulties in Iran were very real.
As any British activity was likely to be suspect or misrepresented, the
Company took the position that the responsibility for informing the
Iranian public about the Supplementary Agreement rested with the
Iranian government. Though the Anglo-Iranian Company did not
deserve to be a scapegoat for the ills of Iran, it served as one. Dr.
Mossadegh, the leader of the newly formed National Front, blamed

[43] In 1947 the royalties and taxation received by the Iranian government from
the Anglo-Iranian Oil Company amounted to $19,880,000, whereas the British
government got $56,000,000 in dividends and taxation.

[44] The Shah's Minister of Court, Hazhir, intervened in these elections (1949)
even in Teheran. As a countermeasure, Dr. Mossadegh and some colleagues, the
victims of the intervention, claiming the privilege of *bast*, took refuge at the Court
and proclaimed their intention to remain there until the intervention by the
Shah's agent ceased. The Shah yielded and these leaders of the future National
Front were triumphantly elected (Mossadegh re-elected) as members of the Majlis.
See T. Cuyler Young, "The Social Support of Current Iranian Policy," *The
Middle East Journal*, VI (1952), 143.

even the slums of Teheran on the oil company. The Company was surprisingly resourceless against the initial impetus of the nationalist tide. The Company had been the creator of modern southwest Iran, and its refineries on the sweltering island of Abadan offered possibly the best working conditions in the Middle East. But, in spite of their power and influence, the British remained aloof from Persian life. The whole oil area was removed from informed Iranian interests.[45]

The Iranian background grew darker in 1950 and distress encompassed country as well as town. For two years harvests had been poor, to the point where even seed was lacking and livestock had had to be slaughtered. Inflation was followed by a policy of financial deflation which might have been effective if Iranian productivity had increased. By mid-1950 Iran showed signs of disorganization, even of disintegration. Neither Britain nor the United States could adequately respond here. But in their mutual failure in this Iranian situation there may be seen a charade depicting Matthew Arnold's lines about wandering between two worlds, one dead, one powerless to be born.

British policy was based on calculations that applied to a dead world. The British government sought to have the Anglo-Iranian Oil Concession maintained. The Concession, originally made to a private individual, had been vested in a great corporate enterprise in which the British government had a role. As a result, the Concession was the concern both of the Company and the British government. The latter's interest was manifold: its investment and revenue from the Company; the security of cheap oil supplies for the British Navy; the necessity that governments, including Iran, should observe agreements they had made; the protection of British lives and property in Iran.

Now the developing nationalist movement not only prevented ratification of the Supplementary Agreement but was engaged in a skillfully led campaign to nationalize the oil industry and put an end to the intrusion of British power and influence into Iran. This was an old story to the British and the classic response called for firmness. In official and unofficial British pronouncements were expressions of

[45] Critics have suggested that foreign concessions should be organically related to the life of the concessionary nation. But a British authority on Middle Eastern oil, Stephen H. Longrigg, rejects the criticism even in the second edition of his *Oil in the Middle East* (New York, 1961). Thus, he appears committed to the isolated enclave policy maintained by Anglo-Iranian. In turn, this means that the concession readily becomes the subject for ingeniously hostile nationalist mythmaking.

sympathy for Iranian aspirations; of mingled regret and anger that
the Iranians were so unrealistic as to think they could nationalize or
even run the oil industry; and of firmness touched with contempt for
what was looked upon as a characteristic Iranian attempt to use the
communist threat and the United States against Britain in Iran. If
"old Mossy," as Sir Anthony Eden called Mossadegh, were so unrealistic as to try to match his nationalist words with deeds, the
British expected that the good sense of the Iranian people would
assert itself and be ready to accept moderate politicians (pro-British)
in place of "extremist" politicians (the nationalists opposed to Britain). Muslim fanatics assassinated several moderate politicians including Prime Minister Ali Razmara. As the dimensions of the reform movement of which nationalization was a part and the costs of
it became clear late in 1951, there was wavering among some landowners content with the *status quo*, but the nationalization movement acquired an impressive national support to which the Shah himself, with all his misgivings, had to yield.

The Conservative imperialists did not at that time accept such a
reading of the situation. British interests, they argued, were not dependent on a dead or dying cause in Iran. The weakness was at home
and in the unwillingness of the British Labour government to use the
formidable strength of Britain. The argument, of course, cannot be
effectively contravened. As long as Britain was decisive and could
make its strength felt in Iran, there were Iranians prepared to recognize the strength and to accommodate Iranian and British interests.
Perhaps British decisiveness and strength combined might have saved
the day in 1951. But the saving would not have been for long. There
is a threefold explanation of this:

The first is the change in Britain's power position. In addressing the
United Nations Security Council, Sir Gladwyn Jebb observed that in
the past the British government would have responded to such an
action as the British ejection from Iran by using force to settle the
matter. He added: "Some would say this is what His Majesty's Government ought to do now in the interests of the World Community
as a whole." [46] Churchill, who taunted the Labour government for
its Middle Eastern policy of "scuttle," had earlier listed the basic
reason for the British failure to act in the Iranian crisis: ". . . the loss

[46] *News Chronicle*, October 2, 1951; the grounds of the British complaint to
the Security Council are presented in *Yearbook of the United Nations, 1951*
(New York, 1952), pp. 810-817.

of our Oriental Empire and of the well-placed and formidable resources of the Imperial Armies in India." [47]

The second is that Dr. Mossadegh had assumed the leadership of
a nationalist movement of extraordinary proportions. In its nationalization program it commanded the support of the right-wing Muslims
who rejected the West, the growing body of reformers frustrated by
existing Iranian conditions and looking to the end of foreign power
in Iran as the major first step in the regeneration of Iranian politics,
and the fellow travelers and communists of the illegal Tudeh Party.
He skillfully appealed to the range of Iranian complaints against the
Company and the British.[48]

Finally, British policy had to take account of two other foreign
powers, the Soviet Union and the United States, as well as the United
Nations. And this consideration of the two major rivals of the Cold
War conspired to make for British impotence, for in the American
view strong British action would have invited Russian intervention
under the terms of the Agreement of 1921. The American alternative
was to come to terms with the Iranian nationalizers.

The British Labour government adopted its own special response.
Once the nationalization measure had passed both houses of the
Iranian legislature and, after Mossadegh (April 28) became Prime
Minister, had obtained the Shah's reluctant approval (May 2, 1951),
the British government was not in the happiest position for resistance.
Until early 1951 the British government had refused to intervene significantly between the Company and the Iranian government. When
the British government finally took the initiative, the nationalization
movement was all but in orbit. Thus, the British government argued

[47] *Parliamentary Debates*, Commons, 5th series, Vol. 491, col. 2654, June 30,
1951.

[48] In the *Survey of International Affairs, 1951* (Royal Institute of International
Affairs, 1954), pp. 296-297, George Kirk listed some of the grievances. In his
memoirs, *Mission for My Country* (New York, 1961), pp. 82-109, the Shah made
it clear that he too regarded the nationalization campaign and the reduction of
British influence as the fulfillment of the national cause. But he drew a contrast
between the extraordinary negativism of Dr. Mossadegh and his own positive
nationalism. On p. 92 he noted that his countrymen would have been spared
many economic miseries, "if Mossadegh had been willing to enter into rational
negotiations." Against those who have insisted that irrationality and immaturity
had been characteristics of Iranian life for centuries, he described those qualities
as a response to foreign occupation and foreign domination and argued that the
Iranian temper under Mossadegh was in the general pattern of anticolonial nationalism.

that it recognized the Iranian government's right to dispose of territory and property within its own area of sovereignty. But nationalization of the oil industry raised issues more far-reaching. In the first
place, the Iranian government broke a solemn agreement providing
the necessary terms for Anglo-Iranian operations and the inducements
for investing a large amount of capital. The British government could
not accept the Iranian government's unilateral repudiation of its
agreement with the Company, for to have done so would have initiated a series of such repudiations. Secondly, the Iranian nationalizers refused to allow for, possibly to understand, that the oil company made very little money in Iran and accumulated its profits from
a series of international transactions. Perhaps, if the Iranians had
yielded on this point, they could not have moved to satisfy their
nationalist passions.

Under Mossadegh, the Iranian government argued that the Company's nationalization of the oil industry was solely a matter within
Iranian competence. But the government was willing to make use of
the Company's organizations abroad, if the latter would serve as
Iranian agents. Here the mistrust of each party for the other is most
manifest. The Iranian government insisted upon the primacy of its
own control over the Company. But in the British demands the Company was to be entirely free of Iranian influence in its functioning
on the international market.

The mistrust of each party also rested upon a serious miscalcula-
tion. With the parochialism of extreme nationalism, the Iranians
appear to have believed that the British had to make use of Iranian
oil. This error is all the more inexplicable in that the possibilities of
rapid expansion of oil production elsewhere were known or knowable.
On June 12, 1951, Anglo-Iranian's Basil Jackson emphasized that
capital for new pipelines would only be forthcoming from the Company and that the loss of Iranian oil and even of Abadan's refining
capacity could be made good elsewhere.[49] More justifiably, the British
government believed that the Iranian government had to have the oil

[49] Alan W. Ford, The Anglo-Iranian Oil Dispute of 1951-1953 (Berkeley,
1954), pp. 64-65, and Marlowe, The Persian Gulf in the Twentieth Century,
pp. 151-164; additional material may be found in George Lenczowski, The Middle
East in World Affairs (Ithaca, 2nd edition, 1956), pp. 192-201; Longrigg, Oil
in the Middle East, 2nd ed.; Henry Longhurst, Adventure in Oil: the Story of
B.P. (London, 1959); L. P. Elwell-Sutton, Persian Oil: A Study in Power Politics
(London, 1955); Shwadran, The Middle East, Oil and the Great Powers; and
Nasrollah S. Fatemi, Oil Diplomacy: Powderkeg in Iran (New York, 1954).

revenue and would have to sell the oil through Anglo-Iranian facilities. What the British calculation did not allow for was the play of the irrational. Mossadegh's triumph was the ejection of the British from Iran, though the price was the stoppage of oil production and of the refineries and the termination of the Company's payments to the Iranian government.

Though British vigilance and foresight had been insufficient to forestall nationalization, British nerves were strong enough to sweat through the crisis. As the Company's agreement with the Iranian government explicitly provided for arbitration, the British brought their case to the International Court of Justice, which asked both parties to refrain from action pending the Court's deliberations. Premier Mossadegh, however, refused to admit the competence of the Court in this matter. In 1952 the Court finally rendered its opinion that the case did not fall within its jurisdiction. Meanwhile, the British government brought the matter before the United Nations Security Council, which urged the two parties to continue negotiations and to await the verdict of the International Court.

The British Labour government, which resigned after electoral defeat in October 1951, found the issue peculiarly embarrassing. It had so many other preoccupations, including the issue of financial stability, that it had no policy for the Iranian crisis other than the maintenance of the British oil interests there. Those interests had been challenged by an Iranian nationalization campaign. Was the Labour government to step forward as the opponent of Iranian nationalization and the armed defenders of British interests? The Labour government finally decided against playing such a role. It insisted that British lives in Iran would be protected by force, if necessary, and disposed forces in readiness for such an eventuality. But it also accepted the principle of nationalization and sought to negotiate a new agreement with Iran that would have enshrined this triumph of Iranian assertion of sovereignty. These later negotiations foundered on the issues of compensation.

Throughout the summer of 1951 the Iranian oil industry remained idle. By early October 1951 British personnel had been totally evacuated from the refineries and oil fields. While the British calculation that Iran had to market the oil abroad did not allow for the economic irrationality of Mossadegh, the calculation was entirely realistic. Iran could not market the oil over British opposition, and the oil company, supported by the British government, informed interested parties that, as it regarded Iranian oil as its property, it would bring legal suit against the purchasers of Iranian oil. The British policy was to bring conspicuous economic pressures against Mossadegh so that his difficulties and failures would serve as a generally recognized warning to other countries against following the Iranian course.

The lesson was a grim and dangerous one. The oil fields were unproductive and unemployment there was general. The loss of the oil revenue impaired the government's finances just when unusual demands were placed on the government. But the British and the West were, perhaps, fortunate in the man, a conservative and elderly landowner, Dr. Mossadegh, with whom they had to deal, for the Iranian Premier was no ruthless social revolutionary. If he had been, the lesson might have gone awry. Mossadegh apparently had little more in mind than the nationalist triumph. In short, the very negativism that may have induced him to spurn any possible settlement also prevented him from exploiting his victory. He was ignorant and provincial, and he created favorable opportunities for the Tudeh revolutionaries upon whom he had to depend. But, as for himself, he apparently sought to go nowhere.

Nevertheless, he reached for ever-greater political power, not as the dynamo of a revolution but in response to dynamics which he had helped to set in motion. By 1953 he had done away with the Senate and the Supreme Court, he had turned against the Shah, and was seeking to make the Majlis his own instrument. His coalition of left, center, and right was in disarray. The left were eager to replace him; the right mistrusted him; and the moderates were full of alarm at a prospect that seemed to promise anarchy or revolution.

The Mossadegh regime came to an end in August 1953 in a series of actions in which the American Central Intelligence Agency played a role, though the Shah in his memoirs has emphasized the primacy of the Iranian actors. The Shah replaced Mossadegh with General Fazlollah Zahedi. In the subsequent struggle the Shah left the country for a few days but the army, which in Iran had remained aristocratic and decidedly not reformist, gained control.

General Zahedi's victory was followed by substantial grants of American aid; under Mossadegh aid had been limited to Point Four Assistance on the grounds that Iran could not refuse to arrange for oil revenues and seek American aid at the same time. The oil dispute, also, was settled within a year. The new arrangement provided for an international consortium of eight companies in which Anglo-

Iranian had a 40 per cent share, American oil companies a 40 per cent share, Royal Dutch Shell had 14 per cent and a French company 6 per cent. The consortium was to produce, refine, and market oil as agent for the National Iranian Oil Company. One half of the consortium's profits were to go to Iran, which in turn agreed to pay $70,000,000 a year for a decade as compensation to the Anglo-Iranian Oil Company for the facilities in Iran which had been nationalized.

The oil dispute was settled but at a considerable cost for Iran, not merely in the decline of its economy. In the meantime the lost Iranian production had been more than made good elsewhere, notably in Saudi Arabia and Kuwait, which became Iran's rival as oil supplier. New oil discoveries in Iran, however, assured Iran's continued prominence as an oil supplier and the flow of oil revenue to the Iranian government.

Once again, the Shah had the opportunity to resume the onerous task of moderate reformism in Iran, this time in firm alliance with the West. But behind him—his seriousness, pettiness, and, in crisis, vacillation—there lurked the strange specter of Mossadegh and the nationalization crisis that did not become a revolution. Plaguing the Shah and the West was the fear that an Iranian nationalist revolution, once aborted, might yet explode.[50]

Soviet policy-makers were encouraged by this fear which they could see as a hope. Yet, just as British policy was inhibited by the interests of other powers in the Iranian crisis, Soviet policy was perhaps equally influenced by similar fears. Indeed, the failure of the Iranian communists to seize power in 1953 points to a considerable caution in the new Soviet leadership, which in succeeding to Stalin did not have an assured position in 1953. But the Iranian experience also pointed the way to a new and intensified Soviet policy in the Middle East. For the Soviet program of rendering the Middle East insecure for Western interests, the phenomenon of Mossadegh argued that the Soviet Union did not have to seek communist control. Soviet policy could look for spectacular gains simply by encouraging Middle Eastern nationalism against the West.

For the United States the Iranian crisis has posed the relatively unanswered challenge of defining the scope and purpose of its aid program and of giving it both consistency and flexibility. When Mos-

[50] Here it may be well to recall the confident words of Khrushchev to the Twenty-Second Congress of the Communist Party of the Soviet Union: "Events in Teheran are moving our way—there is no need for us to act."

sadegh created difficulties about compensation, the United States supported the British position concerning Iran with loyalty and some misgiving, prompted by the fear that Iran would pass under a communist-dominated regime. Thus, the United States was not as unrelenting to Mossadegh as British policy-makers would have wished. And to promote mistrust among allies, the American oil companies were the beneficiaries of Britain's ejection from Iran.

The spectacular aspect of the British ejection from Iran is properly heightened if it is recalled that only ten years earlier, Britain, engaged in war, had occupied Iran. The memory of that quite recent triumph made the experience of 1951 all the more puzzling, and even infuriating, to many Conservatives. They recognized that in the later years the British government had not surrendered to the extremists and had rendered the Iranian nationalization less an inspiring model than a cautionary example. But there remained the insistent doubt that the Labour government's policy had weakly invited disaster. Yielding to the simplification of situations that appear to make them comprehensible, they overlooked the complex play of forces that added to the inhibitions of the Labour government's will. They were understandably resolved to prevent any similar challenges that might interrupt oil production and transit. As they read the Iranian lesson, they were also prepared to use force. Such a line of thought contributed to the decision to launch the Suez expedition. And the Suez experience suggested that the Tory charges of "scuttle" at Abadan were not the true lesson of the Iranian crisis. But it is always possible to propound a new simplification to sustain an older one, to suggest that the proper will was lacking at Suez—and this, too, forms part of the continuity of history, though fortunately not of the continuity of British policy.

E. EGYPT

FAILURE OF FIRST ATTEMPTED SETTLEMENT

The war had transformed Egypt's economic position. The sum of £450,000,000 stood to Egypt's credit in Britain's blocked sterling balances. The metamorphosis of a country in a dependent relationship into a creditor of the imperial power might have provided a fruitful basis of cooperation between the two countries. Two other developments, however, blighted this prospect: Britain had to concentrate on her own economic recovery and was unable to release sterling to

Egypt in any but initially insignificant quantities; and, in spite of substantial British concessions to Egypt, Britain was unable to reach an accord on Egyptian nationalist demands.

These two developments are interrelated. The war had gravely dislocated the Egyptian economy and the war's end terminated the work of planning and allotment of necessities carried on by the Middle East Supply Center. Inflation compounded the dislocation. Funds for serious work were not available and no Egyptian party advocated tax policies to provide them. Thus, the bare possibility that Egyptian governments might have undertaken extensive and constructive work became wholly illusory.

Politics as usual, then, prevailed in Egypt. Substantially, this meant a continuation of the intrigues and maneuvers of the Wafd, other parties and personalities, and King Farouk for influence and extended power. Farouk is a typical pre-deluge figure whose achievement in reigning was the negative one of not forestalling the deluge, and, thus, of making himself a scapegoat, along with Britain, the West, and Israel, for Egypt's ills.[51] A self-centered pragmatist lacking in the subtlety his ambitions imperiously demanded, he played with forces, Arabism and anti-Zionism, of which he could not take the measure. His irresponsibility in failing to do what could be done was matched by his rival, the Wafd Party, then the most effective political organization in Egypt. The Wafd pretended to be the trustees of Egyptian nationalism but had actually become a racket. Other groups and personalities gained power for short periods. All were united in seeking the same nationalist ends, but the Wafd, notably, had almost mastered the art of substituting nationalist agitation for government. And in its determination to allow no other Egyptian group to achieve the national goals, the Wafd had effectively doomed any non-Wafd Egyptian government to impotence. Yet, there were new elements on

---

[51] The Shah of Persia, *Mission for My Country*, mentions his father's belief that most Iranian politicians intrigued with foreign powers. A similar view is expressed of Farouk and his dynasty "which was cooperating with foreign elements for the sake of its selfish interests, oppressing the people and causing corruption and instability in the country." Abd El-Fattah Ibraham El-Sayed Baddour, *Sudanese-Egyptian Relations* (The Hague, 1960), p. 151. In the individual this kind of talk is evidence of an advanced neurosis. The individual, projecting his blame on external conditions, is inhibited from achieving the goals he professes to seek. Nationalism plays a similar role for some social groups. Although the Egyptian nationalists, for example, could have undertaken many constructive works, they only too readily argued that they were inhibited by the presence of the imperial power.

the Egyptian scene: the nationalist assertiveness was more resolute
and less frequently shaken by self-doubt and inward despair; a powerful support of anti-foreign nationalism appeared in the Muslim
Brotherhood; and a small but distinct communist penetration of
Egypt, among intellectuals and some trade unionists, had taken place.

The British government was well aware that British control in wartime would produce explosive reactions after the war. In support of
this was the experience in Egypt and Iran after the First World War.
The Labour government, which had made a memorably generous
offer to Egypt in 1929, also recognized that its victory had raised
Egyptian expectations. As the British government had resolved to
head off the explosive reactions by fostering Arabism and appealing
to the Arab nations as partners, it sought to come to terms with
Egyptian nationalism in 1946.

Even then, critics of Bevin's policy argued that he had been dilatory
in removing occasions of irritation to Egyptian nationalities. Lord
Altrincham charged that the British government had been advised
as a matter of immediate urgency to remove its troops from Egypt at
the end of the war: but "they took no action until much too late." [52]
In Bevin's defense it may be argued that the unexpectedly early conclusion of the Japanese war placed a temporary strain on British
shipping resources that made difficult the evacuation of British forces
from Cairo and the Delta. Lord Altrincham's criticism of Bevin's
timing, however, may be valid, and in the dismal conditions of
retrospect, optimism can supply the rueful comfort of self-vindication.
It is, however, unlikely that a rapid evacuation which did not include
the Canal Zone could have satisfied postwar nationalists.

Premier Ismail Sidky, an independent who raised some British
hopes that he could be the strong man of Egyptian politics and, thus,
might conclude an agreement with dispatch and similarly have it
ratified, came to England to negotiate with Ernest Bevin. With the
Wafd in unrelenting opposition the task would not be easy. But
Sidky decided against an all-party delegation and essayed the role of
single champion of Egypt.

Bevin, Sidky, and their staffs worked understandingly and ingeniously. They drafted and initialed (October 1946) an agreement
which was a triumph of the traditional diplomatic art. It satisfied all
interests and each *amour-propre*. But it required an eighteenth-

[52] *Parliamentary Debates*, Lords, 5th series, Vol. 141, cols. 347-350, May 21,
1946.

century audience to appreciate unquestioningly the neatness of its algebra.

The British agreed to evacuate Cairo and the Delta and later (in 1949), the Suez Canal Zone. Egypt agreed to make with Britain defense arrangements whereby Egypt would maintain the workshops of the Canal Zone and would concert plans for joint defense and the re-entry of British troops if aggression took place against Egypt or her neighbors. This great British concession was made because other bases in Gaza and Kenya were being considered. Britain also recognized that the Sudan was under the common crown of Egypt and Egypt, in turn, agreed that in due time the Sudan would be free to choose its future status.[53]

How then did the Agreement fail of ratification? It had apparently provided for the satisfaction of the two Egyptian nationalist demands: the evacuation of Egypt and the unification of the Nile Valley. The difficulty arose over the second issue. Egypt sought control of the Sudan in order to assure for herself the supply of Nile water and to gain *lebensraum* for her growing population who might be used to divert the economy of the Sudan away from competition with Egyptian cotton and to the production of food supplies. Egypt's historical claim to the Sudan was based on Mehmed Ali's conquest (1821), but in the 1880's the Sudanese had successfully revolted. In theory, Egypt shared with Britain in a Condominium over her neighbor to the south. "The Unity of the Nile Valley" could be construed as the dictate of geography and economic rationality. But it also was an Egyptian imperialistic slogan in the familiar guise of geopolitical rhetoric. The British government was not eager to see the Sudan, a staging post and major approach to East Africa, under exclusive Egyptian control. Such an enhancement of Egyptian power might have made formidable an Egypt hostile to Britain. But British policy did not exclude the merger of the Sudan and Egypt. It only insisted upon the keeping of earlier British pledges and agreements to allow the Sudanese to determine their own future. In countering the Egyptian slogan with the demand of self-determination for the Sudan,

[53] Sir Harold Nicolson, connoisseur of the old diplomacy, who cannot repress his distaste for the strident style of intercourse of contemporary states, relations which he cannot dignify by the name of diplomacy, noted that in devising a satisfactory solution the wit of man could not have worked out terms other than those of the Bevin-Sidky agreement. *Spectator*, CLXXXVI (April 13, 1951), 478. The later agreements on the Sudan (1953) and the Canal Zone (1954) confirm his judgment.

the British could put the imperialist onus on the Egyptians who, for their part, compounded their suspicions of Britain; for British influence dominated the administration which managed Sudanese affairs and which was to prepare the Sudanese for making their choice.

The finesse as well as the weakness of the Bevin-Sidky agreement is that both the Egyptian and British claims were affirmed, although the inclusion of the British claim in effect meant that Egypt agreed to the *status quo*. In Egypt Sidky boasted that he had secured the full Egyptian case. This, in turn, prompted questions in London, and the subsequent repetition of the official British claim to the Sudanese *status quo* spurred riots in Cairo, soon afterwards bringing Sidky's resignation and the interment of the Agreement in the Foreign Office's large file of unratified Middle Eastern documents, to await transfer to the Public Record Office in 1996.

APPEAL TO THE UNITED NATIONS AGAINST THE BRITISH
PRESENCE IN EGYPT AND THE SUDAN

Al-Nokrashy, Sidky's successor as Prime Minister, sought in 1947 to encourage American interest in Egypt. He apparently hoped that Egypt could cash in on the containment policy and secure loans and military assistance. But the United States refused to respond to this effort to undercut British influence in Egypt.

In the summer of 1947 Al-Nokrashy brought Egypt's grievances to the United Nations Security Council. The case he presented was that British troops were occupying Egypt against the will of the Egyptian people, that they had used the occupation of Egypt to participate in the control of the Sudan, and that the British administration in the Sudan represented a frustration of the unity of the Nile Valley. As this quarrel was a danger to the peace, he asked the Security Council to order British forces out of Egypt and their administrators out of the Sudan. The Egyptian government, in recognizing the Labour government's desire to place British relations with Egypt on a new basis, hoped that under pressure in the United Nations the British would make further concessions. Bevin, mindful of severe Tory criticism of the agreement he made with Sidky, told the House of Commons that "we cannot go any further than the offer we have made." Whether the Egyptians took the matter to "the Security Council or anywhere else," the British government would not appease Egypt at the expense of the Sudanese people.[54]

[54] *Parliamentary Debates*, Commons, 5th series, Vol. 437, col. 1963, May 16, 1947.

The British reply, presented by Sir Alexander Cadogan, was quite effective, for it denied that the issue posed a threat to peace, and rested upon the Anglo-Egyptian Treaty of 1936, though sympathy for Egypt was widely expressed. British forces were evacuating Egypt and the British position on the Sudan was almost unassailable. The Egyptian counter-reply was that the Treaty dated from an earlier day had been abused, and had no validity in the age of the United Nations.[55] Al-Nokrashy was no innocent in international politics and law. He, of course, shared Egyptian national aspirations, but he essayed the United Nations appeal, emulating earlier complaints of the Soviet republics, because domestic considerations compelled him to be nationalistically active. His failure in the United Nations arose from his linking the British military presence in Egypt with the issue of the unity of the Nile Valley, on which even the Soviet bloc did not support him.[56] His failure in the United Nations, as well as the United Nations' handling of the Palestine issue, prepared the ground for Egypt's declared neutralism in the Korean War.

THE END OF BRITAIN'S ARABIST POLICY

The Palestine War marks a decisive turning point in Britain's relations with Egypt and in Britain's Arabist policy. The Arab League urged on the war against Israel. The Egyptian government, with strong encouragement from Farouk, launched two ill-equipped Egyptian armies against the Israeli forces. Although Britain sought to maintain her own positions in the Arab states by supporting the latter at critical moments, it became quite clear that the British government had little to look for from Arabism. First of all, the animus of Arab nationalism turned all the more sharply on Britain as the excuse for Arab failure. Secondly, the incompetence of general Arab policy and military effort doomed any expectation of fruitful cooperation. Finally, there was the new situation created by an Israeli

[55] Nationalism in its aspiring form has posed a heated challenge to the order based on treaties. Implicit in the Egyptian case was the argument that the Treaty was invalid because Egyptians were opposed to it. A striking example of the same line of thought may be found in a protest of Rumanians against the Treaty of Bucharest. A copy of the protest dated from Paris, May 1919, is in the National Archives, 763.72119 1750. "In this twentieth century, the liberty of nations as well as the liberty of citizens, should be sacred. No power, no treaty may suppress the right of a nation to aspire to national unity and independence. Any convention which sets aside this unwritten right is valueless before history."

[56] The arguments are summarized in *Yearbook of the United Nations, 1947-1948* (Lake Success, 1949), pp. 356-362.

state and the persisting Arab divisions. It was against this background
that Britain became a party to the Tripartite Declaration of May 25,
1950. As the Declaration accepted the existence of Israel, it was
anathema to Arab views. Thereafter, Britain had little hope of success
in regional and broad Arab policies. Middle Eastern problems loomed
as intractable difficulties over the reaches of the future. Such a prospect inspired renewed efforts to promote cooperation with the United
States. At best the Middle Eastern problems required patient and
persistent effort. But persistent effort implied policy clearly defined
in agreement with the United States. In July 1949 Bevin called a
London meeting of Britain's Middle Eastern diplomats to consider
the possibility of such an approach. But, as Iran and, later, Egypt
provide witness, British-American cooperation in the Middle East was
more fitful than persistent.

REJECTION OF REGIONAL DEFENSE PROPOSALS AND ABROGATION OF THE ANGLO-EGYPTIAN TREATY

The British loss of any hope in an Arabist policy appeared to underline the importance of holding the Suez Canal base, for, if the Middle
East remained disturbed and Britain was unable to concert defense
arrangements with the Arab states, the existing base and treaty arrangement with Egypt had served well in the past. British plans to
develop alternate bases had not been pursued. When the Korean War
erupted to preoccupy American and British leaders with defense
preparations, the facilities in the Suez base were again prized at their
old value, which actually proved to be inflated.

In the Wafd return to governmental power (January 1950), the
British government optimistically saw the possibility of a new settlement. The Wafd had the responsibility of governing and, at any rate,
would not have the freedom to disrupt negotiations as it had in
opposition. Indeed, its majority was large enough to encourage the
hope that its leader, Nahas, might be willing to seek a settlement.
Nahas, however, was inhibited by his own past, for the appeals he
had used had fostered a popular temper and expectations that could
be directed against himself.

The way for the discussions was prepared by Bevin who visited
Cairo early in 1950 on the invitation of Farouk. A new British Ambassador, Sir Ralph Stevenson, later came to take a major part in the
continuing talks. From the beginning the Egyptian conditions were
the total evacuation of Egypt and the unity of the Nile Valley under

the Egyptian crown. Three features of the conversations are worthy of note. The first is the unwillingness of Nahas and his government to settle for less than their full demands. This prolonged the talks and deferred a decision. In Middle Eastern politicians there often appeared an unusual aversion to a final end of bargaining, to definite conclusions, and to affording the means of assessing responsibility. In the present instance this may have been increased by Nahas' awareness that Russia and the United States were likely to loom more prominently in the Middle East and that a settlement might well be deferred until their roles, likely to lessen Britain's stature, had become clearer.[57] In the face of British insistence that provision had to be made for the defense of the Middle East before Britain could leave the Canal Zone, Nahas, unencumbered by technical consideration of the problem, argued that, if Egypt were given arms in quantity, the Egyptian Army within one year would be able to defend Egypt and the Canal Zone. To British proposals of a phased withdrawal of troops lasting until 1956, the terminal date of the Treaty so far as Britain's rights to station troops were concerned, he simply averred that the only decisive question was the supply of Egyptian arms.

The British case was that the Anglo-Egyptian Treaty could be replaced only after Egypt joined a regional defense organization. The British representatives argued that the Egyptian demand for evacuation as the measure of independence was old-fashioned. In the world of the Cold War, states had to enter alliances for self-preservation and to allow, as the NATO nations did, the stationing of foreign troops within their country. The Egyptian Premier, Nahas, replied out of the mistrust that made the negotiations unfruitful: the case of the European powers differed from that of Egypt, for they and Britain knew that upon request American troops would leave their

[57] In November 1951 the British government published a *White Paper* (Cmd. 8419) on these conversations. Shortly thereafter, the Egyptian government published a more extensive *Green Book: Records of Conversations, Notes and Papers Exchanged Between the Royal Egyptian Government and the United Kingdom Government* (March 1950-November 1951).

Farag Moussa, in *Les Negociations Anglo-Égyptiennes de 1950-1951 Sur Suez et le Soudan* (Études d'Histoire, Économique, Politique, et Sociale, Number XVII, Geneva, 1955), has presented what he called a historical critical study of the texts of the negotiations. He is sometimes more ingenious and ingenuous than convincing. From the *Green Book* he quoted the reply of Field Marshal Sir William Slim, then Chief of the Imperial General Staff, to Nahas, who referred to growing American interests in the Near East: "America has nothing to do with the Middle East."

soil, and, anyhow, the arrangement was presumably a short-term one.
Egypt was not at all sure that upon request the foreign forces would
leave her soil and the British presence in Egypt, originally an emergency measure, had become an occupation lasting more than sixty
years.

A second feature of the conversations was the rather ingenuous way
in which some British spokesmen, notably Field Marshal Slim, argued
the Russian danger. The days were anxious enough, but Slim's
specter of the Soviet Army reaching out quickly to Africa evoked the
charge that the British used the Soviet threat as a pretext for pre-
serving imperial influence in Egypt. Thirdly, it is notable that as early
as October 1950 the Egyptian government gave notice that it proposed to abrogate the Anglo-Egyptian Treaty. Despite this impatience, the protracted discussions are testimony to the momentary
moderation of both sides, and their endurance is a tribute to the
diplomatic skill of British representatives in gaining time.

The nationalist campaign in 1950-1951 acquired an obsessive momentum that effectively doomed the British effort to reach a settlement. The American government publicly supported the British
position when treaties were threatened, but privately, American
influence was exerted to press for greater British concessions to
Egypt, especially on the Sudan, where, as British representatives
have heatedly noted, the Egyptian case was weakest. The Wafd
government, which apparently knew moments of fear of the consequences of the demonstrations and riots its course involved, persisted in the nationalist drive, urged on all the more by the hope of
diverting attention from its own corruption, for example, the speculations of some of its members in cotton.

As the British parliamentary elections approached in October
1951, an interesting counterplay of Western and Egyptian policies
took place. After consultations of which Egypt had knowledge, on
October 13 Britain, the United States, France, and Turkey invited
Egypt to become a founding member of a Middle East Command
to be located in the Suez Canal Zone. If Egypt accepted, the British
occupation in the Zone would cease along with Britain's rights under
the Anglo-Egyptian Treaty of 1936. In place of the British forces
in the Zone, there would be an Allied Command and Allied forces
of which the British would form but one of five contingents. Once
again, ingenuity had been in vain and the Wafd government curtly
rejected the proposal. In making all allowance for Wafdist irre-

sponsibility, it may be said that vocal Egyptian opinion was for the moment against any signed commitment to Britain and other foreign powers. The experience of the past argued for mistrust of such commitments, and for their part many Egyptians criticized the effort to sign, seal, and deliver them, as being based on the very mistrust of them that excused imperialist domination.[58]

Five days prior to the Middle East Command proposal to Egypt, the Wafdist Premier Nahas presented decrees to the Egyptian parliament, which passed them unanimously on October 15. The decrees abrogated the Treaty of 1936 as well as the Anglo-Egyptian Agreement (1899) on the Condominium of the Sudan and provided Farouk with the title King of Egypt and Sudan. The decrees, then, required the eviction of the British Sudanese administration and of British troops from the Canal Zone. The Egyptian legislation also provided a constitutional framework, cabinet and legislature, for the Sudan. Egypt had thus embarked on a course from which retreat would be difficult. The Iranian imbroglio profoundly influenced each party, though in different ways that compounded the difficulties of agreement. The maintenance of the Canal Zone base appeared all the more necessary for the assurance of the oil supplies and British influence in the Middle East. The Egyptian reaction to Mossadegh's triumph, however, was: "This is the example that we must follow in our struggle with the British. It is only the weak whom they oppress. Their prestige in the Middle East is finished." [59] The Egyptian Foreign Minister, Salah Ed-Din Bey, said that the "troubles of the British government are endless" and to defer a settlement because of Britain's difficulties meant that "we shall

---

[58] With the Command were to be associated, but not as founding members, Australia, New Zealand, and the Union of South Africa. After the Egyptian rejection, the four sponsors indicated to a number of Middle Eastern governments their intention to establish the Command. On November 10, 1951, the same states explained that forces under the Supreme Allied Commander would be moved into and within states only with the consent of the governments concerned. The Command, they also explained, would not interfere in the disputes of the area, for example, Arab-Israeli Armistice quarrels. Finally, the Command would be concerned with integrated regional defense and not with pursuing the national interest of any particular government. Nothing came of all this. Possibly the proposal had acquired a certain momentum and had to be urged on even amidst the most certain shades of futility.

[59] *Bourse Égyptienne*, October 4, 1951, quoted in L. A. Fabunmi, *The Sudan in Anglo-Egyptian Relations: A Case Study in Power Politics, 1800-1956* (London, 1960), p. 289. Fabunmi's work is comprehensive and valuable.

never finish." "We have been talking with Britain for twenty years. They know our point of view. We know theirs. Further talks only mean more British occupation." [60]

The new Conservative government declared the unilateral abrogation invalid and repeated the firm stand of the Labour government which, Nahas had decided, made the Egyptian action imperative. Prime Minister Churchill deftly elaborated: Britain would maintain her Treaty rights, "using, of course, no more force than is necessary." [61]

In the past Egyptian nationalist campaigns had not disturbed the functioning of the Canal Zone base which made use of a large Egyptian labor force. This time, however, some Egyptian labor was withdrawn and volunteer as well as official Egyptian forces harassed British soldiers and the remaining Egyptian workmen. On January 25, 1952, after days of tension and bloody incidents, a showdown took place at Ismailia when British forces sought to disarm and expel Egyptian "auxiliary police" there. The Egyptian forces, displaying unexpectedly valorous endurance, lost forty dead and had seventy-two wounded. By this time the Egyptian government had lost control of the situation. The next day saw destructive rioting in Cairo, which revealed so great a measure of conspiratorial planning and such irresponsibility on the government's part that Farouk replaced the Wafd government. As a portent of later developments, the riot in Cairo was not brought under control until the army, which had not acted in the Canal Zone, appeared on the streets.

THE REPUBLIC AND THE ANGLO-EGYPTIAN TREATY (1954)

Middle Eastern disasters plagued the Labour government in its last months—and, indeed, the timing of the Egyptian abrogation of the Treaty may have been influenced by the Egyptian government's apprehensions of a Conservative victory in the elections. The Conservative government was fortunate in that the Egyptian political scene soon changed. In July 1952 the army stepped in and took control of the Egyptian government.

This *coup d'état*, which finally claimed the status of a revolution, replacing the monarchy with a republic (June 18, 1953), meant that

[60] The first remark appears in the British White Paper (Cmd. 8419), p. 31, the second is in *The United States News and World Report*, October 19, 1951, p. 18.

[61] *Parliamentary Debates*, Commons, 5th series, Vol. 493, col. 70, November 6, 1951.

the Egyptian government would be for a time relieved of the use of popular demonstrations and volunteer forces which it could not control. But the change had a greater significance than that. The army *coup* was the expression of a confused recognition, not confined to the army officers, that the nationalist cause, which could not be abandoned, had been used in such a way as to discredit and endanger Egypt. Thus, the nationalist cause itself required domestic reform.

The Free Officers who eventually formed the new Council for the Revolutionary Command had their origin in the Palestine War, but their associations and opposition to British imperialism date back to the Second World War. Embittered by their inadequate preparation and supplies for the Palestine War, they were generally torn between two courses. On the one hand, they vaguely favored reform, the purging of politics, and an end to "feudalism." But— and this is the course they pursued as late as March 1952—they believed that the achievement of the national goals came first and was a necessary preliminary.[62] The *coup* was made only very hesitantly and was precipitated by the Wafd's and Farouk's maneuvers to rearrange the government, by Farouk's attempts to secure control of the military organizations and clubs, and by rumors of other actions planned by Farouk in order to forestall the *coup*. Nasser is credited with the remark that, if not true, is *ben trovato*: "If it is to be a battle of liquidation, why not start a revolution?" [63] The officers acted, arresting most of the General Staff and installing Ali Maher as Premier. Finding themselves unexpectedly successful, they compelled Farouk to abdicate but did not proclaim a republic until a year later.

The proclamation issued by the officers at the beginning of the *coup* is very revealing: "Led by fools, traitors, and incompetents, the army was incapable of defending Egypt. That is why we have carried out a purge. The army is now in the hands of men in whose ability, integrity, and patriotism you can have complete confidence." [64] Even the leader installed by the *coup*, Mohammed

---

[62] Rashedel Barawy, *The Military Coup* (Cairo, 1952), p. 201. See, also, Jean and Simone Lacouture, *Egypt in Transition* (London, 1958). There is valuable material in Mohammed Naguib, *Egypt's Destiny* (New York, 1955) and in Anwar el Sadat, *Revolt on the Nile* (London, 1957), and in the first chapter of Keith Wheelock, *Nasser's New Egypt* (New York, 1960).

[63] Lacouture, *op. cit.*, p. 146.

[64] *Ibid.*, pp. 150-151.

Naguib, was not its true leader; he was selected by the young Free Officers as an older man with high rank in the army, who had a good reputation and was sympathetic with their movement.

The new government acted in a number of fields, more quickly than effectively. To cut down large estates and redistribute land, an agrarian reform law was passed. Various efforts to reorganize and purify political parties were made. But, almost inexorably, in response to the early dynamics of dictatorship, the results were always, generally with good reason, pronounced unsatisfactory. Indeed, the Egyptian political parties were in a sorry state and the government, fearing the divisive and inhibiting effects of political parties, became the dictatorship of a military junta. Significantly, Naguib early appointed a committee to formulate the lines of a national Egyptian foreign policy and to end "the auction of national aspirations" that had characterized the previous regime.

In January 1953 a plot against the government was revealed and, in consequence, decrees established a three-year period of military dictatorship and dissolved political parties. On January 23, General Naguib proclaimed the formation of the Liberation Rally, and, two weeks later, indicated that the Rally was to replace the political parties. At the same time (February 6, 1953), he stated that "the struggle for evacuation needs education and coordination. We have to consider evacuation as a very distant target for which we must mobilize our material and spiritual resources. At the same time we must be prepared, if evacuation were realized tomorrow, to play the great role expected of us after liberation." [65]

The fear of relaxing the army's control and the inability of Naguib and, initially, of his successor, Nasser, to deal substantially with Egypt's many and long-unattended problems, so many deriving from pervasive and enduring poverty, help explain the activism of Nasser's foreign policy after the early months of 1955. But even in the beginning the regime was concerned with reform as a step towards settlement of the national questions. The new regime could hardly settle for less than the Wafd had demanded.

Yet, Naguib acted circumspectly, especially in the matter of the Sudan. He himself had a Sudanese mother and other associations in the area, which led him to believe that he would have great influence there. In dealing with Britain over the Sudan, he turned to a new course. He did not reaffirm the Wafd government's abrogation

[65] Quoted in *The Annual Register, 1953* (London, 1954), p. 259.

of the Condominium but sought to hold on to the right which that
arrangement with Britain afforded Egypt. The deposition of Farouk,
however, permitted Naguib greater flexibility in maneuvering, for
he no longer had to demand that the Sudan be under the Crown
of Egypt.

Britain had resolutely adhered to the principle of Sudanese self-
determination and had rejected the Egyptian counterproposal of
immediate Sudanese elections with universal suffrage on the grounds
that some Sudanese education in politics was a necessary preliminary.
Naguib saw an opportunity here and invited the representatives of
Sudanese political groups to Cairo. By 1952 Sudanese political education—for a small group at any rate—had made considerable progress. It had been notably hastened after Egypt's appeal to the Security
Council, for in 1948 over Egyptian opposition, Britain had afforded
a further measure of self-government to extend the beginning made
with the Northern Sudan Advisory Council of 1944. Egypt had
protested the 1948 measure on the grounds that it gave the British
Governor-General too much power. In 1951 the Governor-General
had summoned a Constitutional Amendment commission as a step
towards establishing wider Sudanese autonomy. He dissolved the
Commission later in the year and, drawing on its work, drafted and,
with amendments, had ratified a new Sudanese Constitution.[66] With
the representatives of the Sudanese political parties, Naguib came
to an agreement whereby after a transitional period of three years
a Sudanese Constituent Assembly would vote on self-determination.
Elections to a legislature would take place at once, the civil service
would be quickly staffed with Sudanese personnel, power would
gradually pass to Sudanese hands, and British forces would withdraw
from the Sudan one year prior to the election of the Constituent
Assembly.

Two features of Naguib's policy here deserve mention. The first
is that he separated the issue of the Sudan from the Canal Zone, a
piecemeal approach that may have made the British concessions
more acceptable to the British Conservative Party. The second
feature is even more important: Naguib, hoping thereby to win an
Egyptian victory in the Sudan, accepted the principle of Sudanese
self-determination. Furthermore, Naguib's acceptance of it, com-

[66] Abd El-Fattah Ibrahim El-Sayed Baddour, *op. cit.*, pp. 133, 146-148. In its
political judgments this is a black and white book. British administration in the
Sudan was self-seeking and colonialist, whereas "Egypt was always helping the
Sudanese both materially and morally." *Ibid.*, p. 186.

bined with the agreement he secured from the Sudanese political parties, in effect, called Britain's hand and the British government quickly came to a settlement of the Sudanese issue.[67]

In the Sudanese elections (1953) the pro-Egyptian party won a majority, but in 1954 Nasser's Minister for Sudanese Affairs, Major Salah Salem, acted arrogantly while the British government sedulously courted Sudanese officials. Thus, in 1956, the Sudan became independent and promptly joined the Arab League and the United Nations.

The Egyptian government, in separating the Sudanese and Canal Zone controversies, contributed to making each soluble. But before detailing the negotiations and agreement concerning the Suez base, which many Conservatives thought to be as much a part of British geography as Gibraltar, it may be useful to characterize the approaches of Churchill and Eden in this matter and to consider the state of Anglo-American relations in the Middle East.

Churchill profoundly regretted the whole dismantling of Empire as very premature. Against Labour's efforts in India, Iran, and Egypt, he had hurled the charge of "scuttle." This charge was to haunt him in 1954 when his government came to terms with Nasser. At that time his best defense was that he was yielding to a necessity created by the policies of his Labour predecessors. But Churchill also managed to merge his repeated call for a summit meeting with a vision of an apocalyptic and strangely Hobbesian world of deterrence imposed by nuclear weapons, which were likely to render the

[67] Only a certain defensive tone in *The Memoirs of Anthony Eden: Full Circle* (Boston, 1960), pp. 272-274, provides a hint that Naguib could be described, to use John Marlowe's words, as "having therefore trumped the British ace." *Arab Nationalism and British Imperialism* (London, 1961), p. 73. But the Egyptian leaders might also have recognized that Eden honorably adhered to his previous pledge about self-determination. To do so was not easy, for he himself noted that the Sudanese issue provided a rare instance of his disagreement with Churchill, pp. 273-274. The Egyptian victory was a tactical one, achieved by adopting the British position.

On Churchill's opposition to Sudanese self-determination he suggested that "Sir Winston was influenced on this occasion by his own memories of the Sudan many years before." On the witness of the memoirs, Churchill apparently supported the Suez expedition and after its collapse did so publicly in a speech to the Primrose League. *Manchester Guardian*, May 4, 1957. Both men were unduly influenced by memories of an earlier Middle East that had vanished with the sandhills of yesterday.

Suez base untenable. Churchill hoped to see the squabbles of the former colonial world settled before the summit meeting met to deliberate the cosmic and European issues.

Eden, too, was a Conservative as well as a student of Persian and other Oriental languages. Unfortunately, his understanding of the Middle East did not grow. He was capable of deftness, patience, even imagination, when he recognized a problem as diplomatic rather than imperial. But in the Middle East he was a victim of the old interwar charade of mistaking figures under British influence for representative Middle Eastern leaders. His good words are mainly reserved for Nuri of Iraq, Abdullah of Jordan, Ali Razmara of Iran, and Abdul Rahman al-Mahdi of the Sudan. Egyptian and Iranian leaders, among others, were strangers to him. As likely as not, they would have gone to French schools. Iraqi King Faisal had gone to Harrow, whereas Farouk did not have the advantage of being toughened at Woolwich.[68] Eden did not like such people as old "Mossy" or Nahas but he had some understanding of them. Naguib and Nasser, soldiers who had not been out of Egypt, were a more puzzling generation. They affected an enigmatic sincerity and friendliness to him, but Eden did not know them at all. From 1951 to 1953 he believed that an arrangement for Middle Eastern defense centered on the Suez base was a necessity. The security of British oil supplies and Western influence in the Middle East made this necessity and required the use of British bases in the Middle East. The key to his thinking was that for the Middle East Britain had the primary responsibility. Arab leaders must recognize this primacy and, where they failed to do so, they were sharply reminded of their failure to understand the true situation and their own real interests.[69]

This sense underlines his resentment of Jefferson Caffrey, the American Ambassador in Cairo, as well as some of his impatience

[68] *Full Circle*, pp. 246, 267.

[69] Martin Wight noted that Eden's memoirs, in presenting a collection of aphorisms, also provided a theory of diplomacy. But, where in dealing even with Communist China, Eden was sensitively aware of the other party's interest, he did not have the same awareness in Nasser's case. True, Nasser may be impulsive and not readily calculable. But the injured sense of colonialism is only heightened by an approach which argued that the Arabs must be persuaded "where their true interests lie," that British proposals "meet as far as possible their requirements" (pp. 203, 228). "Brutus in Foreign Policy," *International Affairs*, XXXVI (1960), 305.

with Secretary Dulles.[70] In his eyes the Americans were impatient activists and inveterate courters of popularity. They appeared to be unwilling loyally to support their NATO ally, to provide support "in the only way in which the oriental understood the word." [71] But the full gravamen of his resentment was reserved for the disinclination of the United States government "to take second place even in an area where primary responsibility was not theirs." [72]

Now the whole point was the great trouble in securing Middle Eastern acceptance of Britain's primary responsibility and in making effective disposition to implement it. Some of Eden's criticisms, American activism, optimism, courting of popularity—not always a fault to Eden, who admitted that when in a foreign country he sometimes found his position adapting to that of the foreign country—are fair enough, and for the Middle East he could have added the pursuit of contradictory objectives as well as the lack of consistency and persistence. More than that, many American officials did have the sense that the British position in Egypt was a survival of imperialism, as it was, and that it would not last long. This judgment had its own complex consequences, for some British Conservatives argue from it that the United States did not want the British position to last, that the United States was an inconstant ally.

When major negotiations were initiated concerning the Suez base, the British government asked the United States to join the negotiations. The Eisenhower government agreed on condition that the Egyptians asked the United States in, as they understandably refused to do. As the British were here conceding so much, the United States probably should have made stronger efforts to be a party to the negotiations. But how could it have forced the issue? Above all, how, apart from force, could the United States have compelled the Middle Eastern states to admit the primacy of British responsibility and interest in the Middle East? That was the very thing in question and the American government and public were averse to any com-

---

[70] He criticized Ambassador Caffrey in Full Circle, pp. 255, 259, 264, 280. On one occasion, in response to American pressure for a British concession on the Sudan as a way of heading off revolution in Egypt, Eden "had to say bluntly that we could not keep the Egyptian Government alive by feeding the Sudanese to them." Ibid., p. 260.

[71] The expression, quoted in Full Circle, p. 264, is that of a Foreign Office spokesman.

[72] Ibid , p. 284.

mitment of American forces to British positions challenged by local nationalism. Churchill faced a momentarily stonewall American Congress when he suggested on January 17, 1952, that American troops be stationed in the Canal Zone.

Harold Macmillan is quoted as having said twenty years ago that the British had the mission of being Greeks to the American Romans. The aspiration is perfectly legitimate and expresses an admirable and healthy self-assurance. But as historical parallel it is somewhat deficient, for this appears to be a case of Greek imperialists seeking the aid of Romans, who, with some naivete, are opposed to imperialism, although having had their imperialistic moments and with a maddening appearance, sometimes, of innocence, sometimes, of crusading righteousness, and sometimes, of regret about the shifts made necessary by life in this world, they have used power in ordering the world. But in the Middle East and elsewhere the Americans have encountered the opposition to imperialism which strikes a responsive chord in them. With the British position under fire, on grounds that appeal to Americans as well as on grounds that seem to prevail in the contemporary world, American policy-makers have been tempted to look for the side that is to prevail.

When Churchill's government assumed power, to describe the Middle East as a vacuum was a commonplace. But the void was created by the disintegration of a British order, and before that, of an Ottoman order. To preserve the remnants of that order and to extend it was the aim of British policy. As the disintegration, in part, issued from Middle Eastern opposition to Britain, the resources for the work of reconstruction were somewhat questionable.

But the proud British memory of ascendancy was still strong in the Middle East, which by reason of its transit facilities, strategic location, and oil was "vital to the very existence of the Commonwealth." Late in 1951, a thoughtful and anonymous commentator sought to state the dimensions of the British task without apparently being aware of the enormity of the problem he put into words. Britain would have to use to the full its experience of the Middle East and the prestige of British leaders in the area—for the writer assumed that the Arabs considered the British to be the most understanding and least objectionable of foreigners—"to revive, over against the present temporary tumult, the abiding sense that the British Commonwealth of Nations is in the long run the most tried and trustworthy friend to Islam and the peoples of the Middle East."

The author added: "It goes without saying that here, as elsewhere in the world, the material resources of help can be predominantly supplied only by the United States." [73] The writers for the Commonwealth journal, *Round Table*, occasionally indulge in forms of satisfied self-contemplation of the British Commonwealth, and when they do, they also exaggerate the political effectiveness of Middle Eastern and Asian recognition of British experience and, for example, the willingness of Arab leaders to look on Britain as the trusted "family solicitor."

In this view there is, misleadingly, the appearance of Britain in the middle, Britain the mediator. But the British policy here involved seeking an Anglo-American front, involving British experience and American resources. The purpose of the front was to work out an adjustment to the Middle Eastern revolution that would make unnecessary capitulation to the revolution. This is a well-tried Tory policy, at home and abroad, to save a number of interests by adjustment that in turn holds off revolution.

At any rate, though the United States and the Middle East had much to learn about moderation and consistency from Britain, the necessary coordination of the two powers at the topmost level did not take place. The lack of coordination was unfortunate. But was it at all even a good bet to assume that a great power would use its resources to buttress a lesser power in positions that were of declining value? All the more, was it a good bet when the most powerful political sentiments of the Middle East were directed against Israel and those positions? Above all, why would the Arab peoples, not at all insensitive to power as even the Conservative stereotypes about the Oriental mind suggest, continue to accept the British in these positions?

Indeed, Anglo-American coordination appeared early (March 14, 1953) in the negotiations when American Ambassador Jefferson Caffrey accompanied the British Ambassador on his first call on General Naguib and Dr. Fawzi. After the Egyptians indicated that they did not want trilateral diplomacy in these matters, Caffrey said that he would not seek to be present against Egyptian wishes. The American government also promised substantial aid to Egypt when

[73] "Mr. Churchill's Return," *Round Table*, XLII (1951-1952), 5, 7. Churchill had made the same point in reference to Persia. *Parliamentary Debates*, Commons, 5th series, Vol. 591, col. 2667, July 31, 1951. Earlier *The Economist* had expressed the same view in "New Start in the Middle East," July 16, 1949.

the dispute with Britain should be resolved. Finally, Ambassador Caffrey took a most significant, though not public, role in attempting to mediate the differences between Britain and Egypt.[74]

If Britain was to have Middle Eastern bases, even bases for the West, it had become clear—but not indisputable in political debate —that she required the consent of the host nation. Eden and Churchill believed that the bases were necessary not only for the defense of the Middle East against attack from the outside but as a source of influence in the domestic life of the area's states, especially for dealing with riots and rebellions. But the very search for consent, as well as the bases themselves, proved to be a source of instability, for the prospect of serious negotiations or a treaty with Britain was often met by rioting and demonstrations. In the minds of many British officials the palpable insecurity of these conditions appeared to confirm the necessity of bases and the arrangements that provoked the violent protests. How then were stability and security to be achieved? In the Far East and Southeast Asia British policy was to give way to Asian nationalism and to hope for the best from cooperation with the Asian states. Was it solely the vital nature of British interests in transit and oil that impeded British leaders from envisaging a similar solution for the Middle East? Or was it that British policy-makers having less confidence in the leaders and people of the Middle East thereby justified continued British dominance? But while India and Burma were relatively inaccessible to the Soviet Union, the Middle East was more exposed to the Soviet Union and readily opened to other areas.

The difficulty and, finally, the costly near-futility of holding a base against the wishes of the host nation helped to induce the British government to seek an agreement on the Canal Zone base. There, after the withdrawal of Egyptian labor and occasional harassment by Egyptian activists, an ever larger number of troops were stationed under extremely trying conditions. Both the British and Egyptian leaders faced domestic difficulties in seeking a settlement. The Conservative Party had cheered Churchill's charges of "scuttle" against Labour, and the government had to make allowances for the susceptibility of its supporters, who might not prove so responsive to changing political realities as the officials of the Foreign Office or

[74] Eden's acknowledgement of the American role in helping to reach the Anglo-Egyptian agreement is printed in *Department of State Bulletin*, XXXI (1954), 234.

the military servants of the Queen. Indeed, a segment of the Conservative Party rebelled against the government's policy, and, subsequently, this split probably weighed heavily on Sir Anthony Eden
when he became Prime Minister.

The government's courage, however, was one of necessity. Time
was running out, for the Anglo-Egyptian Treaty would expire in
1956, although a more legalist and less anti-imperialist world might
have thought that unilateral Egyptian abrogation of the Treaty
restored rights in an earlier *status quo*. Thus, negotiations gave promise of something, whereas delay might leave the government with
nothing or, if the government tried to keep forces at Suez, a very
tense and embarrassing situation.[75] Against these arguments was
the special mistrust of Egypt for invoking in the Canal measures of
contraband control that meant interference with Israeli shipping in
the Canal. Here the British legal case was not an assured one, but
the action might be considered a portent that Egypt would not
permit free navigation through the Canal.

The Egyptian leadership had an even less stable base. In 1954
Nasser succeeded to the primacy held by Naguib. As the latter was
popular, there was the real danger that he would seek to rally forces
of opposition against Nasser. An agreement with Britain might be
dangerous, for any agreement could be criticized as a sell-out. But
an agreement might also be presented as a triumph and the achievement of the national cause.

Negotiations began in Cairo, April 27, 1953, and, though Britain
was conceding much from the imperial past, British bargaining was
hard and skillful. Indeed, on May 6, 1953, Colonel Nasser felt impelled to warn that this time the Egyptians were not "prepared to
waste time in allowing the discussions to drag on as the previous
ones did for a year and a half." [76]

In the face of Egypt's challenge the forces at the base had been
increased to about 75,000 men, far beyond the number permitted

[75] An article, "Cross Purposes in Egypt," in *Round Table*, XLIV (1953-1954),
228-229, argued that Britain had engaged herself so much to follow legal principles in international affairs that it is not practicable for Britain just "to sit tight
and ignore Egyptian protests." "The choice is between arranging the withdrawal
of our forces decently, by agreement, giving us such rights as we can obtain, or
staying on until we have to go, as the result of an arbitral decision with which we
shall be bound to comply." Such a withdrawal "would be far more damaging to
our prestige than any agreement that can be reached now."

[76] Quoted in Fabunmi, *op. cit.*, pp. 306-307.

by the Treaty. With its armories, warehouses, and airfields, the base represented an investment estimated at about £500,000,000. The negotiators agreed that parts of the base should be maintained in condition ready for use. To that end, for the period covered by the Treaty, Britain should be free to move material in or out of the base at her discretion. There was a long dispute about the forces designated to maintain the base. In the face of Egyptian opposition the British negotiators reduced the number asked for to 1,200 and, finally yielding on the point that they had to be in uniform, agreed that they should be civilian personnel. The British forces would be withdrawn within twenty months of the signing of the agreement and, thereafter, the civilian personnel would keep the base in readiness for a period of seven years. Here it should be noted that the agreement in effect did not require the British forces to leave much before the date of expiry provided in the 1936 treaty. During the seven-year period—Britain had asked for two decades—Britain had the right of re-entry to the base if any member of the Arab Collective Security pact or Turkey were attacked by a power outside the region. Britain had sought to add Iran to the list of countries but here Egyptian objections had prevailed, although the Egyptians did yield to British insistence on the inclusion of Turkey. So, Britain had gained Egyptian consent to the British use of the base until 1956, and, under certain conditions, until 1963.

The Minister of State, Anthony Nutting, put a firmly triumphant face on the matter, when he argued: "The most important point is that we now have for the first time a legal right to maintain a base in Egypt." [77] Captain Waterhouse, the leader of the Conservative rebellion over Suez, used language that the Tories usually reserved for Labour: the agreement was not so much a sell-out as a give-away.[78]

The demon of consistency between past, even recent statements, and contemporary statements of Conservative leaders embarrassed the government in the Commons debate on the Heads of Agreement. Attlee did not spare Churchill the lesson in continuity which the Conservative leader had read to Labour in 1952 and 1953: "There is an immense difference between the Prime Minister in office and the Prime Minister in opposition. When he comes into office he has to face realities, he has to take responsibility instead

[77] *Parliamentary Debates*, Commons, Vol. 631, col. 1607, October 25, 1954.
[78] *Ibid.*, col. 739, July 29, 1954.

of indulging in merely facetious attacks on those who are bearing responsibility." [79] The Labour leader quoted the speeches of Conservative leaders in 1946 to the effect that the Canal Zone base was essential to the Canal's security and to British interests. But within the partisan arguments there was a substantial measure of agreement and a revelation of the continuity of British policy as analogous to the continuity of living. Churchill had formidably opposed "scuttle" in 1946, 1947-1948, and 1951, because he believed that British concessions and renunciation would leave Britain weak in the face of further demands and in upholding vital interests. His criticism has a somber, Gibbonian charm but it was mischievous, for he was in opposition and had the misguided optimism about British resources and strength that sometimes made for British daring (and once gave Britain an advantage over cautious and dilatory powers) but which was gravely unsuited to the postwar world. In the same years, 1946-1951, the left-wing of the Labour Party criticized the Labour government for following a Tory foreign policy laid down by the permanent officials of the Foreign Office. When the Tories returned to power, they had to face the realities of international politics and could argue that the direction of events could not be reversed. On the Egyptian Treaty the charge of "scuttle" was hurled again, merely as a self-satisfying taunt by the Labour Party, but in grim earnestness by the Suez Rebels, who could readily quote Churchill against the present action of the Conservative government.

In defending the proposed treaty, the government leaders argued that it made possible both financial economy and military efficiency. The costs of maintaining the once beleaguered base would be greatly diminished and the troops from the base could be used to form a strategic reserve and to overcome the almost congenital inclination of British governments to scatter their forces around the world and end up with almost no effective army in readiness for action in a crisis. The government leaders also emphasized that Egypt had reaffirmed the Canal Convention of 1888, a guarantee of derisory value according to Conservative speakers in preceding years.

Moreover, the government was able to support its case by referring to the impact of nuclear weapons on strategic views, for the H-bomb had made a great impression on British thinking at that time. The government argued that the H-bomb had revolutionized strategic thinking and compelled the recognition that the military base at

[79] *Ibid.*, col. 737, July 29, 1954.

Suez would be unusable in war. But would not the H-bomb be as revolutionary on the new British headquarters in Cyprus, which the government had said could not look forward to sovereignty? And if the base would be unusable, then why the elaborate discussion about the rights of re-entry? Finally, the argument that the Suez base could only be useful if the Egyptian population was cooperative evoked a query about the value of the Cyprus base in the light of the Greek Cypriote demand for *enosis*.[80]

On the whole the agreement was well received in the Commons debate, though many speakers thought parts of the government's case, the H-bomb, the strategic reserve, and economy, to be special pleading. The debate followed Eden's triumph at the Geneva Conference on Indo-China. Thus, he enjoyed Labour's good will and the benefits of Conservative sense of well-being, strengthened by the recently made decision to hold on to Cyprus.

The Secretary of State for War, Anthony Head, insisted that "the main consideration, strategically, is our relations with the Egyptian people and with the Egyptian government in the future." With the agreement, the prospect of better relations with Egypt appeared. But there was little more than a cautious and almost unbelieved hope of improvement in the official presentation. Indeed, an alternative course was hinted by Head when he referred to Turkey's membership in NATO. Foreshadowing the Baghdad Pact, he believed that Turkish membership meant that "the likelihood of our being able to take part in a more forward strategy on Turkey's right flank in the defence of the Middle East is very much increased." [81]

In withdrawing from the Canal Zone, the British government made a compulsory gamble on the continuing good faith of Nasser and Egypt. The government's reply to its Conservative critics was that in the face of Egyptian hostility the base could only be maintained on an ineffective level and at great expense. As the government's case was drawn from recent experience, then the security of the Canal rested on Nasser's good faith, reinforced by his interest in not provoking Britain to severe retaliation. Nasser, in making the treaty with Britain, claimed a triumph and received the heady ac-

[80] *Ibid.*, cols. 726, 728, 743, 744, July 29, 1954. Captain Waterhouse rejected the argument that a hostile Egypt would tie down tens of thousands of British troops. Against cogent government objections, he insisted that a small force could do the job. "All over the world we have been doing that for hundreds of years." His conclusion was that "we are really losing our will to rule."

[81] *Ibid.*, col. 726, July 29, 1954.

claim of a victor over imperialism. Indeed, this may have given the hitherto uncertain Egyptian leader with his chameleon affability the taste for the spectacular triumphs he sought in the succeeding years. Those gestures, exploiting British-American divergences and reducing British influence to its lowest point, have tended to bury in oblivion the triumphs of British diplomacy detailed here. Britain held on to a nearly untenable position for a long time and in withdrawing salvaged, at first, a great deal.

6: THE BAGHDAD PACT

Between 1952 and the spring of 1955 British diplomacy had actively attempted to settle outstanding differences between Britain and Middle Eastern states. The approach, in accordance with Eden's *modus operandi* of one problem at a time, was successful as long as it remained a piecemeal one. But when British policy sought in the Baghdad Pact—this time following an American lead along the lines of the unsuccessful Middle East Defense Organization—to establish regional defense arrangements that would provide for the discharge of the British claim of primary responsibility for the Middle East, this active enterprise ran into challenges and storms that gathered momentum towards the Suez expedition.

Agreements had terminated the Iranian and Egyptian disputes. The Governor of Aden, hoping to end frontier disputes, even visited the Imam of Yemen. In 1954 Britain also agreed to arbitrate her differences with Saudi Arabia over Buraimi Oasis, where the villages respected, if recognized is too formal a word, the indirect authority of the Sheikh of Abu Dhabi and the Sultan of Muscat and Oman, both of whom received British protection and, in external matters, were advised by British political officers. In August 1952 Saudi forces, basing their claim on the fact that the Wahhabis had conquered the oasis and for many years between 1800 and 1869 had received from the inhabitants of the oasis a religious payment presented in the Saudi case as a tax, occupied one of its eight villages. On behalf of Muscat and Abu Dhabi the British government submitted the dispute to arbitration in Geneva.[1] But in 1955 the tribunal broke up without a judgment in the wake of the resignation of the British member, who charged that Saudi bribery in the oasis was an act of bad faith and that on Saudi initiative attempts had been made to influence members of the tribunal. Thereafter, the British-officered

[1] On July 29, 1954, Eden noted the agreement to arbitrate. *Parliamentary Debates*, Commons, 5th series, Vol. 631, col. 818.

Oman Levies and Trucial Scouts reoccupied the oasis and Saudi Arabia broke diplomatic relations with Britain.[2]

In the new state of Libya, on the other hand, Britain acquired a special, but, as Suez was to reveal, limited position. During the war Britain had pledged to the Senusi exiles from Italian Cyrenaica that they would not again fall under Italian rule. After the territory of future Libya had been under British and French military administrations for some years, the United Nations in 1949, for want of any more readily acceptable disposition of the territory, resolved that Libya should become an independent state. As the new state (December 24, 1951) could not at first afford even the usual trappings of a sovereign polity, the British government on July 30, 1953, signed with this new member of the Arab League and the United Nations a treaty whereby Britain provided an annual subsidy, trained the Libyan army, and was, in turn, afforded a military base there, to which a number of the troops withdrawn from the Canal Zone were sent. On September 9, 1954, the United States signed a base rights agreement with Libya and so secured the use of the Wheelus airbase.

But the search for new and pacific settlements may encounter old or new forms of conflicting interests. The most spectacular new conflicts emerged as consequences of the membership (February 18, 1952) of Greece and, notably, Turkey, in NATO.[3] In describing (December 17, 1953) Anglo-Egyptian negotiations, Eden argued that

[2] Saudi Arabia branded the British attack as a retaliation against a Saudi-Egyptian defense pact. Eden was shocked to learn that the United States government regarded the reoccupation of Buraimi as an act of aggression against Saudi Arabia. According to Eden, President Eisenhower told him that the British must "take account of world opinion," and Dulles told other diplomats that Saudi public opinion considered Britain as an aggressor. Eden had more than little reason to complain of the willingness of American policy-makers to do on occasion almost anything for a questionable ally rather than an old one. *Full Circle*, pp. 373-74. After the agreement to evacuate the Canal Zone, the British position in the face of challenges in the Persian Gulf was delicate. Many people, however, glibly saw the dispute as solely an issue of oil imperialism. See J. B. Kelly, "The Buraimi Oasis Dispute," *International Affairs*, XXXII (1956), 316-326.

[3] On August 7, 1953, Britain and Turkey signed an agreement whereby in return for the British military equipment supplied before and during the Second World War Turkey undertook to pay £7,500,000 over a period of seven and one-half years. The original British bill had been more than £50,000,000. Up to Turkey's suspension of payments in the summer of 1951, Turkey had made a return of about £17,000,000.

"the position of Turkey is decisive in this Near Eastern theatre" and that an agreement with Egypt was desirable because it would permit Britain to redeploy her forces for more effective defense of the Middle East. Such a rearrangement, his words imply, would make very clear that the British position was no longer an imperial one but was concerned with defense of the area as an interest both of the area and the West. Eight months later, in defending the heads of the Anglo-Egyptian Agreement, he described his critics' charge of "scuttle" as ludicrous, "when, by the arrangement we are trying to make, we shall get nearer to the possible enemy than we were before." He added: "I hope and believe that under this Agreement there will be other bases." [4]

Turkey, then, as in the Middle East Defense Organization, was to be the key to Middle Eastern defense. But, though Turkey had made earlier treaties of friendship with Iraq and Abdullah's Transjordan, there were difficulties in the close association of Turkey with Arab states. Turkish leaders, too clear-sighted to make allowances for the illusory political rhetoric of Arabism, had even recognized Israel and established close relations with her. After 1953, however, Turkish Prime Minister Adnan Menderes sedulously cultivated other Muslim states and showed a new sensitivity to the Arab world.[5] Now, if regional defense was to be established, Turkey and Britain would have to consolidate their positions. In particular, Britain would have to secure the use of the Iraqi bases beyond 1957, which she had failed to obtain in 1948. The approach of the new Eisenhower administration, which had sparked Turkish initiative, eventually appeared to present the means of solving the Iraqi problem.

In the spring of 1953, Secretary of State John Foster Dulles made a tour of Middle Eastern states. One of his purposes was to sound out the possibilities of extricating the United States from the consequences of its earlier support of and close association with Israel. There was to be no repudiation of Israel, but Dulles hoped to acquire a certain capacity for maneuver and some influence with Arab leaders by loosening the ties of an intractable Israel with the United States. The approach was not quite happily symbolized in his presentation

[4] *Parliamentary Debates*, Commons, 5th series, Vol. 631, col. 811, July 29, 1954.
[5] On February 20, 1954, the Turkish Prime Minister Koprulu declared that his government would be neutral in Middle Eastern disputes not affecting Turkish interests. But neutralism in the Arab-Israeli struggle was often given a very hostile interpretation by Arab leaders who professed neutralism in the Cold War.

of a pistol on behalf of President Eisenhower to General Naguib.[6]

Dulles expounded the new approach in a TV-radio address (June 1, 1953). His words gave no endorsement to the view that the Middle East was a primary British responsibility. Instead, he noted that the difficulties in organizing Middle Eastern defense arose from the grievances of the Middle Eastern people against colonialism. Britain and France, the allies of the United States in NATO, were the targets of this mistrust based on their persisting imperial interests and, as a consequence, the United States had to follow a cautious policy that took account of the interests of its allies. As the United States had also incurred the suspicion of some Middle Easterners, "I am convinced that United States policy has become unnecessarily ambiguous in this matter." Thus, American policy must be geared to a major force in Asia: the opposition of Middle Eastern and Southern Asian people to the colonial powers and their demand for independence.

Then, apparently answering a British argument that such an American course was oblivious to the immediate requirements of defense and to the ensuing vacuum, Dulles argued with an optimism not later vindicated that his course would not mean a sudden breakup of colonial holdings, for even the people of the Middle East did not call for such a disruption of the world. But to this argument the British government might have replied that only those Arab leaders with whom they worked showed such prudence. Dulles concluded this section of his speech with remarks that the British would have endorsed as objectives but probably found disquieting in their context. All powers concerned, he observed, aspired to extending "the

[6] President Eisenhower also wrote to General Naguib (July 15, 1953), expressing the willingness of the United States to supply economic and military aid to Egypt after an accord on the Canal Zone had been made with the British. Upon this intervention, though there is no certainty that it was largely because of this intervention, the Anglo-Egyptian negotiations advanced rapidly for a time. The prime obstacle on the Egyptian side, then, was the British insistence on the right of re-entry to the Canal Zone base, in the event of an attack on Turkey.

Here the United States used its full resources to support the British position. In succeeding months Nasser attacked the United States for following with Britain "a common, predetermined policy" and for using aid as an opiate to induce enslaved people to forego struggles for liberation. Naguib's formulation was that the United States administered "the anesthesia, while Britain applied the scalpel." The quotations appear in Keith Wheelock, *Nasser's New Egypt* (New York, 1960), pp. 214-215.

orderly development of self-government." Thus, without endangering Western unity, "we can pursue our traditional dedication to political liberty." [7]

Partly because of the mistrust incurred by colonial powers, a general regional organization for the defense of the Middle East was not feasible for the immediate future. For some time, at any rate, it would not be able to rest, as it would eventually have to, on the will and consent of the people and states, for the project of alliance with a Western power was unpopular. The same sentiment, however, did not prevail in the northern tier of states adjoining the Soviet Union. With those states, aware of the Soviet menace and willing to concert measures of defense, the United States could hope to establish relations that would involve military and economic assistance possibly culminating in some cooperative gathering of strength.

This American approach was decidedly piecemeal. It looked to extending cooperation with Turkey and Pakistan as well as with Iran and, probably, Iraq, which, of course, was viewed as a special interest of Britain. It also had the advantage that in dealing with the northern tier, American policy-makers were able to bypass the Canal Zone dispute as well as the Arab-Israeli conflict. But the bypassing, also, called attention to the West's difficulties in the area to which in 1955 the Soviet Union leap-frogged.

[7] The quotations are from the text of the Secretary's talk in *Department of State Bulletin*, XXVIII (June 15, 1953), 833,835. Dulles' remarks about colonialism are noteworthy because Sir Anthony Eden and others later made it a reproach to Dulles that he thought the British position in the Middle East was imperialist. Dulles' words may present a reality with some roughness but it was a reality. The expression of his views may also have been designed as a tactic to urge the British government to concessions in the Middle East by warning of the limits of American support for Britain. The curious way in which the British and American roles in the Middle East were reversed in Southeast Asia is strikingly illustrated by the following remarks concerning American policy in Southeast Asia in *Round Table*, XLV (1954-1955), 115: ". . . the greatest need of Americans today is to understand and meet the challenge of the anti-imperialist revolutions. It is the American failure to understand these revolutions which more than anything else is preventing a constructive programme of peace and social politics to counter the further spread of Communism to the underdeveloped and uncommitted peoples." Thus, it appears that the United States criticized Britain for imperialism in the Middle East, where Britain claimed special responsibility; and Britain criticized the United States for failing to understand anti-imperialism in the Far East. But—an important qualification—American power greatly exceeded British in both areas. And another qualification: Dulles spoke broadly of the unpopularity of the colonial powers but not about the unpopularity of the United States for its role in the creation of Israel.

The American government pursued its policy by continuing military aid to Turkey, by concluding with Pakistan an agreement concerning mutual assistance (May 19, 1954), and finally by providing military assistance to Iraq.[8] The Iraqi-American agreement (April 21, 1954), on which negotiations were begun after Iraqi initiative in March 1953, was a crucial measure in gaining Iraqi willingness to take part in regional defense arrangements.[9] On April 2, 1954, after a good deal of discussion in Middle Eastern countries resulting from the Turkish and American efforts to extend the initial membership, Turkey and Pakistan signed an agreement concerning friendship, cooperation, and mutual assistance to which other powers sharing their purposes were invited to adhere.[10] Iraq wavered in the early stages of this agreement. The wavering resulted from three considerations: the first and simplest was the desire to make a good bargain and to increase the benefits that might be offered to her; the second was the instability of the Iraqi government in the first half of 1954; the third was the threat posed against the Iraqi government from Arab leaders who might denounce Iraq's joining with Turkey and Pakistan as a sell-out of the collective Arab cause and, thus, increase political instability.[11]

In the changes of the Iraqi government during 1954 Nuri es-Said again became Prime Minister. This time, to consolidate his position, he had political parties dissolved and imposed a censorship as well as other far-reaching controls over his countrymen. After such preparations Nuri received very substantial support in a subsequent election.

The problem posed by Nuri's difficulties in Iraq emphasizes the

[8] In the fall of 1953 Pakistani Governor-General Ghulam Mohammed had visited Washington. On February 22, 1954, Pakistan formally asked for American military aid. At the same time the American government adopted the policy of fostering the defensive capacity of the Middle East by aiding Pakistan and encouraging a Turco-Pakistani alliance. Strenuous but vain efforts, which included the prospect of military aid to India, were made to reassure Nehru. The Turco-Pakistani Pact was relatively loose both to discourage criticism and retaliatory action and to promote the adhesion of other members.

[9] Department of State Bulletin, XXXI (1954), 401, 772-773.

[10] The text is in Denise Folliot, editor, Documents on International Affairs, 1954 (Royal Institute of International Affairs, New York, 1957), pp. 185-186.

[11] In an important and revealing speech after Suez (December 16, 1956), Premier Nuri es-Said noted that the violent Cairo radio attacks on Iraq began not after the signing of the Baghdad Pact but in March 1954. The text is produced in M. Khalil, editor, The Arab States and the Arab League (Beirut, 1962), II, 255-279; for Nuri's charge see, p. 268.

limited political effectiveness of economic development programs. Nuri es-Said's government, like its predecessors, had invested a large part of the government's oil revenues in long-term development programs. Nevertheless, many Iraqi nationalists thought of him as a reactionary and as the tool of Western imperialism. His undercutting and suppression of opposition faced him with a generation of frustrated rivals who had come to hate him. Nuri, too, however, was an Arab nationalist, and, thus, an enemy of Israel and, even had he not been, would have had to act like one in calling for the abrogation of the Anglo-Iraqi treaty. But he understood well that Iraq was a near neighbor of the Soviet Union and had to look to the West for aid in defense as well as in the profitable exploitation of oil and the development of her economy. For these plans and for the maintenance of Iraq's position among the Arab states as well as for his hopes of Fertile Crescent unity, he saw no other practical source of assistance than Britain, familiar to him since 1917, and the United States.

Britain, thus, ranked first with him, and his dilemma consequently was how to behave as an Iraqi nationalist without destroying wider reaches of pan-Arabism. How far was Arabism compatible at all with an alliance with a Western power? The question was a difficult one, for, on occasion, Nuri made full use of pan-Arab rhetoric. The pan-Arab sentiment may not have been a constructive political force in many respects but it was a force.

Britain, in turn, had to reach new terms with Iraq, for the Treaty under which Britain held bases in Iraq was to expire in 1957. The bases could then serve a Middle Eastern defense arrangement, although they had originally been selected and developed primarily to play a part in maintaining the domestic order of Iraq. So, Britain, also, faced a dilemma: how to hold on to privileges in Iraq and, at the same time, yield them to satisfy Iraqi nationalism, for, after conceding so much to a less friendly Egypt, Britain would have to be at least comparably generous to the government of a staunch friend, the Iraq of Nuri es-Said.[12]

For both parties the solution ultimately appeared to be in an extension of the Turco-Pakistani agreement, for this alignment had

[12] Iraq on one occasion suggested to the British government that the Anglo-Iraqi Treaty be replaced by an agreement similar to the Anglo-Egyptian arrangement concerning Suez. Thus, in an emergency Britain could reoccupy the Iraqi bases. Richard P. Stebbins, *The United States in World Affairs*, 1954 (New York, 1956), p. 345.

the apparent advantage of involving Muslim states as partners. As Arab nationalism had involved identification with Islam and the Arabic language, the alliance would have that link with Arab nationalism. Earlier in 1954, when Mohammed Fadhil al-Jamali was Iraqi Premier, he had expressed qualified approval of that agreement and had affirmed that Arab collective security depended upon Arab rearmament and, accordingly, Iraq would continue to purchase Western arms. But before breaking the front of Arabism, Nuri attempted to deal with the opposition of Nasser. In August 1954 Nasser had sent Major Salah Salem to dissuade Nuri and Iraqi leaders from acting independently of the Arab League. Salah Salem may have offered more inducements than he was authorized, for upon his return to Cairo he fell into apparent disfavor. The temporary downgrading of the Major, however, was so public and brief that it may have been a gesture to support a denial of the reported inducement. The latter, an Egyptian promise not to block Nuri's efforts to promote a federation with Syria, had to be denied, if the offer failed, because the rumor would then hamper Nasser's promotion of Arab unity by alternate means. Nuri himself stated that the Major and he had approved an Arab defense arrangement and Iraq's adherence to the Turco-Pakistani agreement, which would have remained a Muslim alignment.[13]

The following month Nuri went to Cairo and vainly sought to persuade Nasser of the desirability of broadening the Arab League Collective Security Pact by including Pakistan, Turkey, Britain, and the United States. After this failure Nuri in October went to Turkey where he agreed that the project of a Middle Eastern defense arrangement be pursued at once, that Iraq would bring her policy into line with the objectives of the Turco-Pakistani Agreement, and that Iraq would not act definitively until she had consulted the Arab states. Menderes of Turkey, too, sought to persuade Nasser to favor a practical regional defense arrangement but soon found that Nasser had reversed his views on the Turks and had replaced the Turks as brothers with the Turks as Ottoman enemy.

On January 12, 1955, Turkey and Iraq announced that they would conclude a treaty "with a view to enforcing and expanding the existing cooperation for the stability and security of the Middle East region."[14] Radio Cairo's "Voice of the Arabs" unleashed a vitriolic

[13] Wheelock, op. cit., p. 219.
[14] Official Communique in Noble Frankland, editor, Documents on International Affairs, 1955 (New York, 1958), p. 286.

campaign against Iraq. The latter, in arguing before the Arab League, had a good case. Nuri argued, for example, that Egypt should have made the provision in the Anglo-Egyptian Treaty concerning British re-entry to the Canal Zone a matter for regional agreement; for if British troops had to come to Turkey's assistance, they would likely have to cross Arab territory. Nuri further recalled Iraqi support of Egypt's case and complained of Egypt's failure to help get rid of Iraq's treaty with Britain. Nuri and Fadhil al-Jamali both noted that Egypt had no suggestion likely to be helpful to Iraq in the immediate future. Indeed, they also noted Egypt's attempt to use the Arab League in a dictatorial way, overriding the sovereign rights of members.[15]

At Cairo, in December 1954, a meeting of the foreign ministers of the member states of the Arab League Collective Security Pact made another effort to settle differences and agreed only on the necessity of strengthening the pact and developing a military organization to assume responsibility for Middle Eastern defense. But in casting the play of Arab unity, Egypt and Iraq were working from separate scripts which involved different plots and protagonists. The first two months of 1955 were full of rumors of plans and retaliatory and conciliatory projects.

On February 24, 1955, the true ancestor of the Baghdad Pact appeared with the signing of an agreement by Turkey and Iraq. In pledging themselves to cooperate in defense and the provision of security, they declared that membership was open to any member of the Arab League or to any other state recognized by the two countries and actively concerned with the peace and security of the Middle East.

This was the opening that permitted Britain to resolve the problem of the Iraqi bases. The opening involved a repetition of the settlement attempted with Egypt in 1951 whereby the British bases in the Canal Zone would have been transformed into the bases of the proposed Middle Eastern Defense Organization. In the present instance the Anglo-Iraqi Treaty of 1930, a bilateral arrangement, was abrogated and under the Baghdad Pact (April 4, 1955) Britain made a special defense arrangement with Iraq, whereby the latter assumed full responsibility for her own defense and control of the former British installations which the British were permitted to use for the purposes of the Pact.

[15] Khalil, *op. cit.*, II, 230-236, 255-279.

In signing the Pact the British government professed to be adopting an American idea and to be responding to the initiative of Turkey and Iraq. But the British role in the prelude of the Pact is not at all clear. Although on January 28, 1954, the government had expressed support for the Turco-Pakistani Agreement, the degree of British initiative is not now assessable. Certainly British leaders did not publicly express any notable interest in the northern tier, for the British government argued that the northern tier failed to take account of British interests in Egypt, the Canal, and the Persian Gulf. In his memoirs Eden, exploiting a sophisticated literary convention (by omitting the background he here achieved the naive charm of a pastoral), reported that he "was delighted to hear at the end of 1954" of Nuri's plans "to strengthen the Arab League Pact, by the inclusion of Turkey and with the help of the United Kingdom and the United States." Perhaps, Eden thought, Pakistan, Iran, and Jordan would also join the revised arrangement.[16]

In signing the Pact over Egyptian opposition the British government entered a course which risked the advantages gained in the Anglo-Egyptian Treaty. True, that Treaty meant in the mind of the British government that Turkey would be the core of Middle Eastern defense planning. But in providing that Britain could re-enter the Canal Zone base, if a member of the Arab League Collective Security Pact were attacked by a power from outside the Middle East, the Treaty also provided an important link to the Arab world. Nasser, in effect, claiming a veto over Arab states, regarded the Pact as a challenge to himself, and his response threatened the Pact from the start. As he had expressed vehement criticism even to the preliminaries of the Pact early in 1954, his opposition should have been and possibly was anticipated.

A deficiency in Eden's calculations was in underestimating Nasser himself and the resources which Arab nationalism made available to him. American policy, as formulated by Dulles, professed greater sympathy for Arab nationalism than British policy-makers did at this time, but supported the Baghdad Pact and uttered no public misgivings. In recognizing the insecurity of Nasser's position, Eden might perhaps indulge in the hope that if Nasser was not compliant, he might be replaced by a more amenable leader. Like Curzon, Eden knew the Middle East, but his knowledge was out of date. Eden himself admitted: "I did not then foresee the extent of Egyptian ex-

---

[16] Eden, *op. cit.*, pp. 243-244.

pansionist aims over other Arab states." But even more important was the fact that Eden overrated British influence and the Arab pillar, Nuri's Iraq, on which it rested and depreciated the possibilities open to Nasser. Of the latter's charge that the Baghdad Pact was inopportunely timed, he curtly remarked: "It is never the right time for some." After talking with Nasser in Cairo (February 1955), he reported to London: "No doubt jealousy plays a part in this, and a frustrated desire to lead the Arab world." And, on Nasser's testimony, Eden's attitude was adopted by others including the British Ambassador. In 1961 Nasser declared that the opportunity for a new start in Anglo-Egyptian relations had existed in 1954 and had been missed. He blamed the persisting British attitude of patronage and cited the approach of the British Ambassador shortly after the agreement: "Now we are friends, we hope you will support us over Cyprus." [17] On the personal level, then, there is here a conflict between Eden's judgment that Nasser was behaving arrogantly[18] and Nasser's overreadiness to regard any opposition to himself as the survival of imperialism.

In underestimating Nasser and his resources, Eden felt justified in proceeding to join the Pact. Doubtless, he gained resolution from the reflection that once an objective is adopted, firmness in pursuit of it is likely to be more profitable and successful than the vacillation and irresolution, masking conflicting interests by irresolute professions of universal benevolence, that beginning in 1955 characterized American policy in the Middle East. Above all, the Egyptian attack on Nuri required a firm reply: loyal support of an ally.

[17] Eden, op. cit., pp. 290, 245; Nasser interview with Times correspondent, The Times, May 15, 1961. Eden's misreading of Egyptian and Arab nationalism was shared by the Times commentator on the transfer of the Iraqi bases from British to Iraqi control. He attributed the sharpness of Egypt's attacks on the Baghdad Pact to Egypt's realization that "the leadership of the Arabs is inexorably slipping from her grasp," and going presumably to Iraq. As a consequence of Nasser's participation in the Bandung Conference, the writer thought it likely that Egypt would withdraw into an African, not an Arab, counterpart of India or Yugoslavia. The Times, May 2, 1955.

[18] The arrogance in Nasser's assumption of the position of dictatorial spokesman for the Arab states clearly appears in a communique concerning Arab defense issued on March 11, 1956, by Egypt, Syria, and Saudi Arabia (the last playing a game very dangerous to its own future). The ninth point records that the conferees had agreed on a plan to end the dispute concerning Buraimi oasis and the Oman Emirate. The plan would also preserve the "Arab character" of the areas and prevent "any breach of their sovereignty." Khalil, op. cit., II, 249.

The United States government, which had supported the Baghdad
Pact in its early stages, had a greater flexibility than Britain and re-
frained from membership in the Pact.[19] Of the abstention of the
United States from membership in the Baghdad Pact, and its failure
to support allies in matters of generally agreed policy, Eden was
severely critical. The United States, he argued, "has sometimes failed
to put its weight behind its friends, in the hope of being popular with
their foes." The United States ventured on a course of "uncertain
diplomacy" in inspiring the Baghdad Pact and then holding back.

> Worse still, they tried to take credit for this attitude in capitals,
> like Cairo, which were hostile to the Pact. . . . A strong power,
> rich in resources, once it determines its goal, has a fair chance to
> reach it, if it holds to its purpose. A devious course is disastrous.
> It is a borrower and lender in diplomacy and loses both itself and
> friend.[20]

For a time, indeed, the Pact spurred diplomatic activity that made
it appear to have some promise. Efforts were initiated to link many
Middle Eastern countries in a series of alliances that might form a
defense system.[21] Pakistan and Iran joined the Pact. But its growth
hardly justified Eden's judgment of the period late in 1955: "The
Baghdad Pact was proving a firm stabilizer." [22] A far juster judgment
is that the Baghdad Pact notably intensified tensions and instability
in the Middle East. How much American support of the Pact would
have mitigated the tensions cannot be answered with assurance. Indeed, even the mitigating effect is not certain.

The instability arose not simply from Egyptian opposition to the
Pact but from the grounds on which Nasser opposed it and the

[19] The American diplomatic papers concerning this story are likely to provide
choice material for the student who delights in the stories of cross-purposes.

[20] Eden, op. cit., pp. 374-375.

[21] A high Pakistani official announced that the Turkish President and the Prime
Minister of Pakistan had under way a project that might include Iran, Syria,
Lebanon, Jordan, and Yemen. The Times, February 21, 1955.

[22] Eden, op. cit., p. 370. Citing the British position in Iraq, Jordan, Cyprus,
the Persian Gulf, and British and American bases in Libya, Turkey in NATO,
and the Anglo-Egyptian Treaty (1954), a writer in Round Table, XLV (1954-
1955), 133, concluded: "By and large the Middle East seems in a better shape
for defending itself in 1955 than at any time since the end of the war." A Russian attack would bring in Turkey, Iraq, and Egypt. But the writer also noted
two monumental qualifications to his optimism: the imperfect coordination of
British and American policy; the persistence of the basic political conflicts within
the Middle East.

weapons he used in attack, for, effecting a sharp definition of Egyptian policy as Arabist against imperialism, Nasser inaugurated an appeal to Arab people against their rulers.

The public argument against the Baghdad Pact advanced by Nasser was that it represented a continuation of the imperialist policy of stationing foreign troops in Arab countries and aligning an Arab people so that they would have to support Western policy. The Pact was characteristic of imperialism in that it was an act of bad faith on Britain's part, and on Nuri's part an act of treachery in that it divided the Arabs among themselves. The charge of bad faith was made because, he insisted, all parties in the 1954 treaty negotiations had understood that he was to be aided in organizing Middle Eastern defense on an Arab foundation. His argument has a limited validity. He was to be equipped with arms and he was encouraged to get on with the organization of regional defense. But in Eden's eyes his regional plans were likely to be too exclusive and too unrealistic, and they were certainly dilatory, to put the most friendly interpretation on his rebuff to Menderes.

Moreover, Nasser argued, the Pact's anticommunism was self-defeating. The Middle East required a time of quiet in which Arab rivalries might lessen, an opinion which supporters of Eden were inclined to regard as hilarious coming from Nasser, unless they judged at once that his definition of quiet was a free hand for himself. Nasser himself, his case continued, had fought and defeated the communists, because he understood the psychology of the nationalists, who then were adamant against foreign alliances. He had warned Nuri that an alliance with the Western powers would give the communists the opportunity they were seeking. So, Nasser's argument ran, the Baghdad Pact should be condemned on anticommunist grounds. Nasser even sought to deal with the objection that the nationalists were blind to the requirements of defense. He explained that he had hoped to strengthen the Arab security agreement and, with a united Arab army serving Arab interests alone, to give the Arab people "the incentive to think strategically." [23]

[23] Speech of Salah Salem, *The Times*, December 29, 1954; interview of Nasser with Ralph Izzard, *Daily Mail*, March 19, 1955; interview of Nasser with Slade-Baker, *Sunday Times*, March 20, 1955. The last interview provided much of the material for the above paragraph.

The interviews were, of course, self-seeking vindications. But the arguments have force and are in accord with the views of some distinguished British Arabists. See the views expressed by Professor H. A. R. Gibb in *United Empire*

Nasser's grounds of attack on Nuri were parochial and took no account of the interests of Turkey, Iran, Pakistan, and Iraq, not to mention the Western powers. The Premier of Iraq was denounced as a traitor to Arabism. To have brought Iraq into the Baghdad Pact was to act incompatibly with membership in the Arab League. But Nasser readily passed beyond the responsibilities of that divided League and talked of the Arab nation, whose people were lying in wait to destroy the imperialists attempting to divide them. For tactical reasons—and, indeed, to speak a partial truth—he declared that Arab nationalism was not represented by any single leader. "It is represented by the whole Arab people who now believe in themselves and in their unity for the sake of security and strength so that they may be able to destroy imperialism." [24]

The key here is the emphasis on the Arab people. The year, 1954, was a time of special challenge to Nasser. He was in charge of a revolutionary government which had successfully achieved the country's prime national goal. In spite of his expressed desire for a quiet time for the lessening of tension, it might have been fatal to indulge in resting on his oars.[25] He could and did turn to the task of domestic reform, and it is at least possible that if large aid in constructing the Aswan Dam had been offered in 1954, he might have become preoccupied with domestic tasks. The offer of such aid, however, awaited Nasser's negotiations to provide for the Sudanese who would be displaced by the artificial lake. But social reform was difficult, slow, and to an insecure dictator seemed to call for more power, which in his case meant a heightening of nationalism. A sense of crisis preoccupied with dangerous tasks abroad is a venerable alma mater of power.

(March-April 1952), p. 73, and in "Anglo-Egyptian Relations," *International Affairs*, XXVII (October 1951), 441-445. In 1950 Lord Strang, interviewing the then Secretary of the Arab League, Abdul Rahman Azzam, was impressed by what he considered Azzam's largeness of view. Azzam said that Britain thought too much of bases and treaties. Lord Strang, *Home and Abroad* (London, 1956), p. 261.

Some two months before the Anglo-Egyptian Treaty (1954), Nasser warned against the pressure for pacts as the source of renewed suspicions which the communists could exploit. Pressure for pacts would be dangerously premature "until the Arabs realize that there is no longer any hidden domination or control in pacts." *The New York Times*, August 20, 1954, quoted in Wheelock, *op. cit.*, p. 217.

[24] Report of a speech, one-hundred and fifteen minutes in delivery, to a visiting group of Syrian students and professors, *New York Times*, February 12, 1955.

[25] Shortly after he made the Anglo-Egyptian agreement, the Muslim Brotherhood made an attempt to assassinate Nasser.

If, then, Nasser joined the Baghdad Pact, he would face domestic difficulties, he would be constrained to work with the representatives of its member states and be inhibited by their separate and even conflicting interests. Its Western members might have checked him in respect to Israel and his approach to Iraq would have to be restrained.[26] In rejecting the Baghdad Pact, however, he could not adopt a position of neutrality. The neutralism he would have to adopt must run counter to the Pact. His neutralism would have to be popular, Arabist, and anti-imperialist, as befitted the Arab hero-victor over imperialism.

The challenge of Nuri's action may be seen in the perspective of a perduring rivalry of the powers of the Nile and the Euphrates. To Nasser it was a menace that had to be thwarted. What he regarded as a breach in the Arab League's front to the West meant that Iraq could look for military supplies from Britain. Iraq, backed locally by Turkey, would be greatly forwarded in her attempt to foster Arab unity in the Fertile Crescent. To be passive meant the loss of Egypt's position of leadership in the Arab League. Nasser's bid for Arab leadership could be effectively supported only by opposing Iraq. The time-honored line of attack was to brand him as the divisive agent and lackey of the imperialists. Thus, events contributed to compel Nasser to act as Arab unifier, a role long in search of its hero, as his ghost-writer, Haykal, had written in the *Philosophy of the Revolution* published under Nasser's name. Arabism provided his cause, the Cold War offered conditions favorable for a bargaining neutral, and Egyptian influence throughout the Middle East—teachers, professional and technical men—furnished agents who could be reinforced by Cairo Radio. Together these forces enabled him to exercise a growing and formidable influence in the Arab world, for with his combination of Arabism, social reform, anti-imperialism, and neutralism, he appealed to discontented Arabs in other states, waging war against imperialism to increase his own influence and to hasten the day when Egypt could command the rich resources of other Middle Eastern states which she so signally lacked.

He became the scourge of Nuri, although his condemnation of reactionaries did not yet extend to Saudi Arabia and the Yemen,

[26] His speeches of July 26, 1956, and later abound in references to British and Western attempts to shackle him.

Speaking at Alexandria, July 26, 1956, Nasser stated that Britain denied arms to Egypt for use against Israel, "this spoiled child of western imperialism in the midst of our heart."

whose rulers lined up with Egypt and Syria in an agreement providing for the cooperation of their staff officers, a unified military command, and financial adjustments among the members to promote military effectiveness.

His neutralism extended his world influence and, as a prelude to Egypt's arms deal with the communist bloc, won him the favorable attention of the Soviet Union. His world influence, as well as his own political experience, widened when in April 1955 he attended the Bandung Conference. There, he was paid gratifying honor as the outstanding representative of the Arab people. There, too, he was able to gauge the support from Asia and Africa that might be attached to his neutralism. In the next years he was frequently in the company of Nehru and Tito. And to them, at first, especially to Nehru, he professed a sense of debt. On his visit to India in 1955, as he said with unusually tactful phrasing, "I learned and realized that the only wise policy for us would be (one) of positive neutrality and non-alignment. Coming back home, I found out from the response it had that it is the only possible policy which could get the broadest support from the Arab people." [27]

To the three circles (Arabic, Islamic, and African) of Egyptian interest which the *Philosophy of the Revolution* described, Nasser added a fourth circle, the neutralist world of former colonial countries and neutralism's fellow-travelers, the communist states which heartily abetted this renewed declaration of independence of the former colonies from the West, the heartland of colonialism and the core of opposition to Soviet expansionism.

As an opponent of the consolidation of the Western position in the Middle East and of extension of NATO through Turkey, Nasser looked like a good bet for Soviet support. Soviet policy in the Middle East was changing. The failure of Stalin's overt actions and demands in the Middle East appeared to call for a new approach that would liquidate the disadvantages accrued by Stalin's forward and somewhat inflexible policy. On May 30, 1953, Foreign Minister Molotov declared that better Soviet relations with Turkey would henceforth be possible because the Soviet Union was relinquishing its territorial and other demands on Turkey. The latter did not take the bait but persisted in her association with NATO and in her effort to construct a Middle Eastern defense establishment. Soviet policy expressed sharp

[27] Nasser, as reported in R. K. Karanjia, *Arab Dawn*, quoted in Wheelock, *op. cit.*, p. 225.

and menacing opposition to the preliminaries and conclusion of the Turco-Pakistani agreement as well as to the Baghdad Pact.

The Iranian experience of 1953 provided its lessons. Mossadegh was a bourgeois nationalist, and Middle Eastern and colonial nationalism had promising possibilities of weakening Britain. In Iran the Tudeh Party had supported the expulsion of Britain and had agitated against American influence lest it should replace the British, for such a result would simply have meant defeat in victory. Middle Eastern nationalism, then, should be encouraged as a means of weakening NATO. But if nationalism was to achieve its goal, it must espouse neutralism, for in doing so it would exclude Western influence, including the United States, which in the neutralist canon was included among the imperialists. The logic of neutralism and the Soviet course was brutally simple: the opponents of their anti-imperialism were imperialists.

Thus, in 1954-1955, Soviet policy was beginning to run parallel with Nasser's policy in opposition to the Baghdad Pact. It was, then, very much in the Soviet interest to strengthen Nasser by providing him with arms. In the light of the forces working against the Baghdad Pact, King Hussain's judgment, possibly based on hindsight, that it was doomed from the start appears warranted.[28]

Nasser's opposition and, notably, his campaign of opposition, were fatal to it, for his tactics mobilized the very instrument against it, popular hostility, that had rendered the Canal Zone a near-wasted asset.

When the Baghdad Pact members first met in formal conference in November 1955, the Soviet Union had already made an impressive break-through in the Middle East. The enmity of Nasser, made more formidable by the Soviet arms deal, the absence of Arab states other than Iraq, and the abstention of the United States make the Pact look like a mouse that caused a mighty uproar. In their deliberations at the conference members stressed the desirability and prospects of economic cooperation as well as the desirability of American membership and of a Palestine settlement. From the first the organization provided under the Pact revealed a lack of clarity, prompting the judgment that the Pact involved obligations but not much implementation. There was to be a permanent Council of Ministers who would be represented by deputies of ambassadorial rank. The Council was to have military and economic committees as well as a secre-

[28] H. M. King Hussain, *Uneasy Lies the Head* (New York, 1962).

tariat. Later, the organization devoted attention to the likelihood of subversion. On such matters, including economic cooperation, the United States was prepared to be associated with the Pact.

The American observer at the Conference, Ambassador Waldemar J. Gallman, presented two grounds to explain the abstention of the United States: the United States sought to prevent the further estrangement of Egypt from the West; American membership would very likely result in an Israeli request for a treaty with the United States, and such an eventuality would worsen Western relations with the Arab states.[29]

The first argument is of very doubtful validity: the American course it prescribed was more likely to convince Nasser that the United States was a push-over. The second argument, which is reminiscent of an unrelenting drunkard's sober account of his affliction or a neurotic's profession of his neurosis, amounts to a confession that the United States was not able to implement a coherent regional policy for the Middle East.

In spite of British complaints against the United States, however, the Baghdad Pact was not a simple development of the northern tier proposal. Dulles had in mind a flexible series of bilateral assistance treaties with Middle Eastern states. His conception assumed not only the bypassing of the Israeli-Arab conflict but some disentangling of the United States from association with British Middle Eastern positions—which he thought impermanent—and the attendant unpopularity of the British. The stress of the northern tier approach was on American military aid and indigenous, regional forces. In accord with British and Iraqi needs, the Baghdad Pact brought in a Western power, intensified Iraqi-Egyptian rivalry—although Nasser's response to the earlier Turco-Iraqi Pact which involved no Western power was also harsh—and engulfed the northern tier in the very difficulties Dulles hoped to avoid. Whether these difficulties were avoidable is uncertain. But in spite of expressions of American support for the objectives of the Baghdad Pact, as well as American Ambassadorial activity in its behalf, Dulles soon had doubts about British participation in the Baghdad Pact and was appalled by its consequences. To explain his attitude, two unflattering possibilities may be suggested: Dulles did not realistically envisage the dimensions of his northern

[29] Article by Kennett Love, "News of the Week," New York Times, November 27, 1955.

tier project, and/or Anglo-American cooperation on the highest level was sadly deficient or fell afoul of Dulles' pragmatism.

The latter is true, not indeed exclusively, and the defective cooperation derives in part from Dulles' realistic unwillingness to recognize unreservedly Eden's interpretation of the primacy of British responsibility in the Middle East. While it is quite possible to agree that the necessity of using American power and resources in the Middle East entitled the United States to initiative and leadership there, American policy lacked the coherence, the comprehensiveness, and the reasonable consistency and firmness required of the leader of allies.

The diplomacy of the Baghdad Pact, therefore, is the story of a substantial achievement for its regional members, Pakistan, Iran, Turkey, and in the long run more doubtfully for Iraq. But the achievement entailed a wholly disproportionate amount of disadvantages. The Pact remained largely a transformed military arrangement involving Britain and Iraq. The strength of Nuri in Iraq had been manifested on occasions and he had displayed an extraordinary capacity for political survival. Momentarily, the Pact strengthened him at home. But the stability provided by the Pact must be weighed against the effectiveness of Nasser's pan-Arab campaigns and his organization of a counter-military organization. Nasser's hostile initiative certainly intensified the difficulties of later Middle Eastern association with Western powers. It is difficult to find advantages large enough to set against the disastrous consequences of the Pact: facilitating (perhaps no more than this) the entry of the Soviet influence in the Middle East, inflaming the divisions of the Arab world, and setting in train events, including the Suez intervention, that eventually destroyed the government of Nuri and eliminated the special British position in the Middle East outside the Persian Gulf.

Some major Middle Eastern tangles were and, indeed, are so knotted and burr-laden that any conceivable course for immediate action can be criticized for its obvious disadvantages. But in the story of the Baghdad Pact one can mark the lack of Anglo-American coordination on the highest level, which may be explained but was, nevertheless, in its magnitude needless and calamitous.

7: THE HARDENING OF LINES

The fifteen months between Britain's signature of the Baghdad
Pact and Nasser's nationalization of the Suez Canal Company may
be divided into three periods: the first extending to December 1955
saw the continuance of British and notably American attempts to
give some measure of satisfaction to Nasser or to offer financial aid
that might turn him from his course of hostility to the British, Western, and Iraqi governments; between December 1955 and the end
of March 1956 the period was marked by Eden's growing alarm at
evidences of Nasser's overt hostility and success and by Eden's efforts
to coordinate a minimum policy with the United States; finally, between April and July 1956, there was Eden's full and heavy recognition that the effort to win Nasser had failed and that, for the
moment, no adequate alternative order existed in the Middle East.
    Late in the summer of 1955 Nasser finally secured supplies of
arms from the communist camp. The ground had been prepared for
the Egyptian-communist arms deal when Soviet policy was reformulated in 1954-1955 and Nasser, in opposing the Baghdad Pact, vigorously reformulated his neutralism. Nasser's Arabist policy imposed its
own dynamism against Jordan and an alarmed Israel ready for aggressive or pre-emptive action. Nasser, indeed, knew intoxicating success,
and a measure of his success and menace appeared in the willingness
of the United States and Britain to aid him in the domestic development of his country and, so, to divert the adventurer from the more
dangerous reaches of Arabism and neutralism. But now the Egyptian
could not be so creditably purchased. His own course had its impera-
tives, and his experience led him to believe that neutralism steadily
pursued would bring still higher returns for him. Some months after
British and American policy had palpably failed, Secretary Dulles in
an attempt to teach Nasser a rough lesson withdrew the offer of aid
to Egypt only to precipitate a new Nasserite challenge as the direct
preliminary of the Suez expedition.
    Britain and the United States had recognized Egypt's need of arms.
But Nasser's neutralist course involved an assertion of Egyptian self-

sufficiency towards Britain and the United States. As the latter powers, then, would have few means of restraining his actions towards Israel or even the Arab states, they could not responsibly provide him with arms on the scale he may have needed, not to mention the scale he called for. The Tripartite Declaration of 1950 was against supplying arms to Egypt without conditions, and American legislation required Egypt to undertake not to use the arms for aggressive purposes but only for internal order and legitimate self-defense.[1] Nevertheless, the two powers were concerned to forestall Egyptian recourse to another supplier, for a change of arms supplier is more momentous than a change of tailors or even bankers, and, if Nasser secured arms from the communist world, the change, with all its political implications, would be irreversible for a time. Now, in this situation, there was charm in positive neutrality for the Soviet Union inasmuch as surplus communist arms could, then, be given without explicit political strings. The likely use of communist arms in Egyptian possessions would be in harmony with Soviet purposes and the mere grant of them would have gratifying political results.

As for Nasser, he needed arms for domestic purposes, for possible use against Israel, and to outpace Iraq. Arms against Israel were an urgent imperative, for Arabism required unrelenting hostility to an Israel which had recently acted very threateningly to Egypt. Nasser, in fact, had charged that France was supplying Israel with planes, tanks, and artillery. Indeed, British and American intelligence was then reported to be more fearful of an Israeli attack on Arab states than of an Egyptian attack on Israel.[2] For two years after the army's

[1] Testifying before a Senate Committee early in 1957, former Ambassador Jefferson Caffrey said that Nasser "wanted military assistance without any conditions." *Hearing before the Committee on Foreign Relations and the Committee on Armed Services,* U.S. Senate, 85th Congress, January-February 1957 (Washington, D.C., 1957), Part II, 785.

Nasser, on July 26, 1956, misleadingly said that to sign a Mutual Security Pact, as American law required, would have required Egypt to accept an American military mission and thus to give up Egypt's control of her own army. M. Khalil, *The Arab States and the Arab League* (Beirut, 1962), II, 750. In the same speech, *ibid.,* p. 754, Nasser said that the British government told him that he could have arms if he remained silent at Bandung and desisted from attacking the British policy of making alliances. The Egyptians also claimed that in the summer of 1955 Egypt got forty Centurion tanks from Britain but without ammunition. Later, in response to protests, Egypt got ten rounds per tank. This is based on an Egyptian-inspired account. Erskine B. Childers, *The Road to Suez: A Study of Western-Arab Relations* (London, 1962), p. 133.

[2] *The Times,* October 6, 1955.

revolution, the Egyptian government had been remarkably unaggressive towards Israel. In that period its leaders mainly confined themselves to references to Israel as their mortal enemy and to assurances that they were concentrating on matters that would make their turning upon Israel assuredly victorious. The Israeli-Egyptian frontier remained relatively quiet. Nevertheless, the Egyptian government argued that it had only concluded an armistice, not its war, with Israel, and, on that ground, prevented Israeli-bound shipping from using the Suez Canal, in defiance of earlier Security Council resolutions.

When under the terms of the Anglo-Egyptian Treaty (1954) Britain undertook to leave the Canal Zone base, Israel professed great alarm. The departure of the British guardians of the Canal would enable Egypt to extend the range of her measures against Israel in the Canal and more freely to stage hostile excursions against Israeli territory. Finally, the prospective British evacuation of the Suez base removed an obvious means of dealing with challenges to the Tripartite Declaration. Early in 1955 Israeli anxieties led to the political return of David Ben-Gurion. Eleven days after he became Defense Minister, this protagonist of forceful action sent an Israeli Army force against the town of Gaza (February 28, 1955). The attack, in which at least forty Egyptian soldiers were killed, served warning of Egypt's inability to help other Arabs, its own soldiers, or the refugees in Gaza. The attack also made notable and educative retaliation for refugee attacks on Israel, for in 1954 Egypt had initiated the organization of the *fedayeen*.

The attack highlighted Nasser's arms problem. First of all, he depended on the army for the maintenance of his domestic position and the army demanded arms. Farouk's government had been blamed for failing to equip the army with adequate weapons. The army's revolutionary Prime Minister could not fail indefinitely in this respect. To be so patently weak before Israel was an intolerable position for the protagonist of Arabism. After impressively long efforts to secure arms from the West, Nasser, having given ample warning that he would seek arms from the communist world, was able to announce on September 27, 1955, that he had arranged to get arms in quantity from Czechoslovakia. The deal was presumably negotiated during the summer when the Western leaders and policy-makers were seeking to penetrate the meaning of the warm Gioconda smiles the new Soviet leaders were flashing at the Summit meeting in Geneva.

The deal had the unwarranted effect of spectacular surprise, in spite of warnings such as Dulles had given in a press conference on August 30, 1955. Politically, the way had been prepared for a long time, and commercially, it had been anticipated by earlier trade agreements between Egypt and communist states including China. Cotton was far and away Egypt's principal export. But, where the United States had its own surplus of cotton and Britain had been using other suppliers,[3] Egypt found the communist bloc prepared to take Egyptian cotton in exchange for arms and other commodities as well as an opportunity to gain political influence.

For Nasser the arms deal had a three-fold importance: it won him the plaudits of the Arab world and substantially strengthened his claims to leadership at home and abroad;[4] it was represented and interpreted as a resounding victory over imperialism and the West and as the first fruits of his neutralist policy; and, apart from the almost symbolic significance that the arms acquired, they also meant strength in the face of Israel and, in prospect, successful efforts against the Zionist enemy.[5] During the summer (August 1955) Nasser openly acclaimed refugee and other volunteer raiders carrying on guerrilla attacks on Israel. These *fedayeen* bands contributed to

[3] Britain turned to other buyers out of dissatisfaction with the marketing policies of the Wafd government during the Korean War. By 1956 Egypt had tied up its cotton crops in trade agreements with the communist bloc. Indeed, the Egyptian government was driven to placing a ban on exports, which principally meant cotton, a restriction that caused Britain no difficulty. The latter had turned for her long-staple cotton to the Sudan and some other African territories. In 1956 British cotton imports from Egypt were only one third of the quantity imported three years earlier and only one tenth of the quantity imported in 1938. *Manchester Guardian*, July 20, 1956.

[4] On October 1, 1955, the Council of the Arab League congratulated Nasser on his arms purchase agreement with Czechoslovakia.

[5] On September 21, 1955, Israeli forces occupied El Auja. The Israeli claim that this key area for control of the approaches to the central part of the Sinai peninsula was under Israeli jurisdiction was in defiance of rulings of the Security Council. Under the 1949 Armistice the area had been demilitarized.

For two of Nasser's accounts of the arms deal see report of an interview, *Life*, November 10, 1955, and Khalil, *op. cit.*, II, 750-758.

In making the arms deal Nasser insisted that he should also immediately receive spare parts for the weapons delivered, in quantities sufficient for five years. Munitions factories were part of the deal. Finally, in Eastern Europe Egyptians were to be trained in the use of the weapons so that there would not be a great influx of Soviet technicians. These generally unnoticed points are presented in Childers, *op. cit.*, pp. 135-136.

heightening the tensions involving the Israeli-Egyptian border. For
her part, Israel, too, continued to mount large scale retaliatory raids
by her army.

For Britain Egypt's acquisition of communist arms appeared to
ratify Nasser's hostility and the blighting of such hopes as attended
the making of the Anglo-Egyptian Treaty (1954). The reaction of
American policy-makers was momentarily one of so great alarm that
an Assistant Secretary of State, George Allen, was sent to Cairo to
bear a note from Dulles sternly warning Nasser of the risks involved
in taking Soviet arms. Under the circumstances, Allen's mission was
more likely to increase Nasser's stature in Arab eyes, but, if Nasser
is to be believed, an American official, undercutting his superior,
Secretary Dulles, even urged that Nasser accept the message, for the
American said: "Nothing concrete will come out of this letter. I
guarantee this to you. Egyptian dignity will be injured in the letter,
but in effect Egyptian dignity will not be injured." [6]

Prime Minister Eden also recognized that the arms deal had un-
dermined the principal sanction of the Tripartite Declaration (1950),
the West's monopolistic position as arms supplier to the Middle
East. This recognition drove Eden to later attempts to coordinate
American and British policy. In view of the likelihood of an arms
race and a perilous mounting of tensions in Arab-Israeli relations,
Eden again attempted to urge a compromise of the major Arab-
Israeli issues. In August 1955 his initiative had been anticipated by
Secretary Dulles who indicated a willingness to guarantee the terri-
torial terms of a settlement mutually agreeable to the Arabs and
Israelis and to contribute financially to a resolution of the refugee
problem.[7]

[6] Nasser described this incident in his speech announcing the nationalization of
the Canal, July 26, 1956. Khalil, op. cit., II, 757.

[7] Dulles' speech (August 26, 1955) was delivered to the Council on Foreign
Relations. To enlarge the possibilities of settling some Middle Eastern quarrels,
Dulles indicated that the United States was prepared to contribute to an international loan to Israel to deal with the refugees and to guarantee by treaty the
territories of the Israeli-Arab states against formal attack. A guarantee of frontiers
would make necessary the difficult task of defining boundaries. Dulles believed
that the over-all advantages of his offer "outweigh vastly any net disadvantages
of the adjustments needed to convert armistice lines of danger into boundary
lines of safety." He several times repeated that he spoke with the authority of
President Eisenhower.

A letter from Eisenhower to Rabbi Abba Hillel Silver, November 15, 1955,
repeated that the President was for a solution by peaceful means and was pre-

Speaking at the Guildhall in London (November 9, 1955) Eden, substantially supported by Secretary Dulles, used "shock tactics" to attempt to break up the rigidity of the Arab-Israeli claims and to get away from irreducible positions. He proposed that the Arabs and Israelis should open negotiations on frontiers, seeking a compromise between the frontiers of 1949 (the Israeli position) and those of the United Nations partition plan of 1947 (the Arab position). If negotiations resulted in a solution, Eden promised a formal guarantee of frontiers and substantial help in settling the refugee problem.[8] The proposals were well received by Nasser and some other Arab leaders. On the evidence of Nuri es-Said of Iraq, Nasser at this time anxiously inquired what Nuri's views would be if Nasser sought a solution of the Palestine problem, presumably on the lines of Eden's speech.[9] But though Nasser saw the proposals as a basis for settlement, Israel grimly held to her own position as irreducible, for Israel had little enough territory for bargaining. But even Nasser's welcome to proposals for a settlement was surprising. Here the intransigence of Israel in rejecting a British proposal formed part of a chain of events that led to the ultimate realignment of Britain and France with Israel.

These proposals, then, were without any but bitter fruit, for Israel's anxieties increased and Arab hopes had been raised. Nasser, also, soon adopted the line of arguing that British policy-makers had played him false, for, he said, they had falsely promised to freeze the Baghdad Pact. This assurance, which would have required British consultation of the Pact's members, was not one Britain could readily give. Even in 1956, after events in Jordan had frozen the Pact's membership, Foreign Secretary Lloyd refused to give it.[10] Eden had made the proposals, out of a kind of dutiful hopefulness, with an impressive diplomatic "follow-up." Eden's proposals also served to remind the Arab

---

pared to adhere to a treaty for the maintenance of agreed frontiers. *Department of State Bulletin,* XXXIII (1955), 378-380, 894-895. In a press conference (April 17, 1956) Dulles noted that his proposals had been previously discussed with a number of nations. *Ibid.,* XXXIV (1956), 712.

[8] Eden, *Full Circle,* p. 368.

[9] Khalil, *op. cit.,* II, 270-276. In this speech Nuri indicated that he had regarded the Western Tripartite policy as an aggression against the Arabs and, in particular, the Western policy of maintaining a balance of arms as keeping the balance in favor of Israel. As Nuri put his case, he differed from Nasser in his estimate of the Soviet Union and in the fact that the Iraqi Premier had to think of Iraqi interests.

[10] Childers, *op. cit.,* pp. 142-143, says that the British assurance was given.

leaders of the role Britain might play in securing an Arab-Israeli settlement. As the proposals, otherwise, were fruitless, the arms race and Egyptian hostility would continue.[11] Eden was thus resolved to continue with support of the Baghdad Pact and Iraq, less perhaps because the policy was positively promising but primarily because retreat in the face of Nasser's opposition would have been disastrous for the range of British interests. American policy, its makers and its agents, pursued no one course at all. Eisenhower was ill, Dulles mingled high-principled utterances with the appearance of unmasterful drift, and, on lower echelons, there were hints that the United States might supply arms to Israel.

A further effort to turn Nasser from adventurism to domestic construction was made. The lure was a twentieth-century style pyramid, the Aswan Dam, and this was the second fruit of neutralism. The dam, long discussed, debated, and supported by preliminary studies, was designed to store Nile waters and to regulate their flow in accordance with the needs of agriculture. As Egypt is truly the gift of the Nile, the dam was to make the Nile's largesse more munificent. Storing and regulating the waters would permit the productive use of more land and at the same time endow Egypt with electric power in abundance. By early 1953 the Revolutionary government had undertaken soundings on the financing of the project.[12]

By the fall of 1955 rumors of Soviet aid for the project were as numerous as a flight of crows and, in Dulles' eyes, as ominous. Moving very rapidly, the United States and Britain in December 1955 expressed willingness to make Egypt an advance of $70,000,000 for the first stage of work on the dam. The first stage, in itself, was rather a fiction than an economic and engineering reality, but the fiction was designed to meet the American government's inability to make

[11] Colonel Anwar es-Sadat, Egyptian Minister of State and close associate of Nasser, wrote an editorial in the Egyptian paper, *Al-Gomhouria*. His thesis was that the Soviet Union "respects our revolution and does not stand in the way of the people's victories." Britain, France, and the United States, however, were "actuated by a single motive," to "wreak their vengeance upon" Nasser. He charged, possibly in reference to the Guildhall speech and its preparations, that the Western powers hoping to promote Israel's survival and the dispersion of the Arabs had tried to compel an Arab-Israeli peace. *New York Times*, February 10, 1956. This expression of the common Arab attitude that the survival of Israel should be anathema makes Nasser's receptivity to the Guildhall speech all the more interesting and puzzling.

[12] Keith Wheelock, *Nasser's New Egypt* (New York, 1960), pp. 7, 173-205, provides a useful account of the project and its history.

long-term financial commitments. This inability prevailed even though President Eisenhower in his State of the Union Message (January 1956) had urged the Congress to approve long-term agreements, which would involve future appropriations and, thereby, would make possible longer-range planning in administering foreign aid.

For the first stage of construction, estimated to cost about $280,-000,000, some $200,000,000 was to be provided by an International Bank loan. The United States was prepared to make Egypt an initial advance of $56,000,000 and Britain to supply $14,000,000. As the estimated cost of the dam was $1,300,000,000, more aid would be necessary later. For her part Egypt would have to supply over three-quarters of a billion dollars in materials and labor.

These engagements would have enforced economic austerity and political moderation on Egypt for ten to fifteen years. The International Bank, considering the loan from the standpoint of conservative banking practice, proposed as conditions that Egypt should secure the Sudan's agreement, that Egypt should act to avoid inflation, that Egypt and the bank should periodically review Egypt's investment program and expenditures in relation to the dam's requirements, and that the Egyptian government should not incur foreign debt obligations in excess of amounts agreed by Egypt and the bank to be provident. These stringent, but necessary, conditions were peculiarly difficult for a dictatorship to accept.[13] The conditions were acceptable in principle, but not formally by Nasser, although the efforts of his regime to be dynamic had already resulted in commitments that may have made these conditions and the construction of the dam at that time impossible.

The American and British governments were at one in offering aid to Egypt but they saw different colors in the same scene. Eden favored the aid as a means of further testing Nasser's intentions. Rather hopefully, American policy-makers looked on Nasser's position as bearing some promise. If Nasser's government succeeded, then there would be a powerful and indigenous Middle Eastern source of resistance to communist expansionism.

The last month of 1955 and the first months of 1956 revealed

[13] Nasser's alternation of moods must have been quite disturbing to those who had to deal with him. Clearly, he changed greatly from interview to interview. In the nationalization speech delivered at Alexandria, he recalled that Eugene Black of the International Bank in speaking to Nasser appeared to be de Lesseps. Simon Malley, "—And the Answer was Suez," *The Reporter*, September 6, 1956, 31; Khalil, *op. cit.*, II, 737-738.

Nasser still in pursuit of his anti-Baghdad Pact and anti-Western policy. In this respect, Jordan, with its largely discontented populations, provided an inviting and dangerous arena. British influence there rested on treaty relations which also provided for bases as well as a British subsidy, on occasion amounting to one-half of the Jordanian budget, and on the British Commander of the Arab Legion, John Bagot Glubb.

At this time, the Jordanian kingdom was politically seething. The Israeli-Arab tension, increased by Egypt's acquisition of arms, troubled it greatly, and Egypt was using its *fedayeen* bands to foment trouble for Jordan's ruler as well as trouble involving Jordan with Israel.[14] But the Israeli War had brought a difficult legacy to the bedouin kingdom of Abdullah, Arab Palestine. The annexation of this territory with its literate and nationalistic urban inhabitants doubled the population of Jordan and presented that kingdom with a range of discontent that intensified Arab nationalism. Abdullah's successors, Talal and then, Hussain, faced in their newly-annexed subjects grave challenges to the pro-British orientation of the Kingdom. It became a kind of meeting place for the tensions of the Middle East. Here Egypt and Saudi Arabia made common cause against the British. King Saud pursued his father's feud against the Hashemite dynasty of Jordan and against Britain with whom he disputed the Buraimi oasis. Saudi money was generally believed to have been spent lavishly in sparking Jordanian riots. An obvious target for (Arab) Jordanian nationalists was the British commander, Glubb. Another target was the Treaty of 1948 which the government called upon Britain to revise. As the British government had yielded to Iraq and Egypt, it was prepared to do the same for Jordan in an

[14] Eden, *op. cit.*, p. 385, described it "as a twisty way of entangling a neighbor." See also Benjamin Shwadran, *Jordan: A State of Tension* (New York, 1959), p. 326, n. 21. But Eden's account of Jordan also reveals how completely he accepted the British charade structure of Jordan. He saw opposition in Jordan to the British Treaty or the Baghdad Pact as the work of refugees, not of real Jordanians. Where he reports that Jordanian newspapers would accept smaller sums of money from the government for printing propaganda in favor of a British-approved course than they would ask from Saudi Arabia or Egypt, he noted: ". . . patriotism at a price" (p. 384). What kind of patriotism did he expect in Jordan? John Marlowe's account of the dilemma of the pioneer Arab nationalists of Syria as well as of the Baathists applies much more to Jordan: ". . . they turned to Arab nationalism because there was no principle of unity or of nationality resident in a truncated and divided Syria." *Arab Nationalism and British Imperialism* (London, 1961), p. 95.

arrangement involving the increased arms supplies requested by the government of Jordan. Eden saw Jordan as an "outpost of Iraq." If it passed under Egyptian control, "the United Kingdom's influence would be shattered." [15] Thus, British policy favored an eventual association, if not union, of Jordan and Iraq. With Jordan under pressure, association of the two in the Baghdad Pact began to look promising.

Early in November the Turkish President, Celal Beyar, visited Jordan and urgently pressed membership in the Baghdad Pact on Jordan. In line with Turkish suggestions Jordan coupled her armaments requests and a call for revision of the Treaty with a proposal (November 16) to join the Pact. As the issues raised by the Jordanians were mainly military, Sir Gerald Templer, the Chief of the Imperial General Staff, came to Amman on the invitation of the King, though for the occasion he was presented "as a plenipotentiary not as a general." [16] As Eden in his memoirs made it clear that Templer was not chosen lightly, the plenipotentiary was doubtless sent to indicate the seriousness of British intentions.

Templer received an encouraging response, but there followed a cabinet crisis during which the new Jordanian Prime Minister suggested that it would be prudent for Templer to leave. When the new Jordanian government expressed favor to the Baghdad Pact, rioting (December 16), encouraged by Egyptian and Saudi Arabian agents, ensued.[17]

In January 1956 the Jordanian government indicated that it would not join the Baghdad Pact. Although Jordan's entrance would have increased the Arab membership of that defense organization and have allowed a revision of Britain's alliance with Jordan, the riots and difficulties should have been expected. Jordan, maintained by British subsidy and the British-trained Arab Legion, appeared to illus-

[15] Eden, *op. cit.*, pp. 391, 395. On p. 382 Eden noted that Foreign Secretary Macmillan expressly urged that Jordan then should join the Baghdad Pact.

[16] Shwadran, *op. cit.*, p. 326. But consult Commons Debate, Vol. 548, col. 12.

[17] See the account of the military correspondent of the *Daily Telegraph*, H. G. Martin, "The Soviet Union and the Middle East," in *Middle Eastern Affairs*, VII (1956), 49-55. The memoirs of John Bagot Glubb largely confirm his story. Martin states that many of the Jordanians did not know what the Baghdad Pact was and believed the story that Jordan's adhesion to the Baghdad Pact would have meant the immediate sending of the Arab Legion far from home. A characteristically Middle Eastern touch is the fact that the Jordanian Premier who first turned against the Pact was Circassian and fearful for the safety of his own small community.

trate Nasser's anti-imperialist propaganda about British control. The effort to bring Jordan into the Pact gave Nasser an advantage which he continued to pursue in 1956.[18]

Against this background of difficulties in the Middle East there appeared a surprising amount of domestic criticism of the new British Prime Minister, who had perhaps had too long an experience as crown prince to Churchill. As heir apparent to party leadership and to the Prime Ministership for many years, he may have missed some of the political education that a less assured position might have made inescapable, and he may have failed to develop the tougher qualities of leadership. As expected, he became Prime Minister on the day of Churchill's resignation (April 5, 1955). Less than two months later, a relaxed budget and the prospect of a summit meeting helped the Conservatives to win the elections and increase their parliamentary majority. For a time, the Geneva summit atmosphere, the absence of Churchill, and the new leader induced many Conservatives to believe that more normal, less demanding and frustrating, days were at hand. In the fall, however, with a meeting of the French, British, Russian, and American foreign ministers, the "spirit of Geneva" turned more somber and a supplementary budget with new restrictions and increased taxes was introduced. Hardly anything appeared to be going well, in Europe, the Middle East, and relations with the United States.

For the first time in his life Eden had to endure the atmosphere of unpopularity and severe criticism within his own party. Among the severest critics were the Suez Rebels, who insisted that the Anglo-Egyptian Treaty had been a sell-out and urged a course finally involving Britain's return to the Suez Canal base. Under this ordeal

[18] In the January troubles the British government sent two parachute battalions and one light-infantry battalion to Cyprus. The British representative in Jordan urged the dispatch of two British brigades to Amman. The Jordanian King, Eden has recorded, also asked for help from Iraq. Nuri called for American pressure to compel Nasser to desist in Jordan. Anticipating Suez, Nuri also urged that Britain and the United States threaten Egypt with the removal of the protection of the Tripartite Declaration from Egypt. Eden, *op. cit.*, pp. 385-386.

In the tangle of reports and counter-reports in power struggles, it is almost always possible to make a case for anyone by judicious omissions. Erskine B. Childers in the *Road to Suez*, pp. 142-143, is concerned to make a case against Eden and Nuri and in behalf of Nasser. Thus, he emphasized an alleged (no documentation offered) British assurance to Nasser that membership in the Baghdad Pact would not be extended and is all but silent on the rest of this affair.

Eden's stance of imperturbable mastery began to collapse. On the home front, the criticism of his political deficiencies received, as it were, support from Eden himself. On January 7, 1956, his own office issued a denial of the rumor that he would resign, probably in May —an unusual action and a revealing indication of his sense of being pressed and of being almost resourceless to divert the criticism.[19] The incident may have confirmed Eden in the hardening of his views on Nasser and in the espousal of a course that for a time gained him the support of the Suez Rebels.[20]

In November 1955 Eden had arranged for a visit to the United States. His purpose was to persuade the United States that the Middle Eastern situation had become so menacing that a dramatic affirmation of American-British cooperation was necessary. Prior to his departure a two-day conference on the Middle East at the Foreign Office assessed British policy and provided a review of it for the new Foreign Secretary, Selwyn Lloyd. There, during a press conference, the possibility of a change of British policy was raised. With engaging *hauteur*, for the question was being asked at the wrong time, the Foreign Office spokesman replied that no new policy was in prospect, as Britain already had one.[21]

It might have been more accurate to say that British Middle Eastern policy was in a peculiar state of transition. Immediately, Britain was eager to maintain the peace of the Middle East, and to do so by strengthening Nuri, Hussain, and the Baghdad Pact and by dissuading Nasser from hostile courses. But the long-range calculations of British policy-makers could not but have their foreboding

[19] The story on which he acted appeared in *The People*, January 8, 1956, a left-wing and sensational Sunday paper. It was picked up by Reuter's and Eden quickly put out his denial. Butler, the Conservative Leader of the Commons, reacted oddly when interviewed on Sunday. First he denied knowledge of the rumor. Upon being told of Eden's denial, he also denied the rumor, adding: "I have always supported the Prime Minister as my leader and I shall continue to do so as the best Prime Minister we have." *Manchester Guardian*, January 9, 1956.

[20] Eden does not allude to the incident in his memoirs. The *Daily Telegraph* was a severe critic. In *Punch*, CCXXX (January 25, 1956), 133, the following appeared: "Even the political cliché fancier was left unsatisfied by the Premier's speech last Wednesday." *Spectator*, CXCVI (January 13, 1956), 35, in a comment headed "Leading from Weakness," was hard put to find Eden doing any major thing right. In the issue of February 17, the harsh judgment was maintained: "British Middle Eastern policy is a failure. That is the lesson of the Washington talks" (p. 203).

[21] *Manchester Guardian*, January 4, 1956.

quality. Clearly, there was the danger of increased *fedayeen* raids against Israel, and even more likely, of an Israeli attack on the Arab states. In this situation, Egypt was the key state, and, equally clearly, Nasser was dangerously challenging the structure of British power in the Middle East.

British interests in transit and oil depended, in Eden's mind, on the retention of bases. Later in the year he put it quite strongly: "No Cyprus, no certain facilities to protect our supply of oil. No oil, unemployment and hunger in Britain. It is as simple as that." Earlier he made the same point: "The lives of our people depend on Cyprus as the position, guard, and stage post to take care of this vital interest of ours—oil. This is not imperialism, it is the plain duty of any government and we intend to discharge it." [22] If so much importance attached to an island base which Eden sought to hold with a kind of desperate determination, how much more compelling was the British position in Iraq and Jordan.

Britain had already yielded much to anti-imperialism. The prospective danger was that past concessions and American wavering would encourage more extreme and dangerous demands on Britain.[23] British interests and the positions on which they depended had encountered rivals, the Soviet Union and Nasser, who were exploiting the Middle Eastern difficulties for ends disruptive of British interests. Thus, Eden had described the Egyptian-communist arms deal as "a move to gain popularity at the expense of the restraint shown by the West." In the center of his difficulties was Nasser, who attacked the British positions, was bidding to unite the Arabs and, so, apparently to wipe out the British bases, had made possible effective Soviet penetration of the Middle East.[24] Now, if Nasser were specified as the prime enemy, and equated with the future of communism in the obsessive

[22] Speech at Norwich, June 1, 1956, *The Annual Register*, 1956, p. 29; *Manchester Guardian*, March 15, 1956, account of Commons debate.

[23] A leader in *The Times*, June 25, 1956, commented on the visit of the Yemeni Crown Prince to Moscow and on the Imam's policy towards Aden: "Much of his policy he probably regards as a prudent insurance against the risks of a rapidly changing situation." The rumor of a Yemeni grant of oil and uranium-prospecting rights to the Soviet Union "accurately reflects the growing feeling that nothing is to be lost by annoying her [Britain]."

[24] "Our general policy in the Middle East was founded on the need to protect British interests in Iraq and the Persian Gulf. The main threat to these interests was the growing influence of Nasser with his anti-Western ideology and collusion with Soviet Russia, especially in arms supply." Eden, *op. cit.*, pp. 393-394; for Eden's approach to the United States at this time, *ibid.*, pp. 369-375.

manner for which American policy was often criticized by British politicians, then a British reversal on Israel might very well be in order, for the Middle Eastern proverb that the enemy of my enemy is my friend is no limited regional maxim. To specify Nasser as the enemy made it possible to think of cooperation with France in the Middle East, for France, too, had been infuriated by the Egyptian leader's espousal and support of the Algerian rising.

Thus, in January 1956 Eden sought to arouse American policy-makers to his sense of the seriousness and dimensions of the Middle Eastern crisis. The United States should warn Nasser of the dangers of his course and should attempt to instill a sense of responsibility in the ruler of Saudi Arabia. To head off likely Arab-Israeli fighting, Eden called for a reaffirmation of the Tripartite Declaration (1950), supported by visible preparations to take action in its behalf. Finally, as a counter to the anti-imperialist speeches of Bulganin and Khrushchev in Burma and India, Eden hoped for an Anglo-American Declaration of Purpose, a manifesto, as it were, for the free world.

Eden's quest for cooperation and vigor did not take place at an auspicious time. There were differences between the British policy and American approaches to the Middle East, and it is difficult to find coherence in the latter. President Eisenhower had recovered from his illness but his diplomatic performance on occasion, as here, took the form of riding herd smilingly on a passel of mavericks. The American government was aware of the contradictions and conflicts of its Middle Eastern policy: it was not able to solve them. Vigorous action, it was argued, might give the Soviet Union a pretext for extending its intervention in the Middle East. Thus, as the President put it, the United States sought to be "friends with everybody," although Dale Carnegie offered no guidance for the interstate problem of neutralism.

The year 1956 was also to be a presidential election year in which vigorous action was reserved for erupting emergencies—not for heading off crises. Communications between Dulles and Eden, never pleasurable, had already suffered the inhibitions of mutual mistrust. The United States was allied with Britain and France but a large part of American opinion shrugged uneasily before the colonial onus borne by its partners. It listened with a deaf ear to talk about Britain's Middle Eastern sphere and wondered about the unacceptability of that British view to the Arab people. At times it dreamed of the opportunities that might develop when British imperialism was liquidated. It favored an organization for the defense of the Middle East but, partly out of deference to Saudi Arabia and Egypt, was not prepared to join the Baghdad Pact. It favored the security of Israel but would not itself provide arms to that state. It solicited the cooperation of Nasser, the enemy of Israel, Britain, and France. Finally, American and Western European oil groups shared some interests and were rivals in other respects.

The United States did agree to closer association with the Baghdad Pact and later joined its Economic and Anti-Subversion Committees. American officials encouraged Eden to make another effort to negotiate problems with Saudi Arabia. Eden, however, recognized that American official utterances—many, portentous, and hortatory—barely disguised a paralysis of action so far as his reading of the Middle Eastern situation and its immediate dangers were concerned. The Bricker Amendment even cast its paralyzing shadow on implementing the Tripartite Declaration, for the new situation in the Middle East indicated that implementation might be more costly than originally anticipated. The Eisenhower administration, further, had promised during the hearings on the Amendment in 1953 that American troops would not be involved in overseas fighting unless Congress consented. As the only exceptions made were an attack on American forces or an extreme emergency, and as the government had not asked for Congressional approval of the use of troops in the Middle East, arrangements for implementing the Tripartite Declaration—for the conference in Washington had announced the establishment of a French, British, American working group to make military plans for its implementation—were not formidable.[25]

The joint communiqué issued on February 1, in reaffirming the Tripartite Declaration against violations and preparations to violate the Arab-Israeli armistice and the frontiers involved, added little by way of deterring a crisis. The two leaders said: "We have made arrangements for joint discussions as to the nature of the action which we should take in such event." But in a conference-ridden world the threat to meet for discussion was an all but unintended downgrading of the crisis.

In the Middle East Britain and the United States had reversed the roles they played in the Far East in 1954 and later. Sir Anthony Eden,

[25] *Ibid.*, p. 372. Eden noted that even precautionary concentrations of forces were ruled out. So, "joint movements of our forces" to support expressed concern were not possible. See, also, John C. Campbell, *Defense of the Middle East* (Revised edition, New York, 1960), pp. 90-91.

thinking in terms of immediate British interests, sought joint action with the United States to head off an impending crisis. Although American leaders agreed on the difficulties and dangers, American policy-makers could not acceptably resolve conflicting American interests, and, here the reversal of its Far Eastern role, the United States professed unwillingness to agree to action that ran counter to Arab nationalism. In the crisis immediately following the nationalization of the Suez Canal the United States worked for an international action rather than national action to protect Western interests. More immediately engaged in this instance and linking British Middle Eastern influence with the security of British oil supplies, Eden was willing to act unilaterally or with available allies. And here, too, the British government sounded the urging trumpet against Soviet communist expansionism.

The communiqué issued during Eden's visit to the United States represented a very minimum consensus. As events developed, it appeared that the worst British fears were being realized. *The Spectator* argued that the communiqué underscored the failure of British Middle Eastern policy.[26] At a Washington press conference, Eden, in replying to an Arab reporter's question about the failure to consult the Arab states in making the Tripartite Declaration of 1950, expressed a view that was to guide him increasingly in the coming months: it was not possible to discuss with everybody as to how to discharge obligations "that were ours." [27]

Eden's unhappiness with the United States and the Middle East was intensified by the ousting from Jordan of General John Bagot Glubb, Commander of the Arab Legion. On March 2, 1956, he was cursorily dismissed on the charge that he worked for British and against Jordanian interests. The timing of the dismissal, which coincided with a visit of Foreign Secretary Lloyd to Cairo, was Hussain's own doing. It was done in response to intense external and internal pressure upon the King exerted by the rulers of Saudi Arabia and Egypt but using Arab nationalism as the agent. Late in 1955 they had challenged Hussain to do away with British influences and had promised him a subsidy equivalent to that paid by Britain. The King, recognizing the weakness of a position that had compelled him to nullify a call for new elections, had to come to terms with the dissidents in his own kingdom and to lessen external pressure by

[26] "No More Appeasement," *Spectator*, February 17, 1956, p. 203.
[27] *Manchester Guardian*, February 4, 1956.

making a gesture in favor of Arabism. Glubb himself professed a genuine love of the Arabs and was inclined to attribute the attack on his influence to foreign, that is, Egyptian and communist as well as Saudi influence. The lover of the Arabs did not understand their latest political passion. Hussain himself had resented his tutelage and paid tribute to the demands of Arabism, but he was fearful that a blow to his British connections might also be his own undoing.

Hussain, however, carefully sought to present the dismissal as mainly a personal matter. Eden, in spite of the fact that Glubb's dismissal seemed like the fall of a major pillar of British influence, did not react heatedly. So, for a time, the British subsidy and the Anglo-Jordanian Treaty continued in effect. Britain still had bases and troops in the country. Not until the aftermath of the Suez invasions did Jordan move firmly against the British connection.

At this juncture, Eden in his worry became more anxious and increasingly reserved the direction of policy to himself.[28] His own formulation of his difficulties was a strengthened affirmation of his earlier position that the effort to protect British interests in the Middle East had encountered the continuing hostility of Nasser's government. Relations with Egypt and the Arabs were embittered by the persisting Israeli-Arab feud, likely to become explosive if forceful action was not taken soon. The Soviet Union abetted the discord and the United States afforded him little help and appeared to be urging him to appeasement of Nasser.

A new and official hostility to Nasser appears in many forms: first of all, in the remarks of a spokesman of the Foreign Office;[29] secondly, for ten weeks in the spring of 1956, the British Embassy in Cairo ceased to have any but the most routine administrative contacts with the Egyptian government.[30]

The British Prime Minister sought to remove any uncertainty about British policy. In Cairo Selwyn Lloyd had warned the Egyptian gov-

[28] Aneurin Bevan said in a speech at Newcastle: Eden's administration is in the same semi-Fascist mood that led us into the world war and could lead us into another. The Tories, he said, were so angry to find themselves in the twentieth century that they determined to be tough in Cyprus. New York Times, May 28, 1956.

[29] "In spite of the Sudan agreement, the treaty over the Canal Zone, the offer of British help for the Aswan Dam, and consistent British efforts to establish better relations, Egypt has not ceased from actions and propaganda directed against Britain and governments in treaty relations with Britain." Foreign Office spokesman quoted in Jewish Observer and Middle East Review, March 30, 1956.

[30] Tom Little, Egypt (New York, 1958), p. 281.

ernment that Britain would use force to resist any attempt to interrupt the oil supplies and revenue from the Persian Gulf.[31] When
Bulganin and Khrushchev visited Britain in April 1956, Eden told
them that Middle Eastern oil was so vital to Britain that "we would
fight for it." [32] At the same time, in recognizing that the Soviet Union
might have fears concerning the Baghdad Pact, Eden assured them
that the Pact was nonaggressive and entertained the hope that the
Soviet leaders might accept the Middle Eastern situation if the
Western powers pledged that they would seek no further bases from
the Middle Eastern members of the Baghdad Pact, a concession that
might also appeal to Nasser.

So far, then, and with admirable firmness, Eden was prepared to
go to meet the interests of the Soviet Union in the Middle East.
Later, as the prospect of an Arab-Israeli war may have alarmed the
Russian leaders, Foreign Minister Shepilov in Cairo told the Egyptians that the Soviet Union did not intend to support hostile actions
of the Arabs against the Western powers. Khrushchev himself told an
Egyptian journalist that an Arab-Israeli war would mean the Third
World War.[33] But the Soviet view of peace in the Middle East called
for the acknowledgment of Soviet influence there. Indeed, on February 13, 1956, in commenting on the Washington communiqué of
the Anglo-American talks, the Soviet Union supported the Arab
League's criticism that Western policy for the Middle East, if it was
concerned with stability, should first secure Arab approval. The Soviet
Union argued against any unilateral settlement and demanded that
in seeking a Middle Eastern settlement the Western powers should
consult the United Nations and gain the participation of Middle
Eastern states. On April 17, 1956, the Soviet government again urged
a settlement of the Palestine problem without outside interference
and indicated its own willingness to promote such a peaceful settlement.[34] But Bulganin also said at the end of his visit to England:
". . . the British side does not share our views on this question."

---

[31] Wheelock, op. cit., p. 235, report of his interview with Anwar es-Sadat.
[32] Eden, op. cit., p. 401.
[33] The Observer, June 17, 1956; The Times, July 2, 1956.
[34] Soviet News, February 14, and April 18, 1956, and The Times, April 18,
1956, cited in Geoffrey Barraclough and Rachel Wall, Survey of International
Affairs, 1955-1956, Royal Institute of International Affairs (New York, 1960),
pp. 276-277. This section of the Survey reflects Barraclough's belief that these
Soviet statements contained promising professions that should have been ex-
plored.

Nevertheless, in April and early May, there were persisting reports from Washington that a Middle Eastern Pact involving the Soviet Union was possible. Speculations about the contents of such an agreement included a recognition by Britain, the United States, and the Soviet Union of their concerns in the Middle East and, possibly, an agreement on maintaining a balance of arms there.[35]

Eden met a measure of success when he asked for increased and open American support for the Baghdad Pact. A senior official, Deputy Under Secretary of State Loy Henderson, represented the United States at the Pact's Teheran meeting (April 16-19, 1956). The abstention of the United States from full membership and the refusal of Jordan to join the Pact, by minimizing the Pact's political and military aspects, had contributed to a special emphasis in the Pact's meetings on economic cooperation and aid. The United States became a full member of the Economic Committee and the Counter Subversion Committee of the Pact. Secretary Henderson informed the Pact's Ministerial Council that the United States was prepared to discuss the supplementing of "bilateral aid programs through a program of broader economic cooperation coordinated through the Pact Organization." For its part, the British government also supported economic aid, for it offered, among other things, to establish a training center in atomic energy at Baghdad.[36] But, for example, it was difficult for the members of the Pact to discuss officially the Arab-Israeli crisis, even though the Council's communiqué urged a solution of the Palestine problem. With Iraq, notably, but with Iran and Pakistan as well, there could be no discussion of supplying arms to

[35] The Times, April 12, 1956; New York Times, May 5, 1956. A spokesman for the Foreign Office firmly denied (May 4) that such an agreement was in prospect. Britain stood by the Baghdad Pact and welcomed the increased support of it by the United States government. With unusual crispness he said that the real extent of Anglo-Soviet accord on the Middle East was reflected in the communiqué issued at the end of the Russian leader's visit to Britain. Drew Middleton's report, New York Times, April 13, 1956, also referred to Dulles' consideration of such a Middle Eastern agreement and to the opposition of the British government to it.

To support his thesis of a British, American, Israeli, Iraqi plot against Nasser, Erskine Childers, op. cit., pp. 148-149, has argued that this frequently denied rapprochement with the Soviet Union contributed to Nasser's very hasty recognition of Communist China (May 16, 1956) so that he could hope to secure arms from China, if the other major powers resolved against an arms race in the Middle East.

[36] Department of State Bulletin, XXXIV (1956), 753-756.

Israel.[37] Here, as in other matters, there was genuine cooperation between the United States and Britain. But in spite of the assurances of full cooperation from American Ambassador Aldrich and the British Ambassador, Sir Roger Makins, there is, behind all this, evidence of bad temper in both countries and, on occasion, lack of communication, in spite of their greater accord against Nasser.[38]

Like Khrushchev, Eden saw that the crisis in the Middle East might mean war, possibly general war. But a new aspect of British policy-making in the spring of 1956 is that after Nasser had been specified as the British enemy, the Foreign Office began to reverse its views on the likely originator of a Middle Eastern war. Formerly, many British diplomatic spokesmen emphasized that the Arabs would not dare risk a war against Israel. The connection between the two points was made by the veteran correspondent, Drew Middleton:

> This may seem extreme. But in Whitehall, the assumption is that if Nasser is encouraged, he will sooner or later create a situation that will cut the oil supplies. . . . It is symptomatic of the new British attitude toward the Middle East that more attention is being paid now to a war arising from Arab ambitions than from a preventive campaign by Israel.[39]

The puzzle is, why the change? It is perfectly true that Arab statements, even by Iraq's Nuri, frequently menaced Israel with war.[40] British spokesmen usually had discounted such remarks as Arab rhetoric and, of course, Britain had some means of restraining Iraq. The restraint on Jordan's Arab Legion had been removed, for Glubb's

[37] *The Observer*, April 15, 1956. Even critics of the Eden government blamed, as Robert Stephens did here, the United States for the Pact's unreality.

[38] In a debate on Cyprus after the Tories had cheered the deportation of Archbishop Makarios by the British authorities, Aneurin Bevan disclaimed the role, assigned to him by the Tories, of the poisoner of Anglo-American relations. If the role were his, he said, he could not have done a better job with it than the present British government. He described the deportation as a concession to the Tory Right Wing: ". . . one would have thought that when the announcement was made of the deportation of the Archbishop we had heard news of a new Battle of Trafalgar." The Conservatives did not look on the breakthrough of colonies to independence as "the progress of mankind but as a liquidation of their imperial inheritance." *Parliamentary Debates*, Commons, 5th series, Vol. 550, col. 401, March 14, 1956.

[39] News of the Week, p. 5, *New York Times*, April 8, 1956.

[40] Nuri, in speaking to the Iraqi Parliament, January 9, 1956, announced that Iraq was building a modern radar network and was receiving the most up-to-date military weapons. Every gun, he boasted, will help solve the Palestine problem in the interest of the Arabs. *The Times*, January 10, 1956.

successor in command of the Legion, Ali Abu Nuwar, was working to
put the Legion under Egyptian control. The communist arms deal
had freed Egypt from Western influence. But, and here the published evidence is inevitably slight at the present time, British policy
was being considered in a broad and long-range context. It was not
simply and passively reacting to events. Here I am speaking of calculations rather than the immediate day-to-day policy, which was
particularly concerned not to become embroiled in the Arab-Israeli
mess. Eden was studying Middle Eastern affairs passionately and
obsessively. If a warlike initiative from Israel was feared earlier, was
not such an initiative even more likely in view of the growing
strength of Egypt?[41] And was not such an initiative so likely that
account must be taken of it in making future plans? I do not mean
to suggest that Suez represented the long-working out of a carefully
nurtured plan. I do suggest that as Eden saw his duty in facing this
problem—compounded, as it was, by his inability to secure a firm
American provision against an Arab-Israeli war—it was his duty to
use such a war to the advantage of British interests in Egypt and
the Canal Zone.

Violent Arab rhetoric, once discounted, sounded more menacing
when it came from a military dictator in whom Eden saw the shades
of the Fuehrer and the Duce. It was possible to shrug aside such
extravagances as the following from the Egyptian weekly, *Rose el
Youssef*: "Our dispute with the West is fundamental and deep-
rooted, has been continuous since the Crusades, and will never cease
except by the decisive defeat of one side or the other." [42] But
Egyptian opposition was more galling and less contemptible where

[41] The retired Sir Winston Churchill sounded a note that forecast this change
of policy. The occasion was an address to the Conservative Primrose League of
which Churchill was the Grand Master. As an early friend of Zionism, Churchill
could appropriately urge the change to support of Israel. Moreover, he more
than any British figure could in effect appeal for American support by expressing
confidence that in behalf of the Tripartite Declaration President Eisenhower
"will make the will power of America felt clearly and strongly—and felt in time."
In relation to Israel he said: "If Israel is dissuaded from using the life force of
their race to ward off the Egyptians until the Egyptians have learned to use the
Russian weapons with which they have been supplied and the Egyptians then
attack, it will become not only a matter of prudence but a measure of honor to
make sure that they are not the losers by waiting." *New York Times*, April 13,
1956.
[42] *The Times*, May 15, 1956. The comment was occasioned by reports of
Canadian, French, and British arms deliveries to Israel.

there was the suspicion that it had managed to foment an anti-colonial demonstration that greeted the Colonial Under-Secretary, Lord Lloyd, upon his arrival in Aden, or, two months earlier, Selwyn Lloyd in Bahrein.[43] Nasser attacked British efforts to promote an association of the states of Aden as well as a British promise of protection to them. The Egyptian dictator declared for the liberation of all such strategic footholds on the Red Sea and the Indian Ocean. Such "foreign positions may always jeopardize the military, economic, and political independence of the Arabs in the hinterland." [44]

This Arabist campaign genuinely menaced British positions. Eden, justly concerned about it, saw it as illegitimate and sinister and behind it the hand of even more powerful agents, the communists.[45] His view made him impervious to new information—and to new courses. He had become a difficult man with whom to deal. A writer for *The Annual Register, 1956*, tersely characterized the situation: ". . . the sun never sets on the headaches of British imperialism in retreat." [46] The dilemma was: "It has been Britain's insistence that her strategic interests should be secured independently of the future willingness of the local majority to cooperate. . . . The truth is that, in this age of nationalism, the priority of strategic considerations cannot be enforced—except in time of war." [47] The not very easy answer was that Britain would have to foster conditions and relations so that the local populace in a strategic area could be loyal and cooperative in the future. Eden, however, insisted that the bases must be held in the present and near future, as Britain's loss of them in that period would be disastrous for Britain and the West.

Presumably to contribute to the balance of arms in the Middle East, arrangements were made to supply arms to Israel. The public announcement of the provision of Western arms to Israel was oddly timed, so far as a lessening of tension was concerned. The United

---

[43] *The Times*, May 12, 1962.

[44] *Daily Telegraph*, April 5, 1956, quoted in Barraclough and Wall, *Survey of International Affairs, 1955-1956*, p. 301.

[45] In his memoirs Eden has carefully noted Hussain's suspicions of communist activity in Jordan. He cannot allow that there is Arabist sentiment in Jordan, or in Iraq against Nuri, or anything but demagoguery and communism in Egypt. Selwyn Lloyd ineffectually spoke from the same kind of brief in New Delhi, when he denied that the Baghdad Pact hampered Arab unity and affirmed that though Arab unity did not exist, Britain sought to bring it about. *New York Times*, March 6, 1956.

[46] P. 29.

[47] Editorial, "Bases," *The Observer*, May 20, 1956.

Nations Secretary-General Dag Hammarskjöld, had just returned
from the Middle East, his second of three journeys there in 1956.
The April-May journey had been made in response to a Security
Council Resolution. In spite of his earlier cautions that there were
problems in the world that could not soon be solved or reduced to
tolerable dimensions, the Secretary's mission was unexpectedly successful, by which is meant that his efforts provided a respite. He
secured a cease-fire agreement, this time signed not by local commanders, as in the case of earlier conciliatory efforts, but by the governments involved.

In the aftermath of this success the French government indicated
that it was going to supply more planes to Israel, and the Canadian
government was described as considering the sale of jets to Israel.[48]
In reply to this, Nasser quickly recognized Communist China.

At the end of June the last British troops left the Canal Zone,
and their departure was the occasion for a grandiose celebration in
Egypt in which the Soviet delegation was notably prominent. Indeed,
Nasser had risen high in the world. And to Eden and Dulles he appeared to have committed himself very heavily to the communist
camp. These commitments posed a grave political problem in maintaining the offer of financial aid for the High Dam project. It was
admitted that the dam was most desirable on economic and humanitarian grounds. But these could not be isolated from the political
impact of granting aid to Nasser's Egypt. Nasser, an opponent of
phases of American policy in his espousal of neutralism and the pro-
ponent of courses that menaced British interests, expected to receive
financial assistance from the two countries.

The situation posed genuine difficulties for foreign policy as well
as in American domestic politics. Nuri es-Said complained to Eden
about a policy that rewarded and strengthened Nuri's and Britain's
enemy. If the United States was to be so generous to a more than
uncooperative Nasser, the Philippines and Pakistan were prompted
to ask about the material value of being an American ally. Indeed,
Khrushchev was reported to have claimed credit not only for his
direct aid to Egypt but for American aid, which was prompted, he
said, by emulation of the Soviet Union. Nasser's government, moreover, had observed financial policies that augured ill for Egypt's
ability to carry the dam to completion. He had not secured the necessary agreement of the Sudan about the allocation of waters and about

[48] Arthur Blakely, "Ottawa," *Montreal Gazette*, September 3, 1956.

the Sudanese territory and people to be displaced by the dam's waters.

Domestic pressures, as well, urged Dulles to withdraw the offer of aid. Jewish and other pro-Israel groups were hostile to such aid to the military dictator of Egypt. Some southern senators objected to aiding an enterprise that, so they mistakenly argued, would increase the supply of cotton competing with American supplies. Nasser's recognition of Communist China may have clinched the Congressional case against him. Finally, the Senate (July 16, 1956) amended an appropriations bill to the effect that mutual security money could not, without specific authorization of Congress, be used for aid in constructing the dam. Meanwhile, time had run out on the appropriations originally marked for Egyptian assistance.

While Dulles was sensitive to the divergent pressures, which, in effect, made the loan-offer poison in domestic politics, his manner of withdrawing the offer suggests that the withdrawal was conceived as a grim lesson enjoining neutralists to avoid Nasser's ungrateful behavior, although the warning was the less impressive in that Nasser's arms deal with the communists had heightened the American willingness to aid with the dam. The withdrawal was further grounded in the belief that the Soviet Union was in difficult straits and could not deliver on its hints of promises of aid. If this could be publicly dramatized, Dulles would have scored a notable victory.

The withdrawal of the loan-offer was a gesture not of quiet diplomacy but of open diplomacy. An accompanying explanation, reflecting, justly enough, on the weakness of Egypt's financial position, was clearly more than the mischievousness of a candid friend. It was meant and interpreted as a rebuff to Nasser, a rebuff of global educational value that would be compounded as his weakened position and prospects reduced his influence.[49] Possibly, too, the calculation was that Nasser's attempts at retaliation would further discredit him, although such a willingness to "let her rip," applied to the Middle East, would argue that Secretary Dulles was a reckless gambler with other people's holdings.

Here was a community of ill-will. Nasser knew the American position, too, and yet he sent his ambassador to Washington to arrange for the loan. After he had nationalized the Canal, he provided an explanation of his action, for he had been inclined to tell Washington that he would not accept the aid. "But on second thoughts I felt

---

[49] *Time*, July 27, 1956, which often praised the Secretary in very generous terms, commented: "Chess master Dulles has checkmated Nasser."

this was the occasion we were waiting for in order to unmask before world opinion the duplicity of United States policy towards Egypt. We wanted to show how the Americans had been stalling us for many years while promising aid all the time." [50]

Eden has indicated that the British government had decided against the loan and, although he recognized the importance of "timing and methods," there had been no consultation with the United States, as the matter was not urgent. But the date of July 19 was publicly known as the day for the Egyptian Ambassador's call on the State Department, and the matter was of some urgency. This is not to disbelieve Eden's remark that he "would have preferred to play this long and not to have forced the issue." [51] To Childers, an exponent of a plot theory—usually an attempt to give rational and aesthetic coherence to a historical maze—it is unthinkable that Eden with his obsessive concern for the Middle East would not have known about the Dulles decision. A possible explanation is that Dulles kept his own counsel to add to the dramatic effect of the withdrawal.

At any rate, he could not have avoided the knowledge that the American government was going to deny aid to Egypt and perhaps in a sensational manner. But for clear lack of coordination the American case is the proper example. The American Ambassador to Egypt, Henry Byroade, who had been criticized for being too pro-Nasser and had received notice that he was to be transferred, later testified that the first knowledge he had of the withdrawal of the loan was obtained from the Cairo papers.

On the following day the British offer was publicly withdrawn. As the International Bank loan was contingent on the American-British offer, that loan-offer also lapsed. In this atmosphere of ill-will, with Eden's hostility to Nasser and his lack of communication with the United States, and with Dulles and Nasser deciding to make an issue of the loan-offer, it is not too surprising that so much trouble ensued.

[50] Simon Malley, "—And the Answer Was Suez," *The Reporter*, September 6, 1956, p. 33.
[51] Eden, *op. cit.*, p. 470. Eden deplored that the withdrawal, of which he approved, was done "abruptly" in a way that "gave our two countries no chance to concert either timing or methods, though these were quite as important as the substance."

8: NATIONALIZATION AND THE BRITISH EFFORT TO REGAIN THE PAST

Nasser received the news of the American withdrawal of the loan-offer at the end of his conference at Brioni with Tito and Nehru. The American action was a dramatized rebuff to the Egyptian leader after some five weeks of spectacular triumphs, notably the British evacuation of the Canal Zone (June 13), and with the evacuation the attendant celebrations (from June 18-20), including military parades of Egyptian forces equipped with communist arms and the presence of the Soviet Foreign Minister Shepilov. Nasser had also proclaimed the end of military rule in Egypt; a new constitution had been ratified; and Nasser had been elected President. Brioni appeared to mark his approach to the summit eminence of neutralist statesmen. Dulles, contributing to the spectacular quality, had been willing to make the withdrawal a public and dramatic occasion for warning that neutralism did not pay—at any rate, not as well as alignment—and that American allies such as the Philippines, Turkey, and Pakistan would not have to watch the puzzling spectacle of Nasser, the recipient of communist arms, the recognizer of Communist China, and the enemy of many Western policies, as the beneficiary of lavish American aid.

In view of the lesson imparted it is not surprising that Nehru, who accompanied Nasser to Cairo, supported Nasser's criticism of the American decision and statement issued to explain the withdrawal. Nasser then prepared a spectacular counter-punch, the nationalization of the Suez Canal Company announced July 26, in the course of a long speech in Alexandria devoted to an attack on imperialism. By imperialism, he indicated that he meant dominance, unequal partnership, and even the imposition of such terms as the World Bank had attached to its loan-offer. But Nasser was also careful to pledge that the navigation of the Canal would be maintained freely open and that the shareholders of the Company would be compensated. To link the nationalization with the political rebuff he had received and to appeal to the profound interest of Egyptians in the Aswan Dam, he indicated that the revenues arising from the Canal's operation would be used in building the dam.

His announcement of the nationalization was acclaimed as though it were a work of redemption, a redeeming of Egypt and the Arabs from decades of weakness, inferiority, frustration, and imperialism. Arab leaders and rulers may have been shocked by his audacity and fearful of his progress but a vast majority of the vocal Arab people cheered him as their hero and leader. Indeed, the applause came from the whole colonial world, and Nasser's response to Dulles' teaching on neutralism appeared to be developing into an incitement to imitate Nasser, to defy the bulwarks of imperialism and to take possession of them.[1]

The news of Nasser's action reached Eden in London while he was acting as dinner host to the King of Iraq and Premier Nuri es-Said. He and his guests, agreeing that this was "an event which changed all perspectives," understood how much depended upon the resolution with which this act of defiance was met. The resolution, indeed, would decide "whose authority would prevail" in the Middle East, for the changing perspectives involved Britain's position as a power in the world and the fortunes of Nuri. Of the latter Eden added his recognition that in the Baghdad Pact and Iraq's development plans Nuri was engaged in a race against time and Nasser.[2]

Here could be no retreat, as at Abadan. Eden's own past as well as his reading of present events urged him on. His own speeches recalled that the use of force could not be foresworn where violence was used against vital British interests. Nasser now had "his thumb

[1] An article in the *Manchester Guardian*, August 2, 1956, a foremost critic of Eden's Suez policy, reported that many Asian countries were anxiously watching the issue of Nasser's actions, that, indeed, in some Asian countries there was talk of holding another Bandung Conference to celebrate Nasser's feat. See also *The Times*, July 30, 1956. *The Times*, July 28, 1956, argued that, if Nasser were allowed to act with impunity in this matter, Britain's economic future might be grave. Much of that future depended on the oil fields of the Middle East, which were "mainly in the territories of friendly Middle Eastern Governments. But in the shifting sands of Arab politics extremists in every country would soon be pressing to follow Egypt's lead, if it were seen to be successful."

[2] Eden, *Full Circle*, p. 472. Nevertheless, Nasser's act had so won the public support of Arab nationalism that the government of Jordan and Iraq publicly endorsed Nasser's nationalization. See *The Times*, August 6 and *New York Times*, August 6, 1956.

on our windpipe." [3] A failure "to keep the Canal international would inevitably lead to the loss one by one of all our interests in the Middle East." He resolved that British interests must be safeguarded, "if necessary by military action." The following day he informed President Eisenhower that in the last resort Britain would use force. The decision had a self-fulfilling quality, because, as Eden viewed the situation, there were few prospects before the last resort.[4] Nevertheless, Eden's early watchwords for the situation, firmness and care, expressed in speaking to the Commons on July 27, are more moderate than the French government's reaction. The Egyptian Ambassador in Paris refused to receive the French protest, since its terms were "inadmissible, and unacceptable." Foreign Minister Pineau told .the Egyptian Ambassador: "The French Government has noticed repeatedly that the Egyptian dictator has failed to fulfill his word of honor." [5]

As the British state dinner broke up shortly after the news of Nasser's bold act had been received, Eden by the very early morning had consulted the principal members of his government and the service chiefs as well as the representatives of France and the United States and then held a Cabinet meeting later in the morning of the same day.[6] From the Chiefs of Staff Eden was not surprised to learn that Britain did not have the forces in paratroopers or in any other form for an immediate blow against Nasser, if that had been decided. This meant that for the moment serious efforts to secure American as well as French military support and, thus, their concord in policy with Britain would have to be a matter of urgency.

[3] *The Times*, July 30, 1956, said much the same thing: President Nasser's virulence and his record to date rebuff any thought of a new approach and leave the Western powers with the need to decide on stern measures to safeguard the Canal and all that depends on it.

[4] *Ibid.*, pp. 474, 474-475, 476-477.

[5] The Egyptian government also refused to accept Britain's formal protest against "an act within Egypt's sovereignty." *New York Times*, July 28, 1956. *Ibid.*, July 29, 1956. Nasser said in Cairo: "As to the impoliteness of France and the rudeness of her Foreign Minister, I shall leave it to the Algerian nationalists to answer the French."

[6] A ridiculous part of the effort to identify Nasser with Hitler was the frequently made assertions that Nasser was copying the technique of week-end *coups*. The nationalization was announced on Thursday. If Thursday and Friday along with Monday formed part of the week-end, the week itself would be reduced to two days.

In Eden's eyes British interest required a new and secure arrangement for the Canal and the toppling of Nasser, which, in turn, would
buttress Jordan and Iraq. In subsequent weeks these coupled objectives made it impossible for Eden to agree to proposals that involved
trusting Nasser, such as one made by India. To topple the Egyptian
leader called for pressures, the threat of force, and perhaps the use
of force. This, in turn, meant that Eden sought to present a front of
British inter-party unity and to that end the sense of outrage at
Nasser's nationalization expressed by the Labour Party leader, Hugh
Gaitskell, was much quoted by Conservatives. But after the (July 27)
initial shock and in the absence of a clear British course as well as
of Western unity, Labour returned to a critical and oppositionist
role. The Conservative government, however, eventually acquired
its own momentum and proceeded with little attention paid to
Labourite criticism or to a realistic assessment of its own policy. Even
in his memoirs Eden appears to believe that he had firm general
support in the Commons and the country until September 12. He
sustained this belief only by ignoring the fact of persistent Labour
criticism and questioning of his government.

Pressure on Nasser, therefore, took three forms: economic; political moves including the rousing of British opinion against Egypt and
the announcement of military preparations; and efforts on the international level to concert policy with allies and to rally world opinion
so that it could be gathered in support of demands on Egypt. Eden
did not expect economic pressures alone to have immediate results
or to be effective in the long run.[7] But the British government at
once froze Egyptian funds in Britain and maintained the freeze on
blocked sterling balances until the end of 1958. British and French
ships, refusing to pay tolls to Nasser's Canal authority, continued
to pay them to the company.

The attempt to rouse and harden British opinion against Egypt
began with many advantages and initial success. Just as Nasser's
action made a tremendous appeal to the Egyptians and Arabs, so
for some Britons the Canal, as a vital artery of commerce and communications, had become an emotionally charged symbol of Empire
that made for a widespread sense of outrage against Nasser.[8] After

[7] Eden, op. cit., p. 477.
[8] Erskine Childers, The Road to Suez (London, 1962), p. 212, n. 19, has
argued that there is "overwhelming evidence" to support the sincerity of Nasser's
expressions of surprise at the uproar that followed nationalization. Nasser is described as bewildered at the storm of criticism directed at the taking of what,

the long period of Egyptian nationalist agitation, Egyptians had relatively few public friends in Britain and Nasser had almost none. Indeed, Egyptians were among the least popular foreigners for the general run of the British people, especially former British servicemen. The abruptly defiant manner of terminating a venerable company's concession evoked special and widespread animosity. The hope of the Suez rebels was for the moment shared by many angry Britons. In short order the government and its spokesmen were attributing sinister designs to Nasser and were equating his *Philosophy of the Revolution* with *Mein Kampf* and Nasser with Hitler and Mussolini. Selwyn Lloyd propagated such views, which are also enshrined in the very title of Eden's memoirs, *Full Circle*, that is, the wheel had come full circle from the Rhineland crisis and Hitler to Suez and Nasser.

The military preparations were a more complex matter. To gain immediate effect, some preparations had to be public, but for longer-range purposes, other initiatives had to be secret. The American government was informed that the British Chiefs of Staff had been instructed to be ready in the last resort for the use of force. The Chiefs were also instructed to devise "a plan and a time-table for an operation designed to occupy and secure the canal, should other methods fail." [9]

Moves to strengthen the British military position in the Mediterranean were announced on July 31. Military reservists were also called up. The French military response to Nasser was even more public and threatening. On August 2, French women and children were ordered to be evacuated from Egypt and French naval preparations in the Mediterranean were known to be formidable.

Moderation and restraint did not delay the taking of military action. But, on the military side, two factors made for delay: an expedition against Egypt could not be mounted from Cyprus, which lacked adequate harbors, but would, therefore, have to come from Malta, a sea journey of about six days for an expedition to Port Said; and Britain lacked adequate landing craft necessary for a formidable invasion force. American authorities knew from the very beginning that Eden contemplated the use of force as a possible, even likely,

---

under the Company's concession, would have been Egypt's in twelve years. This is characteristic of the special pleading that vitiates Childers' effort to subject the Suez crisis to a new treatment. The expressions of surprise were at best ingenuous and psychologically cannot be squared with Nasser's charge of Western intrigue and conspiracy against himself and the Arabs.

[9] Eden, *op. cit.*, pp. 476-477.

course. The American government, while not denying Britain's right
to use force, generally argued firmly against the prudence of such a
course.[10] The American view placed obstacles in Eden's path and
American policy-makers had to take account of Eden's determination, for Dulles feared Soviet exploitation of the use of force in the
Middle East. Where Eden thought of the crisis in terms reminiscent
of Munich, the American government thought of it in terms of the
prelude to a war, for example, the assassination at Sarajevo in June
1914.[11] The interplay of such mutual suspicions of two allies helps
explain some of the tortuous character of the attempts to focus
pressure on Nasser by rallying international opinion. As though a
special Middle Eastern djinn were presiding over this crisis, the
actions and policy statements of all the principal actors are unusually
lacking in directness and even honesty.

For the first months of the crisis Dulles was eager to prevent the
British government from appealing to the United Nations Security
Council. There, the Soviet veto might very well give Eden a pretext
for arguing that the futility of peaceful means justified warlike actions.
In fact, when the British government sent (August 30) a draft of
the resolutions it proposed to submit to the United Nations, Dulles
indicated that the British resolution would have American support
"on the understanding that our move was an honest attempt to
reach a solution," and—here Eden quoted Dulles—not "a device for
obtaining cover." [12]

As Dulles has been reproached for failing in loyalty to the British
ally, all the more for having provoked Nasser into his action against
Britain, it would be well here to indicate the difficulties of the American Secretary's course. He recognized that Eden was determined to
follow a line that made warlike action probable. As Eden did not
expect American participation against Egypt, he looked for American
neutrality. Dulles, however, fearing Eden's resolution, sought to deter

[10] All of the early statements of the American government appealed to common
sense against precipitate action or talked about appeals to the interests of the
maritime nations, in short, about internationally concerted action. Eden, *op.
cit.*, p. 484; State Department Press Release, July 27, 1956, August 3, 1956;
Dulles' statement upon his return to Washington; *New York Times*, July 30,
1956; Dulles' televised report, August 3, 1956. The televised report and the
statement of July 27, are in Paul Zinner editor, *Documents on American Foreign
Relations, 1956* (New York, 1957), pp. 291, 294-300.

[11] The Alsops who were somberly critical of American policy mentioned the
Sarajevo parallel in *New York Herald Tribune*, July 30, 1956.

[12] Eden, *op. cit.*, p. 513.

him by urging courses of appeal to international interest which implied exaggerated American agreement with the British case against Nasser, with the unfortunate result that Eden did not appreciate the American position until early September. Dulles told Eden that Nasser must be made to "disgorge" the Canal and endorsed the view that the Canal must be under international control rather than that of a single country. He, too, was averse to Nasser and concerned lest international obligations be repudiated, for the United States had its own Canal in another country.[13]

At first, the American policy endorsed the British view of the injury done Britain. This position was that Nasser's nationalization of the Canal was unacceptable because the Canal could not safely be allowed in his hands. The criterion was a political judgment, involving "broader international grounds" than those of law.[14] Now this was the very difficulty that was to arise in the attempt to rally international opinion against Nasser. Clear law might have been persuasive, but British reason of state was not likely to gain general and effectively implemented agreement.

In international law the British case was not promising for any course acceptable to Eden, and there are two main reasons for the weakness of the British legal case, which Eden himself appeared to recognize, for he urged on Eisenhower that it was British policy to avoid involvement "in legal quibbles." [15] First of all, though the Canal Company as Concessionaire, was international in scope and had its headquarters in Paris, it was technically an Egyptian company and was registered in that country, and the Egyptian govern-

[13] The American Under Secretary of State, Robert Murphy, speaking in 1957 on the Middle Eastern policy of the United States, described pre-Suez policy in terms that reveal the insufficiency of American policy. The "tempo of events had been building to fever pitch." In nationalizing the Canal Company, Nasser provoked the British and French and alarmed the Israelis. But the injured and threatened parties also were wrong, since the action they planned and undertook jeopardized the beginnings of a world order to be established through the United Nations. Indeed, the United Nations was at fault, for it had failed to come to grips with problems from which the crisis stemmed. *Department of State Bulletin*, XXXVI (1957), 515-522. Particularly noteworthy here is the blame cast on the United Nations, for the United States is portrayed as looking to an international solution of the crisis. But if the United Nations would not act, did it follow that a great power should not act? In the days of the League of Nations, predictions of the League's inactivity, which often were the refusals of the states to act through the League, were usually used to justify unilateral action.

[14] Eden, *op. cit.*, p. 477.

[15] *Ibid.*, pp. 476-477.

ment presumably could nationalize it upon the payment of adequate compensation. The Anglo-Egyptian Treaty (1954) had recognized the Canal itself as an integral part of Egypt. The Canal had been constructed and operated under a Concession from Egypt. This Concession was, in effect, an agreement between the Egyptian government and an Egyptian company. The Canal, however, was the subject of an international Convention (1888) which provided for the free and unimpeded navigation of the waterway. British policy had from the beginning of the Convention failed to provide an agreed basis for implementing and guaranteeing the international interest in free navigation proclaimed in the Convention.[16] Nasser had appeared to meet the major legal difficulties by promising compensation to the company's share-holders and by affirming the Convention of 1888. Here, Nasser's case was impaired by his action in preventing first Israeli ships and then Israeli-bound ships from using the Canal on the ground that a state of war existed between Israel and Egypt.

These major points made the presentation of a formidable legal case difficult for the British. The government, of course, was not resourceless in law, for the precedents in international law were not simple. But the British case against Nasser was not so clear as the title of the nationalization chapter in Eden's memoirs, "Theft," suggests. It is also revealing that his memoirs misstated the status of the Panama Canal. The latter, he argued, was a private affair, for the Canal was American and regulated by Treaty between the two governments. The Treaty, however, gives the Panama Canal an international significance that for Suez was to be found only in the Convention.

The second difficulty in appealing to international opinion was the climate of opinion in the former colonial world which on this matter generally received support from the communist states and, more measuredly, from the United States. Many former colonial areas had become, as the phrase goes, members of the community of states. This, however, did not mean that they unreservedly accepted the traditions of Western international law. Their own experience led

---

[16] Of the considerable literature on the legal aspects of the Suez crisis, the following may be cited: Quincy Wright, "Intervention, 1956," *American Journal of International Law*, LI (1957); T. T. T. Huang, "Some International and Legal Aspects of the Suez Canal Question," *ibid.*, 277-307; Paul de Visscher, "Les aspects fondamentaux de la question de Suez," *Revue Générale de Droit International Public*, 3rd Series, XXIX (1958), 400-403.

them to look on parts of international legal traditions as buttresses of power structures which they had rejected, vestiges of a world they had never made and sought in part to undo. This viewpoint was eloquently expressed at the London Conference by an Indonesian delegate, Abdulgani:

> Most of the International treaties which are a reflection of international law do not respect the sanctity of men as equal human beings irrespective of their race, or their creed or locality. Most of the existing laws between Asian and African countries and the old-established western world are more or less outmoded and should be regarded as a burden of modern life. They should be revised and made more adaptable to modern national relations and the emancipation of all parts of mankind. . . . This process of emancipation is sometimes carried out gracefully. . . . Sometimes it creates explosive repercussions. . . . But nobody can defy the process of this emancipation which is the inevitable course in human history.[17]

The "broader international grounds," including, as they did, opposition to Nasser's bid for leadership of the Arab world, his exclusion of Western interests, and his unrelenting hostility to the Middle Eastern friends of the West, meant that Nasser could not be trusted. This is the meaning of Eden's emphasis on "unfettered control of a single power" over the Canal. In the past British forces in the Canal Zone were on hand to protect British interests. But the Convention had not designated them as the guarantors of the Canal. The new demand for international control was, in effect, the continuing British demand that international forces should with Britain take over the former British task of keeping the Middle East stable. It was bluntly and politically a vote of no-confidence in Nasser's capacity to manage the Canal in the international interest and a reciprocation of Nasser's hostility to British interests. For his purposes Dulles (August 2) accepted the British (and French) statement that the Canal Company, technically Egyptian, had been "an international agency" which was responsible for operating and maintaining the Canal, in accord with the Convention of 1888.[18]

Of Nuri, on July 26, 1956 Eden wrote: "I found him deafer, but as resolute as ever and without illusions." [19] In relation to Nasser Eden, too, was without illusions, and resolutely deaf. This helps to explain why he dismissed Egyptian proposals utterly or as offering "nothing

---

[17] *The Suez Canal Problem, July 26–September 22, 1956.* A Documentary Publication of the Department of State (Washington, 1956), p. 84.

[18] *Ibid.,* p. 489.

[19] *Ibid.,* p. 471.

new." If Nasser's proposals meant that he would survive and remain unhumbled, then the proposals were not worth heeding.

On August 1 Dulles went to London to confer with the British and French representatives. His influence carried the day for a Conference that would deal rather more with legal rights arising from the Convention of 1888 than Eden perhaps would have liked. In return Dulles, in the Joint Statement issued on August 2, accepted the British and French arguments that the Canal Company had "an international character" and was "an international agency which has the responsibility to maintain and operate the Suez Canal so that all the signatories to and beneficiaries of the Treaty of 1888" can enjoy their rights in full security.[20]

To gather international opinion into pressure on Nasser, a Conference of the principal users of the Canal met in London August 16. There, eighteen nations, not including India, the Soviet Union, Indonesia, and Ceylon, agreed upon American proposals, much amended, calling for agreement with Egypt and providing for the operation of the Canal by a board composed of Egyptians and representatives of other interested states, as well as for effective sanctions to deal with violations of the Canal Convention. A committee headed by Australian Prime Minister Robert Menzies presented the proposals and, as Menzies had no authority to amend the proposals, they were, in effect, presented for Nasser's acceptance. The Egyptian leader rejected them as unacceptable on the ground that they infringed upon the sovereignty of Egypt.

The London Conference was doomed to failure and this doom was written on the mission of Menzies. The Conference, after all, had not been in agreement and Nasser could count on Soviet and Indian support and on American unwillingness to back Eden by force. The failure derived from the political judgment that inspired the British approach to the Conference. Nasser would not accept his own humiliation without coercion and he was careful to refrain from giving additional occasions of angering Eden or affording pretexts for an Anglo-French attack on Egypt. Eden's political objective made it impossible for him to secure the widest international agreement on the status of the Canal, in particular the adhesion of India to the plan of the London Conference. If Eden's interest had been limited to

[20] Paul Zinner, editor, *Documents on American Foreign Relations, 1956* (New York, 1957), pp. 292-294.

the Canal—and in his calculations it could not be—tolerably satis-factory international arrangements might have been possible.[21] These would have had the full support of Dulles, the full but possibly not the sustained support of India, and such a solution was probably the only one that would have been acceptable to a very large segment of Arab opinion, including the public utterances of Iraq's Nuri. To humble Nasser was quite agreeable to Nuri, but the action would have to be managed in such a way as to avoid offending Arab opin-ion. This ruled out association with Israel and France in an armed attack on Egypt, as well as a lengthy British reoccupation of the Canal Zone.[22] In short, the objective adopted by Eden appeared to be self-defeating, for the prospect of an attempted humiliation of Nasser and strengthening of the Baghdad Pact could hardly control these necessary conditions. For his enterprise Eden required a Bis-marckian capacity for simplicity in complexity, a condition made unattainable by the intractably complex forces with which Eden had to work.

Eden, however, believed that persistent and public American sup-port for the Menzies mission might have shaken Nasser's firmness in rejection. The United States government, less concerned with dis-lodging Nasser and professing a desire for peaceful settlement, fos-tered continued diplomatic contact with him. Dulles publicly rec-ognized Nasser's willingness to receive the Menzies mission as a con-tribution to the solution of the problem. Indeed, Dulles, doggedly repeating earlier American views about the Egyptian Revolutionary government's sense of responsibility, expressed the belief that Nasser's influence and authority were great enough to enable him to accept

[21] On September 3 Eden received from Eisenhower the advice that Britain should separate the Canal issue from the general British policy towards Nasser and the threat he posed to the Middle East and North Africa. The latter, the President argued, was a long-range problem. Eisenhower also noted that present negotiations were unlikely to inflict on Nasser the setback he deserved. Eden, op. cit., p. 518. Later, Eisenhower told Emmet Hughes that the British were furious with Dulles and himself for holding them back. As an example of how little people understand world affairs, the President then cited Senator Knowland, who came to Eisenhower seeking assurance against American involvement in one of Britain's wars. Emmet John Hughes, The Ordeal of Power: A Political Memoir of the Eisenhower Years (New York, 1963), p. 193.

[22] When early in the crisis the Iraqi government supported Nasser's nationali-zation, it also emphasized that the crisis made Israel more dangerous than ever. The Times, August 6, 1956.

a fair plan.[23] Dulles particularly urged a pragmatic approach on Nasser and on all parties the avoidance of slogans.

In the question about who is using whom, Eden clearly believes that Nasser was using the American government. His complaint is that the "uncertain diplomacy" of the American ally compounded the hostility he faced. But an American policy of certainty would have implied Dulles' support for the use of force. When the British Cabinet agreed on August 28 to appeal to the Security Council if Menzies were not successful in his mission, Dulles' reservations appear in the conditions he proposed. In fact, the American government was not prepared to sign or even to support the Franco-British resolution to be presented to the Security Council. Eden's summary of Dulles' refusal is revealing: "We were told that they did not wish to create an identity of interest, which might prove embarrassing to the French and ourselves." [24]

The middle weeks of September were the decisive turning point. Then, the different approaches of the British and American governments became inescapably clear. For some time the representatives of the American government had been pointing to the legal weakness of Eden's case. As Britain prepared to appeal to the Security Council and as invitations to the Second London Conference were about to be sent out (September 14, to meet September 19), Dulles attempted another maneuver. He advanced a proposal for a Suez Canal Users' Association, which, basing its rights on the Convention of 1888, would have an administration of its own and deal with Egypt on matters necessary for maintenance of unimpeded navigation of the Canal. The project, a development of earlier ideas advanced by Dulles and others, was mistrusted at once by the French government as designed primarily to delay action. Eden, however, accepted the proposal out of concern for the American alliance, and in the latter half of September hasty discussions prepared the establishment of the Users' Association. The latter might have been successful if Eden's objectives were centered on the Canal and if the Users' Association had been the fruit of the London Conference. Under the prevailing circumstancs the Association was a device to delay Eden, and to arrange for international control if operation of the Canal should be impeded by the withdrawal of pilots, a device shorn of its effectiveness when Dulles assumed quite correctly that Eden would use it as a means to coerce Nasser.

[23] Dulles press conference, New York Times, August 29, 1956.
[24] Eden, op. cit., p. 531.

When Eden first announced the Association to the Commons on September 12, he was triumphant. The Association would run ships through the Canal under its own pilots. Nasser would presumably have to accept the Association or interfere with the Canal's operations. Eden parried questions about the use of force. The leader of the opposition was effectively critical of the difficulties and inadequacies of the sketchily improvised plan. The triumph ended the next day when Dulles, after having announced the Association, was asked questions that issued from the previous day's debate in the House of Commons. "We do not intend to shoot our way through. It may be we have the right to do it but we don't intend to do it so far as the United States is concerned."

Here, then, was Dulles' "double-cross," a point which was made not only by supporters of Eden but by left-wing critics of Eden's policy.[25] How did this "double-cross" or misunderstanding take place?

There are real puzzles in the story. First of all, it is difficult to understand why Dulles failed to see the possibilities of formidable challenges to Nasser with which the Association project provided Eden. In early September Dulles felt harassed and uncertain about how much the United States could do. He believed that each day without conflict was so much gained and admitted that he simply went on improvising from day to day.[26] While it is true that Dulles was hard put to secure delays, the proposal was trap-laden. Dulles was not thinking of force but, if he was thinking of economic pressure on Nasser, it must be recognized that the United States was not likely to take action in that direction. A further source of trouble is that part of the discussion about the Users' Association took place by telephone. Further, Dulles, in his uneasy relations with Eden, found it difficult to talk frankly with the British Prime Minister. In public he affected exaggerated cordiality and on this private occasion he was trying to persuade Eden. After all, his intent so far as Eden was concerned was devious. Eden, who called Dulles "that terrible man," found Dulles' language lacking in precision. But there is the testimony of another British diplomat to the effect that Dulles' intent was unmistakable if you listened to all that he said. This may very well be the key.[27] Eden was at best a patient listener only through self-discipline. On this occasion, he had that closed mind which may

[25] Paul Johnson, *The Suez War* (London, 1957).

[26] Hughes, *op. cit.*, pp. 177-178.

[27] Roscoe Drummond and Gaston Coblentz, *Duel at the Summit* (New York, 1960), pp. 161-169.

make for sustained deafness. He was looking for support against Nasser and, as he had failed to secure American understanding of the gravity of the Middle Eastern situation, he was looking for a means of gaining an American commitment that could be used for the objectives of British policy. Eden's sense of being let down cannot be fully explained away, for later the United States government indicated that it was unable to insure that all American ships using the Canal would refuse to pay tolls to Nasser. Thus, immediate financial pressure on Nasser would be ineffective. Eden's conclusion, then, was that the Users' Association by displaying American unity with Britain served the purpose of making recourse to force unnecessary. When Dulles, in effect, torpedoed the project, there remained only the alternatives of force or acceptance of Nasser's triumph.[28]

Eden's bitterness on the occasion, however, has led him to a grave overstatement. He has argued that in espousing the Users' Association and delaying an appeal to the United Nations he lost the bipartisan support of the Commons. This is at best ingenuous, for since the second week of August the Labour Party had voiced many doubts and criticisms of Eden's policy. And Eden would have had to do more than appeal to the United Nations in order to avoid a Commons vote of the Parliamentary Labour Party against the government's Suez policy. In dividing the Commons against the government's foreign policy, the Labour Party was fearful of the very objectives and means contemplated by Eden. The latter, however, continued to believe that he had the general support of the British people and became heated when American spokesmen reminded the Prime Minister of the divisions of British opinion.[29] Thus, the jubila-

[28] Eden, *op. cit.*, p. 540.

[29] Eden ignored the serious opposition directed against the government's course in a series of editorials ("leaders") and news stories in the *Manchester Guardian*. On August 31, 1956, a "leader" entitled "To War?" stated that the government seemed to be preparing for war immediately, if the Menzies mission failed. As the government had lulled the country by assuring that its warlike moves were only precautions, the government should be called to answer the following questions: "First, does it make sense to fight alone in defiance of the United States and the Commonwealth? Secondly, are the military operations likely to be quick and cheap or long and costly? Can we be sure of limiting the war to Egypt? Thirdly, shall we be upholding or destroying an international rule of law and will the United Nations order sanctions against us or, instead, let itself disintegrate? Fourthly, shall we in the end make our oil supplies more secure or less?" "Mr. Dulles has saved us once already from an impetuous resort to arms, and he has left no uncertainty that the Americans cannot join in the fighting." I have used the text appearing in *The Manchester Guardian Weekly*, September 6, 1956.

tion—an irresponsible jubilation—of Labour's left-wing, that Labour had finally ended formal, parliamentary, inter-party accord on the government's foreign policy and had repudiated the principle of continuity, rankled.[30] But there were real divisions, primarily on method and procedure rather than ends, within Eden's own party, though Conservative Party discipline and the Conservative tradition of restraint from rocking the boat operated to make Conservative criticism even less effective than Labourite attacks. Nevertheless, on September 13, a former Conservative Attorney General, who, in effect, spoke on behalf of critical Conservative M.P.s, argued that Britain could not rightly use force until she had sought redress through the United Nations.

By accepting Dulles' proposal of a Users' Association, Eden did lose momentum. He had to go through the profitless and painful tasks of preparing for the Association's establishment. This continued to be an occasion of bitter Anglo-American comment. Dulles later said of the Association that "there were no teeth in it as far as I am aware, and as far as all three of us were aware." At the same press conference Dulles emphasized that the United States did not have treaty obligations to Britain concerning Suez. Indeed, the Secretary said that on the issue of colonialism—likely, Dulles said, to be a heated matter for another fifty years—the United States found it impractical to identify itself completely with the colonial powers or with those seeking independence as rapidly and fully as possible.[31] Apart from continuing his warnings to Eden against the use of force, Dulles here reveals how far removed from a directing influence Amer-

[30] In addressing the Conservative Party Conference, October 31, 1956, Eden was particularly critical of those who exulted at the end of bipartisanship in foreign policy. But, he also argued, the broader Socialist criticisms were damaging to Britain, for "they amount to encouragement of Middle Eastern countries to nationalize oil and other undertakings." Such nationalization not only deprived Britons of the reward due to their labor, enterprise, skill, and capital but was harmful to the Middle Easterners themselves. *Manchester Guardian*, Oct. 15, 1956. There is a good study of the role of the Labour opposition in Walter Goldstein, "The Labour Party and the Middle Eastern Crisis, 1956." Unpublished Ph.D. thesis, University of Chicago, 1961.

[31] The text of the press conference is in the *Department of State Bulletin*, XXXV (1956) and the essential part in Zinner, *op. cit.*, pp. 337-338. Perhaps the strain under which Dulles was laboring was responsible for the wording of his original remarks. Two hours later the official transcript of the conference quoted here made a number of revisions of his original remarks. *The Times*, October 3, 1956, in an editorial "Distorting the Issues" commented: "Britain has nothing to learn from anybody about the task of bringing progress, freedom, and self-government to the emerging people."

ican policy was. His statement was less a policy and more an account of the American dilemma. He came closer to the full problem, albeit abstractly, when in speaking at Williams College on October 6, he was very critical of Nasser and argued that world opinion, which was strongly against force, should equally be concerned with justice.[32]

Dulles' statement of October 2 was a warning reply to Eden's message to President Eisenhower sent the preceding day. In it the Prime Minister stated his conviction that Nasser was then effectively under Russian control, as Mussolini had been under Hitler's control. He then referred to evidence of Egyptian plots in Libya, Saudi Arabia, and Iraq, and argued that trouble might erupt in any of those places unless the West provided evidence that Nasser is losing.[33]

Eden's loss of momentum after the Commons debate in early September and the obvious inadequacy of the Users' Association made an appeal to the United Nations necessary. Thus on September 26 the Security Council met to discuss the Franco-British resolution as well as the counter-complaint of Egypt. The principles enumerated by Dulles (August 10) and later elaborated and refined in discussion formed the first part of the resolutions. The second part declared that these principles were satisfied by the proposals of the First London Conference, rejected by Nasser, and invited Egypt to present proposals designed to make the principles effective. The dissenting Yugoslav vote was supported by a Soviet veto. Eden described the result as ushering out the Franco-British proposals, Britain's "minimum requirement for the security of the Canal."

The Users' Association was in Eden's mind the proper successor to the Suez Canal Company as the guardian of the international guarantee of the 1888 Convention. He had said that if the Egyptian government should interfere with the Association or refuse to provide the essential minimum of cooperation, Egypt would have breached the Convention of 1888. The threat here was so patent that Dulles' subsequent and emphatic qualification of American support is understandable. As the reservations of Dulles included basic matters such as the use of pilots, payment of dues, and passage of the Canal, the Users' Association had none of the bargaining power necessary for the attainment of the British objective. For its sake Eden was trying to outmaneuver Dulles who, in turn, was attempting to outmaneuver Eden into involvement in negotiations that would finally head off the

[32] *The Observer*, October 7, 1956.
[33] Eden, *op. cit.*, p. 556.

threat of force and war. For Eden a major and, thus, unlikely concession from Nasser was essential, a concession that would effectively
prevent national control of the Canal. Foreswearing force and believing that Eden was intent on more than "brinksmanship," Dulles then
had to emphasize the optimistic possibilities in pressure and in the
rallying of world opinion to support the work of justice, a point he
also had to stress. Eden, looking at the vista of immediate consequences, thought that time was running out and decision was urgent.
Dulles, viewing force and war at that moment as dangerous and
unwise means, appeared to be thinking of the piecemeal gains pro-
curable by pressure coupled with negotiation.

When the Security Council convened to consider the Franco-
British and Egyptian resolutions, the British government finally
secured American support. At first the American position had been
that the United States only endorsed the Eighteen Powers' proposals
in their broad and general lines. But in return for British willingness
to call for a private session of quiet diplomacy after an initial public
statement of views by members, the United States declared its support for the Franco-British resolution.[34]

On October 9, 1956, Dulles argued in favor of the Franco-British
resolution as the only one likely to win enough support to make it a
possible solution. But he sought both flexibility and independence by
arguing that effective alternatives would certainly be considered. The
core of the Suez problem was, he argued, the necessity that the Canal
be freed from control in the interests of a single nation's policy. Approaching the British position, he added: "If that principle is repudiated, then it is difficult to foresee a useful role for a negotiating
body." [35] The Egyptian delegate, Mohammed Fawzi, approached the
British case in agreeing to the principle that the interests of Canal
Users should be represented and consulted. He also urged the establishment of a negotiating body to be guided by a set of agreed
principles. But the Soviet delegate, Shepilov, argued more negatively
and insisted that an international group would not insulate the Canal

[34] Report from the United Nations' Correspondent of *The Times*, October 6,
1956, and by Thomas J. Hamilton in *New York Times*, October 6, 1956.
[35] With Britain apparently committed to negotiations, Dulles interpolated into
his prepared closing speech an expression of unequivocal support for the Franco-
British resolutions. *The Times*, October 10, 1956. The British delegation to the
United Nations was reported to have no criticism of Dulles' speeches and actions
during the proceedings of the Security Council. Max Freedman's dispatch, *Manchester Guardian*, October 16, 1956.

from politics and that the Franco-British resolution would infringe on Egyptian sovereignty in the name of international and imperialist interests.[36]

During six private meetings of the Security Council the Secretary-General attempted to draw up a list of the principles upon which the conflicting parties agreed. He compiled six principles: free and unimpeded navigation of the Canal; respect for Egyptian sovereignty; insulation of the Canal's operation from the politics of any country; establishment of tolls in consultation with the users of the Canal; assignment of a fair proportion of the Canal's revenue to maintenance and improvement; arbitration of disputes between Egypt and the Suez Canal Company. With good will this considerable area of agreement might have been an augury of future settlement. Such was the reaction of President Eisenhower in an opening announcement to the television audience of an election campaign program. "Most gratifying" progress had been made, and after talking to Dulles he could say that "in his heart and mind there is a prayer of thanksgiving." [37]

These optimistic assumptions were partly belied the next day when, to the reported surprise of some diplomatic representatives at the United Nations, Britain and France pushed for a vote on the two-part resolution. The first affirmed the principles and passed unanimously. The second, pointing to the Eighteen Powers' proposals as embodying an effective means of implementing the principles, invited Egypt to make proposals to give them effect. It invited the three most interested parties to continue their exchanges and in the meantime insisted that the navigation of the Canal be kept open. This second part met a Soviet veto.

American and British diplomatic reactions were illuminatingly different. The American position was that the Soviet veto was a regrettable instance of fishing in troubled waters but that, as substantial progress had been made, private exchanges should continue, as, indeed, was tentatively arranged. Eden noted that American representatives had complained of the suddenness of the appeal to the Security Council. Once it had been made, however, the American line was to insist that Britain had entered upon negotiations and that in spite of the Soviet veto the question was still before the Security Council. Further, American officials were reported to be puzzled by British

[36] *Manchester Guardian*, October 10, and *The Times*, October 10, 1956.

[37] *The Times*, October 13, 1956. The President also said that "a very great crisis is behind us."

insistence that their position had not changed, for they argued that Britain had yielded importantly on the issue of international operation of the Canal and "had approached the Egyptian view." [38]

The speeches of British leaders had made abundantly clear that the principle of international interest in the Canal was meaningless unless immediately buttressed by the provision of effective sanctions to maintain it. The principle without the sanctions, the sum of agreement as the result of the Soviet veto, was an Egyptian victory and in Eden's mind a signal to the world that plundering had paid off. Foreign Secretary Lloyd had insisted that the talk about principles was at best exploratory and that the discussion and definition of principles could not be called negotiations. The United Nations had not displayed any substantial concern with the international interest. This position was well expressed by Sir Hartley Shawcross, who had been Attorney-General in the postwar Labour government. Speaking to the Grotius Society, he questioned the value of submitting international legal problems to the United Nations, where the best to be hoped was a political solution "and more often, because of the veto power, to secure no solution at all save possibly a negotiated compromise." [39] This meant that international investment and contracts were at the whim of local legislatures and that the world economic climate was, therefore, destructive equally to investing nations and states in need of investment capital. "What happens in Egypt today, if not successfully challenged, will happen elsewhere tomorrow."

But neither the American nor British policy spokesmen were addressing themselves solely to the case at issue. The British case about sanctions was concerned with humbling Nasser in the name of the principle. Secretary Dulles had feared the British appeal to the United Nations mainly because he believed that the British government would not obtain there the justice it sought and thus would feel free to seek redress by force, a redress which in principle he had to endorse as a right of last resort. In the present case he believed that the exercise of that right was a dangerous mistake and would probably destroy the frail structure of order represented by the United Nations and the somewhat more lively hopes attached to it. In attempting to check Eden's willingness to use force, Dulles was driven to exaggerate the prospects of a peaceful solution and, thus, consistently foreshadowed the American course pursued after the Suez

[38] Max Freedman in *Manchester Guardian*, October 16, 1956.
[39] *Manchester Guardian*, October 27, 1956.

expedition had been launched. His efforts also provided assurance
to Nasser that he did not have to face united Western powers. As a
result the threatening stance of France and Britain failed to secure
concessions from Nasser that might have been forthcoming. The
lack of coordination was disastrous all around. It even permitted the
Soviet Union to exploit the situation far more than otherwise might
have been possible.[40]

Though there was the possibility of a meeting in Geneva for
further discussions and at the end of the month discussions were
to take place concerning the Tripartite Pact's obligations, Eden now
felt himself reduced to the alternatives of using force against Nasser
or accepting Nasser's triumph. A similar view had been held for a
longer time by French leaders. Foreign Minister Pineau told re-
porters at the Security Council: "We have made no progress at all.
There is no basis for negotiation. There have only been a lot of
words." [41] As the crisis was bringing Britain and France together in
the Middle East, an agreement to station French troops in Cyprus,
ready for Middle Eastern action, had been announced on August
29.[42] On September 26 Eden and Lloyd in Paris had assured French
Ministers that if the Security Council revealed itself incapable of
maintaining international arrangements, Britain would take all necessary steps, including the use of force, to compel respect for obligations
arising from such arrangements.[43]

Finally, Eden and Lloyd on October 16, 1956, met with the French
Ministers in a conference. The meeting took place upon French
initiative and on short notice. Its proceedings have not been revealed,
except in the form of leaks from the French defense ministry. Eden's
memoirs tell us remarkably little about this meeting. From the

[40] In a characteristic gambit of Soviet policy, Soviet First Deputy Premier
Mikoyan appeared at an Afghan Embassy reception in Moscow on October 15.
There he told newsmen that all ships should be free to use the Canal and
expressed the hope that with Egypt's nationalization of the Canal Israeli ships
would no longer be barred from it. It would be interesting to learn whether
British or American action was taken to ascertain the intent of a Soviet declaration made so indirectly and in so odd a place. New York Times, October 16,
1956.

[41] The Times, October 12, 1956. To the Chamber of Deputies Pineau explained, in the style of this crisis, saying the opposite of what he meant, that
France would not behave like "a cuckolded husband," in spite of her disillusionment with the attitude of the United States. The Times, October 17, 1956.

[42] New York Times, August 30, 1956.

[43] Eden, op. cit., p. 554.

memoirs, however, it may be inferred that the British and French governments agreed on joint action under certain circumstances and eventualities. Another Pineau-Lloyd meeting, apparently on short notice, took place in London on October 23. But another cycle of events, propelled in part by calculations based on the obviously divided Western counsels, began to unroll towards war in the Middle East. Over this other cycle of events in the Middle East itself—the fateful cycle—Dulles had almost no control and it is not clear that in his increasing illness he gave it adequate thought. Ironically, it was Dulles' drive to avoid war, the alleged ground for his failure to declare for a policy that took account of Middle Eastern urgencies, that drove Eden on. Dulles had stalled him in negotiations that made no progress of a substantial order. By turning to the Middle East and to France (October 16), Eden was able to formulate a course of action designed, as he believed, to regain momentum, to undo the losses that followed 1954, and to regain a position comparable to that of the past.[44]

Israel was the motive force, and she had the support of France relentless against Nasser because he had abetted the Algerian rebels. French support of Israel included the provision of weapons and, finally, of French-staffed fighter planes. The calculation of Israel was that Nasser had to be humbled dramatically before his forces had learned to use their large and newly acquired stores of communist-bloc arms. The nationalization controversy and Nasser's subsequent fears of an Anglo-French attack had compelled him to withdraw half of the Egyptian forces usually stationed in the Sinai Peninsula. For the moment the Egyptian President was weakened and the military initiative was with Israel. Nevertheless, Nasser's continuing pan-Arabist campaign had acquired a dangerous dynamic. On October 22 Jordan's armed forces were amalgamated with those of Syria and Egypt under Egyptian command. This grave menace to Israel prodded the Zionist state into action, and with French support Israel was prepared to spring. September saw a heightening of friction of Jordanian origin on the Jordanian-Israel frontier. Eden desired to avoid association with Israel, but even he had to think in terms of the existing Middle Eastern realities. On September 15 a member of Eden's cabinet speaking solely on his own behalf told the Israeli-bound Colonel Henriques to inform Ben-Gurion that Israel should refrain from attacking Jordan, that in an attack on Egypt Israel would

[44] Diplomatic Correspondent, *The Times*, October 17, 1956.

not have British support but in the subsequent negotiations would
get full diplomatic support for her objectives.[45]

As Eden spelled out the issue, an attack on Jordan would involve
Britain's treaty with that state, which Eden affirmed after the Israeli
attack on the Jordanian town of Qalquilya (October 10-11). But
an attack on Egypt would open more favorable possibilities for Britain, although Eden here suggests that then, of course, there would
be other worries including that concerning the safety of the Canal.
If Israel attacked Egypt, then Britain and France could intervene to
prevent the spread of fighting and could occupy the major positions
along the Canal to protect it.

In October Israel launched several attacks on Jordan where elections were scheduled for October 21. Instability in Jordan became so
great that its government was prepared to adopt a proposal to admit
Iraqi troops. Israel replied that the entry of Iraqi troops would be a
breach of the armistice. The proposal was dropped. The elections
were held and went in favor of the nationalists. Jordan then agreed
to a common military command with Syria and Egypt under an
Egyptian. On October 27 the Israeli government ordered a mobiliza-
tion of its forces and on October 29, possibly influenced by a desire
to finish with Egypt before the American elections, launched Israeli
forces on a large raid into Sinai.

The Israeli attack on the Sinai Peninsula and Gaza enjoyed rapid
success. The eruption of fighting afforded an opportunity for Britain
to enter the Canal Zone with military forces. British spokesmen have
given conflicting accounts of their reasons for taking action, but the
direction of British forces indicates that the dominant objectives were
to secure the Canal, to topple Nasser, and, thereby, assure Britain's
oil supplies and block Soviet penetration of the area. Britain and
France used the occasion to send an ultimatum to both parties asking
that the latter should within twelve hours withdraw ten miles from
the Canal. For Israel such a withdrawal would have meant an advance. The Israelis, of course, agreed to do so, but the Egyptians
refused.

The execution of the Franco-British action was attended by many
difficulties, partly from dilemmas of British defense policy and partly
arising from Eden's uncertainty about the means and tactics that
should secure his objectives. After an initial stage of British preparation, loaded ships in some cases had to be unloaded. Cyprus lacked
adequate harbors and airfields. Landing-craft and transport planes

[45] *The Spectator*, 203 (1959), 623, 823.

were in short supply and the forces involved were widely dispersed. Some reservists, hastily called up, had been allowed leave. In their planning the British commanders in the Mediterranean had to remain very flexible, for they could not be sure in advance which tasks and military objectives would be assigned to them. Though the necessity of ten days' notice for the beginning of operations was accepted, the notice of the ultimatum allowed the commanders less than half a day. The initial concentration was on the Egyptian airfields and the airborne assault on Port Said took place on the morning of November 5. The Egyptian military commander in Port Said worked out surrender terms which were later rejected on orders from Cairo. The British Commander has recorded that trucks with loudspeakers went through the town "announcing that Russian help was on the way, that London and Paris had been bombed, and that the Third World War had started." French parachutists captured Port Said's twin city, Port Fuad and turned towards Ismailia. The forces had at first restricted themselves to a very limited action which had encountered some formidable resistance. Thus, a sea-borne invasion, preceded by a limited aerial and naval destroyer bombardment, was launched on November 6. Thereafter, the British forces had to face street-fighting with Egyptian soldiers in civilian dress and other Egyptians. The Allied Commander-in-Chief, General Sir Charles Keightley, particularly noted the effective Egyptian use of Soviet self-propelled anti-tank guns and the lavish supply of Egyptian ammunition. Late in the afternoon following the landing the Allied Commanders had received orders to cease fire at midnight. A United Nations Force, they were told, would take over from them. Britain and France, then, had halted the expedition in compliance with cease-fire instructions of the United Nations' General Assembly.[46]

[46] The dispatch of the Commander-in-Chief of the Suez expedition, General Keightley, was published as a supplement to *The London Gazette* (London, H. M. Stationery Office, Sept. 12, 1957). Apparently, the one eventuality he was not ordered to plan for was an intervention following an Israeli attack on Egypt. See *The Times*, September 13, 1957, for its editorial, "Soldier's Story." So, to avoid the charge of collusion even the military command was kept in the dark. But Randolph Churchill has added further information: the Suez expedition did not look for intelligence from Israel, and for its part the Israeli intelligence service did not trust the British government. In the period of the Suez landings, however, Israeli military intelligence was supplied to British military attachés. *The Rise and Fall of Sir Anthony Eden* (New York, 1959), p. 276. The original plan of using Libyan-based British soldiers for an overland invasion of Egypt was overruled by the attitude of Libya. Later, the forces there were completely excluded from the expedition roster.

The British government presented the expedition as a straight military success. A number of military criticisms, however, have been made in detail by Liddell Hart, and in terms of general policy by Randolph Churchill.[47] Britain not only was short of the necessary equipment, but lacked a mobile force in reserve that could be sent to trouble spots. The gravest weakness of all, the long delay between the ultimatum and the invasion of Egypt, during which the most effective pressures and Egyptian retaliation were mounted against Britain, was presented as a military requirement. The critics allege that a more resolute British Prime Minister would have dissuaded the military of this necessity or would have called for another plan, even another policy.

The government's defense was that the military action, though it had been entirely effective, had been halted in deference to the United Nations, which had at long last moved to deal with the problem. This *apologia* was an attempt to blur a more fundamental weakness against which Eden himself had warned in speaking to the Conservative Party Conference (October 13, 1956): "If you are determined to defend your national interests, nothing is more foolish than to do so with inadequate forces." [48] The Suez action, resting in part on last-minute hopes that the Soviet Union would be preoccupied with Hungary and the restless communist bloc, and on expectations that American policy, especially with respect to Israel, would be immobilized by the American elections and that Nasser would quickly be tumbled, proved to be beyond the strength of Britain. Eden's "political algebra" confronted new quantities. Britain could have defied the United Nations—briefly, at any rate—and she might have momentarily discounted Soviet threats as a bluff, but she could not face the pressures generated by the United States and the Soviet Union working to condemn her through the United Nations. At home, too, Eden had to endure the criticism of the Labour Party and the questioning of a section of his own party. Eden's own vacillation concerning the expedition, appearing as late as November 4, suggests that his own resolution was strangely uncertain, possibly resulting from illness and possibly stemming from a realist's sense that his stroke of policy was a desperate gamble.

On October 30 the Security Council met quickly to consider the

[47] Liddell Hart, "Operation Musketeer," *The Observer*, February 24, 1957; Randolph Churchill, *op. cit.*, pp. 278-280, 290-292, 315-318.
[48] *Manchester Guardian*, October 15, 1956.

Israeli attack on Egypt. Before the Council debate was joined, the Anglo-French ultimatum was made known. The United States introduced a draft resolution calling for Israel's retirement to the established armistice lines and the suspension of military and economic assistance to Israel until she had complied with the resolution. France and Britain, arguing that their intervention had done the work of the United Nations, vetoed this resolution as well as one later introduced by the Soviet Union. On the following day a heated meeting ended with a vote in favor of a special session of the General Assembly in accordance with the Uniting for Peace Resolution (1950).

An appeal to the General Assembly meant the elaboration of new instruments of action and supervision, and that likewise involved a considerable broadening of the initiative and authority of the Secretary-General of the United Nations. The General Assembly could order a cease-fire which was imposing because the United States and the Soviet Union supported the resolutions. On November 2 the Assembly called for a cease-fire, the ending of the movement of military forces into the Suez area, the withdrawal of forces behind the 1948 armistice lines, and the reopening of the Canal. To implement this resolution, a United Nations presence was necessary. To supply it, the United Nations Emergency Force was authorized by a Canadian-sponsored resolution of November 5, which had the additional advantage of offering an out to the French and British governments, which had earlier expressed willingness to hand over the Canal positions to a United Nations force. On November 6 the British and French governments ordered the Suez forces to halt operations. In yielding to the order, the British government bowed to the unexpected speed of American and United Nations action and recognized the difficulties of proceeding in a course that had brought British and French forces to the Canal Zone but failed to command the resources for a speedy victory. The most pressing difficulty was that the Anglo-American rift had generated heavy pressures on the pound sterling. Britain's international payments were accumulating in a threatening way and, for the moment, the American government was even prepared to compound the pressures.

In yielding to the United Nations and to American pressure, the British government had a ready scapegoat for failure, for the United States could be blamed for the fiasco. In succeeding days, with Dulles in the hospital and the election ending, the American position wavered, but there is a consistency running throughout its Suez

actions. American policy argued that the use of force in the Suez
dispute was mistaken, and, less convincingly, wrong. In espousing
the cause of international order against the Suez policy, the United
States, however, was compelled to work with the United Nations.
This meant that the Israeli, British, and French presence on Egyptian
territory could not be used for bargaining on other matters in dispute.
The guiding principle was that aggression could not be allowed any
reward and the General Assembly's numerous voices were overwhelm-
ingly favorable to Egypt and against the three protagonists in the
attack on Sinai and the Canal.

The initial failure, in effect, was unredeemable. The delay between
ultimatum and landing enabled Nasser to have the Canal glutted
with sunken ships.[49] For the moment Israel's victory may have chas-
tened Nasser and deprived him of great stores of arms, but he
emerged as a great hero of Arab nationalism. Arabs in public speech,
at any rate, lauded him. He had not been humbled but exalted. In
Egypt he sequestered British and French property. Elsewhere, in
Jordan and even in Kuwait British influence was reduced to a very
low level. In spite of all Eden's precautions his Suez action joined
together the Suez dispute with the Arab-Israeli quarrel. Britain's apparent collusion with Israel seemed to confirm the most extravagant
charges of the Arab nationalists against Western imperialism as the
support of Israel. The position of Nuri in Iraq was undercut and the
Baghdad Pact further discredited. Strikes and riots took place in
Bahrein and Kuwait. In Syria several pumping stations on the pipeline from Iraq to the Mediterranean were blown up, and subsequently
Syria refused to allow the oil to flow again until Egyptian territory
should be evacuated. But Eden's account of Arab reaction to Suez
overlooks this quite incomplete catalogue of disasters and approaches
incredibility. "Not a mouse stirred in Arab lands." [50]

It may be argued that many of the consequences of Suez were
mere accelerations of developments already in process. This consideration may even be extended to the growth of Soviet and communist

[49] This maritime version of a scorched earth policy with the cost borne by
others may not have been wholly a matter of impulse, for Nasser had threatened such action in a speech (July 28): "I warn the imperialist countries that
any interference on their part will cause obstruction of navigation in the Suez
Canal. I hold Britain and France responsible for what may happen to navigation
in the Suez Canal." *New York Times*, July 29, 1956. But a number of the ships
were sunk after the cease-fire, and as a matter of wanton obstruction.

[50] Eden, *op. cit.*, p. 534.

influence in the Middle East and the weakening of Nuri's position. But the failure of Suez was starkly evident in the blocked Canal and the interrupted pipelines. The proclaimed objectives of the Suez expedition were not achieved and the evils it was said to avert became real. But, even with the challenge to the Commonwealth and the rift in the Western alliance, the tale is not solely one of loss.

For a number of years Nasser's expansionism was tempered. The United Nations had been propelled into action. Even more important, the United States was compelled to face the Middle Eastern problems directly and to improvise a minimum policy for some of their more urgent challenges. The Soviet Union urged Soviet-American cooperation against the Suez powers. While the Soviet gestures gained credit in the Middle East, they also hastened the renewal of Anglo-American cooperation. The cost, however, was great and has not yet been fully exacted.

At Suez Britain and France had been convinced that they lacked the initiative and power which the action required. But this recognition was not coupled with any pleasant thoughts about their dependence on the United States. Even when the principled consistency of American policy was allowed—though partisan fervor did not usually permit such justice to partisans of another course—the American performance was found lacking in the largeness, coherence, and realism that should go with a leading position. No concentration on the mistaken calculations of Eden can obscure the fact that the Suez expedition was a vote of no-confidence in American leadership. Eden's resignation consigned him to the company of failures. His successor, Harold Macmillan, proposed his slogans as "Europe" and "Power." But the memory of American failure in 1956 to provide for prospective Middle Eastern threats may have spurred Macmillan in 1958 to his initiative with Khrushchev concerning a summit meeting, and the same memory probably confirmed de Gaulle in his determination to possess nuclear weapons as a necessary basis for independent action.

The failure of American leadership made Suez possible. Under the given circumstances Eden, however, bears responsibility for the attack itself and the attack's inadequacies. Evidence is not at all abundant but it does appear that most British Middle Eastern diplomats were against the Eden decision.[51] So, even with Eden, for so long the

[51] The former Ambassador to Egypt, Sir Ralph Stevenson, wrote in a letter to *The Times*, August 8, 1956: The security of the Canal depended on Egyptian

British Foreign Minister, the old interwar tale of politicians' ignoring diplomats appears to have been repeated.

In British politics the affair provoked a long and strangely ineffective debate. In the new session of the House of Commons the Labour Party transformed the debate on the Queen's Address into "virtually a continuous censure by the Opposition of the Government's intervention in Egypt." [52] The government had to face a storm of criticism from the Liberals as well and, more serious, the less publicly uttered misgivings of some Conservatives who feared that Eden's initiative had jeopardized the United Nations as well as the American alliance and had created a precedent hostile to any prospects of insuring a reign of law in the world. Two Tory Ministers resigned from the government and one Tory M.P., disclaiming his Party's Whip, became an independent Conservative.

Nevertheless, the Tory Party displayed considerable rallying power: its Parliamentary forces well understood that the Party could not afford disunity if effective government was to be maintained. Meanwhile, and more than a little confusingly, government spokesmen argued that the intervention had achieved four ends: it had disclosed the scale of Soviet arms to Egypt and for the moment had halted Soviet penetration of the area; it had put an end to the fighting between Egypt and Israel in the Canal area; it had thereby prevented the outbreak of a general war; it had resulted in the establishment of a United Nations police force in the Middle East. [53] The government, after all, could not simply admit that it had been mistaken. Its course had to be defended and these were arguments in behalf of a course that had been checked, arguments for a time of endurance and sweating out the consequences of failure.

The Labour attack proved to be ineffective in Parliament and in the long run in the country. Labour's greatest difficulties in changing opinion probably derive from the fact that a large body of British

---

cooperation. "The problem is how best to obtain it. Action which would result in a legacy of ill-will would defeat our object; and in politics it is never wise to leave the other side with no loophole of escape from an untenable position." These, of course, were calculations that had supported the Anglo-Egyptian Treaty of 1954. Eden's supporters recall that Churchill had overruled the diplomatic and service chiefs in dealing with the Iraqi *coup* of April 1941.

[52] Political Correspondent of the *Manchester Guardian*, November 12, 1956.

[53] Sir Reader Bullard, long associated with British diplomacy in the Middle East, concluded that the Suez expedition became more difficult to understand the more it was explained. *The Camels Must Go* (London, 1961), p. 279.

opinion either approved Eden's action and grimly regretted his failure or believed that he had made a mistake in dealing with a difficult matter for which his opponents had had no helpful alternatives. Labour also suffered from the tendency of some of its leaders to speak in extreme terms. When Aneurin Bevan in public speeches equated the British action against Egypt with the Soviet suppression of the Hungarian government, he made a point that appealed to his own supporters but abroad was quoted to excuse Soviet action. His remark, however, had a remarkably dissuasive effect on most Englishmen, for there are severe limits to the electoral effectiveness of national self-criticism.[54] The Labour opposition could claim that they had given an example of free criticism to the world, and in doing so had voiced the objections of many Britons to the actions of their government and had contributed to the preservation of the Commonwealth.

The British government, however, also had to consider the temper of Conservative M.P.'s, and "Operation-Sweating It Out" in the aftermath of Suez was quite successful. The demands of "sweating it out" were responsible for concentration on the defects of American policy and for refusing to judge the expedition a mistake or a failure. The British government sought to use the presence of British forces, as the Israelis did more persistently with their own forces, to secure guarantees against the hostility of Egypt. On the whole, however, the United Nations, after ordering a cease-fire and providing an Emergency Force, was neither able nor, for that matter, willing to do more than clear the Canal and patch up the Arab-Israeli armistice. Israel's security rested primarily on the power she could wield against the Arabs and her recognized willingness to use it. Eventually, Egypt opened the Canal and agreed that a portion of its tolls would go to the development of the Canal. But no formal agreement to support the "Six Principles" was exacted from Egypt.

In November 1956 the British government sustained its supporters by maneuvering for advantage in the Canal. When oil rationing was threatened, though it was not instituted, and the government was

[54] *Manchester Guardian,* November 12, 1956. On another occasion Bevan elaborated his argument that some of the Soviet leaders shared Eden's old-fashioned belief in force and explained that the British example probably discouraged the Soviet leaders from following a more enlightened course in Hungary. This argument is in line with the views of Bevan's journal, *Tribune,* which early in 1955 argued that Malenkov fell because Western policy-makers gave his allegedly peaceful policy nothing with which to work.

rumored to be about to withdraw from the Canal, the right-wing
Tories spoke bitterly. Some said a Labour government was preferable
to a Tory withdrawal. Lord Hinchingbrooke said: "The Suez Canal
and the area surrounding it are in some essential sense part of the
United Kingdom. I refuse to allow the government of my country
to throw it away." Such a government decision, he added, would split
the Conservative Party in the Commons and render the government
incapable of ruling the country. Paul Williams referred to Britain as
on the brink of "the greatest humiliation of all time." Withdrawal,
signifying a lack of British will-power, would mean that Britain would
be the "lackey of the United States and the whipping boy of the
United Nations." Indeed, he asked, was the American State Department more anticolonial than anticommunist? [55] But the Conservative Party's will to survive prevailed, with a change of Prime Ministers, some rough and covert disciplining of dissidents, and some
more notorious disciplining of M.P.'s by local Conservative Associations.

Britain failed to gain any new security against possible Egyptian
misuse of the Canal. The government sought tenaciously to make
conditions and, failing to do so, indicated that it would seek to find
alternatives to the Canal and in general to lessen British dependence
on it. When, however, the British government informed British shipping interests that they were free to use the Canal, Lord Salisbury,
in a post-resignation speech in the House of Lords, argued that in the
end Britain had abandoned her guns and allowed unfettered Egyptian
control of the Canal. This, in his eyes, was the kind of appeasement
that encouraged Britain's enemies to edge into courses that really
might mean war. The former Conservative Leader of the House of
Lords believed that Britain should have avoided the use of the Canal
as much as possible. Lord Home, then Commonwealth Minister,
argued against Salisbury that, as no one had proposed a practical
alternative, the government had been compelled to reach its present
decision. As Salisbury's criticisms had been harsh, Lord Attlee replied
in kind: "The Government had to face the results of its own folly.
Lord Salisbury's complaint is that it will not persist in that folly."
Lord Salisbury, however, had reached unusual heights when in the
name of consistency and principle he denounced accommodation to
what were thought to be present necessities. He recalled that the old
Marquis of Salisbury was accustomed to speak of "My old enemy,

[55] *The Observer*, December 2, 1956 and *The Times*, December 1, 1956.

the long run." "Do not, I pray, let us fall into that error today." [56]

Possibly the most revealing statements about Suez were remarks by Sir Anthony Eden and by a former British diplomat. On November 17 Eden, in contrasting Soviet brutality with the restraint of the French and British, said that the British government would make no apology for what it had done. Then referring to the argument that the British government had erred in accepting the cease-fire, he added: "The Government understands that argument. They cannot accept it." [57]

In reviewing a book on the Suez crisis, the British Ambassador in Cairo from 1950 to 1955, Sir Ralph Stevenson, noted the "curious blind spot in the eyes of successive British Governments" in dealing with Arab nationalism. The same people who prided themselves on coming to terms with Asian nationalism vastly underrated its force in the Middle East. "How was it possible that the idea that Britain's oil supplies could be safeguarded only by continued political influence, if not actual control, could so warp our usually sound commercial and economic judgment?" And, he added the further question: how will later generations be able even to believe that we hoped for Arab good will while at the same time we sought to thwart their efforts to undo what they consider the greatest wrong done to them —the establishment of Israel?[58]

The former British Ambassador, however, had his attention concentrated on the necessity of seeking Egyptian good will as the basis for British interest in the security of the Canal. Thus, he may not have sufficiently allowed for the fact that Eden was thinking of the range of British positions in the Middle East, many of which depended on treaty arrangements. Against the system of treaty arrangements Nasser had delivered a formidable blow. Eden's reaction, then, was that Nasser must be humbled, not only to assure the Canal but to buttress Britain's friends and position in the entire Middle East. The British Prime Minister had formulated this position in a broadcast speech on August 8. "Our quarrel is not with Egypt, still less with the Arab world. It is with Colonel Nasser." [59]

In effect, this was a position on which he would not compromise or substantially negotiate. But the nature of Nasser's action was such as to make a successful riposte politically dangerous, for it had won

[56] *The Manchester Guardian*, May 24, 1957.
[57] *The Times*, November 19, 1956.
[58] *The Observer*, March 10, 1957.
[59] *New York Times*, August 9, 1956.

for him the public acclaim of the Asian-African world and the support of the Soviet Union. American policy, in which other less rational but no less real considerations—for example, the 1956 elections—also played a part, was based on the judgment that Eden's objective, a riposte against Nasser, was so politically unwise that an approach of undoubted legality should be tried. The interplay of these differing positions encouraged Nasser in his defiance and, thus, drove Eden to the stern demand that allowed Nasser no out. If, from the beginning, the American government had clearly emphasized its hostility to the British use of force and its awareness of the weakness of Britain and the British position, and had won from Eden an unlikely renunciation of the use of force, perhaps, then a whole-hearted British-American endeavor to win legal redress might have been successful. As it was, Eden's awareness of the political issues at stake ruled out such a course. The consequence was that American policy, on occasion, simply exhausted itself in worrying about its ally and in seeking means of delay. When Eden, without sharing the American view of the general situation, saw through this American game, he turned to his own course of action with France and in doing so engulfed in ruin the political interests he sought to protect.

9: THE AFTERMATH OF SUEZ
AND THE IRAQI REVOLUTION

The failure of the Suez policy hastened the dwindling of British influence and positions in the Middle East. Britain's Empire by Treaty had roused the increasing opposition of Arab nationalism. In 1954 Britain had finally agreed to evacuate the Suez Canal Zone. When, however, she had joined the Baghdad Pact to meet Iraqi demands to terminate the "unequal treaty" association with Iraq and, at the same time, to gain on a new basis the continued use of military facilities in Iraq, Nasser in the name of Arab nationalism gained considerable support for his attack on Britain and the Iraqi Premier. When Nasser, having secured communist arms, persisted in his hostile course culminating in the nationalization of the Suez Canal Company, Prime Minister Eden sought to ward off a menacing future and to undo the present by attacking Egypt in the Canal Zone. His failure meant the triumph of Nasser and the strengthening of his attack on imperialism. The latter all the more involved Britain, for Eden's action appeared to document the darkest suspicions about Britain's imperialism and Empire by Treaty.

Arab nationalism, then, continued to surge against that empire. This meant that it was difficult for Britain, outside the Persian Gulf and Aden, to maintain a special position grounded on a treaty that Arab nationalist sentiment would regard as legitimate. The treaty with Jordan was terminated in 1957. In Iraq the connection with the Baghdad Pact was maintained only by Nuri's dexterity and by frequent removal of army officers suspected of pro-Nasser Arabism.

Eden had claimed a primacy of interest and responsibility in the Middle East. When he backed his claim by force at Suez, the two major powers, the United States and the Soviet Union, worked through the United Nations to check the assertion and, in effect, to undercut the claim to primacy. British Middle Eastern interests, however, remained important. Indeed, the accelerated withdrawal of British power made the danger to Western interests in the area appear more explosive and, to Eden's supporters, provided a vindication of him. With Soviet influence increasing and the pan-Arab prestige of Nasser in the ascendant, the United States was compelled to confront Middle Eastern problems more directly and responsively than it had done in the years before Suez.

As the Arab-Israeli dispute persisted, no attempt to effect a general regional settlement was even conceivable. The threats with which American policy sought to deal were the extension of Soviet influence and, a course often feared to be in cooperation with it, Nasser's pan-Arab drive against such governments as those in Jordan, Iraq, and Lebanon. In a transition from failure Britain's capacity to take the initiative was, for the moment, decidedly limited, all the more in that Britain had no diplomatic representation in Cairo, Damascus, and Riyadh.

Having denied the primacy of British responsibility for the Middle East, the United States was occasionally driven to act as though the primacy of responsibility in the area was now American. While the United States did not have an imperialist Middle Eastern past with privileges and bases resting on treaty relationships, the new American course is not readily distinguishable from the course Britain had pursued in joining the Baghdad Pact. The United States sought to foster the military strength of the region's states as well as to enhance their political stability. In turn, this involved military and defensive agreements and these agreements had to be made with the willing representatives of Middle Eastern states. Here, however, appeared a striking recurrence of the difficulties encountered by Britain. The popular basis of most of these states was uncertain and unsteady and opened into an area of bitter conflict in which the pan-Arabist cause had the widest vocal support. Agreements made with any state were negotiated with a particular government itself engaged in the conflict.

Consent to any alignment with the West was not likely to be forthcoming from Nasser, now freed of the threat from Britain and France. The United States government, moreover, did not seek to cultivate Nasser to the point where it would relax the financial restrictions imposed on Egypt after the nationalization venture or where it would aid the Egyptian dictator-President in organizing Middle Eastern defense. He had chosen a course of positive neutrality and had secured communist arms. The United States, then, sought to encourage King Saud, an unlikely leader, too accustomed to using money for intrigue to develop the art of political persuasion. It attempted to win the adherence of divided Lebanon and of Libya, a paradigm of underdevelopment, and to rely on such positions as

Britain had created in Jordan and the Baghdad Pact. But American action in the Middle East conspicuously sought the consent of the governments of the area.

Nasser increasingly took the position that the American course was but another cycle of imperialism, of a new power playing Britain's role of fomenting Arab divisions, that is, objectives opposed by Nasser. His policy gradually turned against Arab rulers and leaders whom he branded as reactionaries and the stooges of Zionism and imperialism, and to the promotion of pan-Arabist nationalism equated with reform and republicanism.

In this positive neutralism Nasser and pan-Arabism had Soviet support until the Iraqi Revolution.[1] The Soviet line aimed at the elimination of Western positions in the Middle East. To that end it found Nasser's neutralism a valuable ally in that it, also, opposed Western bases and influence. The same end was served by Soviet proposals that a new approach be taken to the Middle East. Under this the Soviet interest in the area would receive official recognition from the West, Western bases and treaty arrangements would be dismantled, and, in return, the Soviet Union professed a willingness to regulate the Middle Eastern arms race.

To deal with this situation the American government proposed the Eisenhower Doctrine, which in turn sparked further trouble in 1957 and the major part of 1958. The reaction against it, and its limitations, obvious from the beginning (since the efficacy of the provision of aid in the manner of the Truman Doctrine was questionable in that the acceptance of aid sometimes added to the instability of the recipient), have given it a bad press and a somewhat undeserved reputation of utter failure.

In attempting to counter communist expansionism, American policy had to begin with the remains of British positions and influence in Jordan and Iraq. Where American policy-makers thought worriedly of a Middle Eastern vacuum, the Arab leaders did not argue the fear away in insisting that the vacuum should be filled by the Arabs themselves. Indeed, the new American course encountered the same

[1] In an interview with an Egyptian reporter Khrushchev was reported as saying: "With unity the Arab countries could destroy the Israeli menace. But from time to time the imperialists will use Israel to sound you out to see whether, after your recent victory, you are still strong." For its part the Soviet Union has no ambitions in the Middle East, Khrushchev continued, but he expected the imperialists "to hire some governments through loans and sometimes unofficially through personal contacts." *The New York Times*, January 2, 1957.

difficulties that had beset the Baghdad Pact, Soviet opposition, the attacks of Syria and Egypt, the criticism of Nehru and the former colonial world, and the hostility of the spokesmen of general Arab nationalism. When Ambassador James Richards visited the Middle Eastern countries in the interest of the Doctrine and with the support of $200,000,000 available for economic and military largesse, he did not go to Syria, Egypt, and Jordan. Although his mission was intended to dramatize for Middle Eastern states the seriousness of American concern with their area, his recruitment was limited to Lebanon, Libya, and the members of the Baghdad Pact. The Sudan and Ethiopia also gave him a warm welcome. King Saud, both in Washington and at two conferences of Arab states in Cairo, gave the Doctrine a highly qualified welcome.

To encourage the members of the Baghdad Pact in their regional defense arrangements, the United States joined the Pact's Military Committee. But in the year after Suez the American government also studiously sought to avoid identification with Britain and to exploit the anticolonial and United Nations cause with which American policy had been recently and conspicuously associated. This cause, as well as constitutional limitations and its own conflicting interests, debarred the United States from any action more forthright than the Eisenhower Doctrine, which was designed to lure the Middle Eastern states away from neutralism and association with communist states. The Doctrine approved by Congress and signed on March 9, 1957, pledged American assistance to any Middle Eastern state attacked by external communist forces, and it offered aid to those nations prepared to accept the Doctrine. To the objection that in the Middle East internal subversion was a more likely prospect than external aggression, Secretary Dulles replied that such internal questions would be the concern of the United Nations, a renunciation to which he did not confine himself in Lebanon (1958). At any rate the Doctrine was prominently and several times given the warranty of the United States Fleet in the Mediterranean.[2]

Apart from the immediate value of offering aid to those who held

[2] For events of the post-Suez period, see John C. Campbell, *Defense of the Middle East* (rev. ed.; New York, 1960); Charles D. Cremeans, *The Arabs and the World: Nasser's Arab Nationalist Policy* (New York, 1963); the yearly volumes of *The United States in World Affairs*, written by Richard P. Stebbins; George E. Kirk, *Contemporary Arab Politics: A Concise History* (New York, 1961); Geoffrey Barraclough, *Survey of International Affairs, 1956-1958*, Royal Institute of International Affairs (New York, 1962).

aloof from neutralism, and of improvising a general regional guarantee, the Doctrine's effectiveness was limited by the fact that it called on states to stand up and be counted. Compliance, that is, abandoning neutralism, evoked the charge of imperialism from Arab groups with the most pervasive appeal. Jordan soon dramatized the vacuum by becoming the scene of a bitter struggle intensified by Jordanian opposition to the prospect of accepting American aid as well as the Doctrine.

Trouble in Jordan followed the exodus of British forces and the termination of the Anglo-Jordanian Treaty of 1948.[3] The Treaty had become objectionable to the Jordanian government and an embarrassment to Britain. No longer did Britain find it advantageous to be associated with an Arab state on terms that might involve Britain against Israel. That game was no longer worth playing. At the time of Suez, British forces had evacuated the base at Amman because of the hostility of the local population. The base at Mafraq was difficult to supply. Early in 1957 Mafraq's oil supplies had to be brought through Syria, which was hostilely disposed to Britain. The Anglo-Jordanian Treaty was a source of expense and unpopularity for Britain and of instability for the Jordanian government. The West Bank (Palestinian) Jordanians, being personally affected by the existence of Israel, provided ready support for Nasser's Arabism, as did the numerous Palestinian refugees in Jordan. Even some of the population of Transjordan think of themselves more as Syrians and, while little attached to their own state, are receptive to Nasser's and Syrian Arabism. The only likely use of the bases, so far as Jordan would allow, was not against Egypt or the Soviet Union but against Israel. But, as Jordan's annexation of part of former Palestine was not accepted by Arab proponents of an Arab Palestine, Jordan's interests even here were not one with other Arab nationalists.

On March 13, 1957, an exchange of notes marked the end of the Treaty under which Britain had occupied bases in Jordan and provided a financial subsidy. At the ceremonial signing in Amman, the Jordanian Prime Minister, Suliman Nabulsi, told the representatives of the press that the moment was the happiest of his life. Jordan now saw an end to the sufferings inflicted by the limitations on her liberty and was free "to join the liberated Arab caravan laboring towards the glory and unity of the Arab nation." His formal talk was

[3] Cremeans, op. cit., pp. 103-104; Ann Dearden, Jordan (London, 1958); Benjamin Shwadran, Jordan: A State of Tension (New York, 1959).

less colorful. The British Ambassador, Charles Johnston, expressed the belief that history would honor the memories of British and native servants of Jordan. The changing times called for a transformation of the former relationship. "We entered into these negotiations in what I might call a spirit of friendly realism," concerned to find a relationship suitable to contemporary conditions.[4]

In ending the Treaty with Britain, the Jordanian government became dependent for more than a quarter of its revenue upon the contributions of Arab states, Egypt, Syria, and Saudi Arabia. On January 19, 1957, in Cairo, King Hussain secured the formal agreement of those states to provide Jordan with £12,500,000 in cash and arms annually for ten years. Only Saudi Arabia attempted to meet this obligation, even for a short period. The agreement appeared to manifest Arab solidarity, embracing republican Syria and Egypt and monarchical Saudi Arabia. But dynamism and large popular appeal were limited to Nasser's Arabism, which was republican, reformist, and pro-Soviet neutralist. Though the King of Jordan sought to prove himself an Arab nationalist by cutting his ties with Britain, the reality of his kingdom's financial dependence persisted. In joining the caravan of Arab unity and repudiating imperialism, Hussain put himself at the mercy of his Arab brothers. He soon discovered that this fraternal independence would very likely cost him his crown and kingdom. In this situation, however, the Eisenhower Doctrine was interpreted flexibly and the King's real courage worked for his preservation. Success, however, was his only when he reverted from anti-Western Arabism to cooperation with the United States.

Hussain had warned against the dangers of communism, but his Prime Minister, Suliman Nabulsi, proposed to exchange diplomatic representatives with the Soviet Union on April 3. On April 10 Hussain asked Nabulsi's nationalist government to resign. Thereafter, Nabulsi sought to rally Jordanian politicians, urging them to compel the King to accept what in effect amounted to Cabinet control in following an Arabist course. As the situation grew tense, Hussain appealed to his bedouin troops. Some nationalist leaders, including two successive Chiefs of Staff working in Nasser's interest, and other Army officers,

[4] *The Times*, March 14, 1957. Jordan agreed to pay £4,250,000 for the British establishments and property, including a newly improved airfield at Mafraq. In the 1950's Jordan began to collect royalties on oil pipelines. On May 23, 1962, Jordan and the Trans-Arabian Pipeline Company agreed that Jordan would receive $10,000,000 for arrears and yearly royalties of more than $4,000,000.

fled to Syria. With the proclamation of martial law the royal government, now under conservative auspices, assumed effective control
when, on April 24, it received the assurance of American support.

Stretching a point in two respects, the American government
used the Eisenhower Doctrine to deal with a threat to Middle Eastern
peace, not necessarily attributable to communism. If Jordan had followed an extreme nationalist course, the consequence might have
been the disruption of Jordan and an Arab-Israeli war. Thus, invoking the threat of international communist aggression, of which
Hussain in his extremity had spoken in his appeal for help, President
Eisenhower sent the American Sixth Fleet to Lebanon in ostenta-
tious readiness to drop forces on Jordan. Further, Jordan was given
additional economic assistance of $30,000,000 under the Doctrine,
even though the Jordanian government was not required to accept
the Doctrine.

The United States, then, had for the moment assumed succession
to Britain in the protection of Jordan, and was soon providing aid on
a larger scale than Britain had done. For self-preservation the King
of Jordan had had to resist the impetus of Nasser's pan-Arabism and
to seek American assistance. Momentarily, Nasser's and Syria's position was weakened. King Saud in meetings with Hussain (communi-
qués of April 29 and June 13) and with Faisal (May 18, 1957)
secured joint statements against interference by the Arab states in
the domestic affairs of other Arab states. Nasser's Arabist front had
been broken. So far, then, had the tide turned against Nasser that
Saud had visited Iraq and broken the Arab boycott of Iraq which
Nasser had attempted to maintain since the signing of the Baghdad
Pact.[5] Jordan and Saudi Arabia likewise on occasion condemned the
mendacity of Cairo Radio and the intrigues of Nasser's agents, but
they were eager to maintain a public front of Arab unity and notably
to emphasize this in respect to Israel.[6]

For the moment Syrian and Egyptian influence in Jordan had been
checked. But again the United States felt impelled to strengthen a
British position. On January 19-20 the Baghdad Pact members had
met in Ankara without a British representative. After the Eisenhower-

[5] Barraclough, *op. cit.*, p. 175.
[6] The Arab solidarity meeting in Cairo, January 19, 1957, saw Saudi Arabia,
Jordan, and Egypt agreed in rejecting any foreign sphere of influence in their
countries. Arab nationalism, they argued, "was the sole basis on which Arab
policy could be formulated."

Macmillan meeting in Bermuda (March 21-24), however, the United States indicated its willingness to participate in the activity of the Pact's Military Committee. A formal invitation was soon forthcoming, and the United States took a more active role in the Pact's Karachi meeting, attended also by Britain.

But Nasser and Syria—and the latter now had special Soviet support—still had capacity for taking the initiative. Syria, capable of great influence in the Arab world but an inveterate victim of political instability, was now surrounded by mistrustful and even hostile neighbors, Lebanon, Turkey, Jordan, Iraq, and Israel. Communists or suspected communists took over some military posts likely to be decisive in a future struggle. Syria also maintained a diplomatic offensive against the United States which included the ousting of American military and diplomatic personnel from the country. Turkey, in particular, feared the growth of Soviet and communist influence in Syria as providing an additional base of Soviet pressure against Turkey's frontiers. Turco-Syrian relations were never good, and they had a historical background capable of sustaining acerb and suspicious relations. The Turkish army proceeded to hold maneuvers near Syria's border. In this atmosphere, with the temperature in Syria heightened by conspicuous war preparations—probably a move in the Syrian domestic political struggle—the American government gave strong political support to Turkey and, repeating the Jordan story, held the Sixth Fleet in readiness in the Eastern Mediterranean and increased its military deliveries to friendly Arab states. In this firm response the United States overplayed its hand. The concentration of hostility on an Arab state and the attempted encouragement of other Arab states to stand against Syria gave Khrushchev an opportunity to champion Arab nationalism and to repeat his Suez performance. Syria appealed to the United Nations General Assembly against the threats directed at her. Egypt came to her support and sent a small military force to the Syrian frontier. But Syria's chief source of support came from Khrushchev. Apparently testing his post-Sputnik I prestige, the Soviet leader dropped the issue at once but not until he had strengthened the impression among the Arabs that the Eisenhower Doctrine was opposed to Arab nationalism and was working, in allegedly British fashion, for the preservation of regimes which were the creation of imperialism.

Syrian instability, having made possible an artificial Cold War crisis, became the occasion for an ambiguous triumph of Nasser's pan-

Arabism. Nasser himself had behaved with some caution in the crisis and appears to have grown mistrustful of Syrian extremism and political ineptitude as well as of communist penetration. The crisis, however, promoted renewed Anglo-American cooperation and maintained Nasser in his opposition to Western policies.

After negotiations extending over several months, Egypt and Syria agreed to join in the United Arab Republic (February 1, 1958). With this association, which added Egyptian control over the Syrian pipelines to Nasser's achievement of the nationalization of the Canal, the major oil transit facilities were in Nasser's hands. The merger of the two countries appeared to fulfill the fears that had impelled Eden to his Suez action. Nevertheless, though the British government was concerned by this extension of Nasser's power and had supported the American interventions in the Middle East in 1957, there was no thought of repeating the Suez line of action. Instead, British interest counselled an effort to resume diplomatic relations with all the Arab states, so that Britain could once again be free to influence those states by means of diplomacy. Moreover, the British government did not believe that the union of Syria and Egypt would immediately increase the military capacity of the two countries.[7] As a token of the realization of Arabism, the new Republic gained Arab acclaim for Nasser. From the beginning, however, the union was based as much on Syrian self-mistrust, fully seconded by Nasser, as on the bond of Arab nationalism. Ironically, then, the first achievement of Nasser's pan-Arabism had not been directly or eagerly sought by Nasser and he may have briefly felt as much the victim as the victor of Arabism. Yemen also associated with the United Arab Republic. But the greatest irony of all—and the irony makes doubtful the policies enshrined in the Baghdad Pact and the Eisenhower Doctrine—is that the Syrian Baath Party asked for the union with Egypt to prevent the onrush of communist influence in Syria.[8]

Arab enthusiasm for the merger gave Nasser great confidence. The initial Arab approval was so great that Jordan and Iraq paid the merger the compliment of imitation. The merger of Syria with Egypt rent the Iraqi script for Arab unity and menaced the interests of the Jordanian government. Thus, on February 14, 1958, the mon-

---

[7] The last point was made in reply to a written question presented in the House of Commons, February 12, 1958. See *Parliamentary Debates*, Commons, 5th series, Vol. 582, col. 46.

[8] This irony is well noted in Cremeans, *op. cit.*, p. 161.

archies of Iraq and Jordan agreed to a complex form of federation, an association warmly welcomed by the British government. Nasser, possibly taken by surprise, at first pronounced this further move to Arab unity a blessed development, a benevolent view that he maintained for rather less than two weeks. But the new federation in its short life developed little promise, for Iraq's wealth, recently reduced by the interruption of the oil pipelines at the time of Suez, did not flow to Jordan, which continued to remain dependent on American aid. The hope that King Saud would join this federation of monarchs was blighted. Indeed, King Saud had to endure a sustained and violent Egyptian propaganda campaign against himself, charging him with efforts to prevent the formation of the United Arab Republic. In April 1958 he yielded the royal initiative to his brother Prince Faisal, who put Saudi influence on the side of Nasser for a time, but Saud publicly resumed full power within two years.

This Egyptian triumph, further reinforcing Nasser's Arabist prestige, greatly strengthened the Egyptian dictator's expansionist drive. This took the form of increasing the support he had given since 1955 to a rebellion against the British-aligned ruler of Oman, virulent opposition to the federation of Jordan and Iraq as a betrayal of Arabism to the imperialist, for the sake of maintaining reactionary rulers, and support by propaganda and possibly arms deliveries (certainly some arms deliveries came from Nasser's agents) to rebels—mainly Moslem but some, Christian—against the Lebanese government.

This rebellion, to some extent even in its primary and decisive Lebanese phases, was influenced by the temper created by Nasser's pan-Arabism. The Lebanese government was the result of an accommodating spirit which secured a consensus on toleration by an agreed distribution of offices among the religious groups of Lebanon. Nasserism and the United Arab Republic created a center of attraction for Lebanese Moslems and intensified their claims, made since 1953, to a larger allotment of offices on the grounds that their numbers were increasing. Their grievances were compounded by the pro-Western policy of President Chamoun's government, which in accepting the Eisenhower Doctrine had set itself apart from the Arab states.

The pro-Western speeches of Lebanon's Foreign Minister, Charles Malik, though recommended to Western statesmen by their recognition of communist dangers and by their proportioned view of Middle

Eastern interests, evoked little effective response in the Arab world. It was, in fact, decidedly questionable of Western policy-makers to use Lebanon with its pervasive pluralism as a source of influence in the Middle East. President Chamoun, on his part, was believed to be seeking re-election and the Lebanese Constitution forbade a president to succeed himself. His tardy denials of such an ambition were not effectively made. Disorder and discontent became civil war in May after the assassination of an Arabist journalist. To use the Lebanese army against the rebellion posed special difficulties, for the army itself was constituted on pluralist lines and reflected the divisions of the country. The opposition to Chamoun and the rebellion drew strength not only from Moslems but from a host of other rivalries so that the opposition included many Christians.

The Lebanese conflict soon embraced Middle Eastern and global Cold War rivalries. Nasser provided propaganda, the lively incitement of Cairo's violent radio. As Chamoun called attention to his plight and sought British and American diplomatic support and American arms supplies, the Soviet Union warned against Western intervention. Despite misgivings in the minds of local British and American diplomats, Britain and the United States decided to promote resistance to the external menace to Lebanon. As the two governments argued, the re-establishment of law and order in an independent Lebanon required for the moment the maintenance of its government, that is, of Chamoun. In addition to arms the United States also increased its Marine forces with the Sixth Fleet.[9]

On May 22, 1958, the Lebanese government formally and urgently asked the Security Council to consider the threat to peace posed by the intervention of the United Arab Republic in Lebanese affairs. The Council's consideration of the matter was postponed until the Arab League meeting in Libya should attempt to resolve the issue. Egyptian ascendancy in the League, as well as Chamoun's espousal of a course counter to Arab neutralism, meant that the League did nothing except attempt to persuade Lebanon to withdraw its appeal from the Security Council. When in June the Council again considered the matter of Lebanon, the Lebanese Foreign Minister docu-

[9] On events in Lebanon, see Charles W. Thayer, *Diplomat* (New York, 1959), pp. 1-33; Fahim T. Qubain, *Crisis in Lebanon* (Washington, 1961); Kirk, *op. cit.*, chap. 7. An eloquent and highly partisan pro-Arabist account of the atmosphere in Lebanon during the early months of 1958 may be found in Desmond Stewart, *Turmoil in Beirut* (London, 1958).

mented his charge of Egyptian intervention. The Council, however, limited itself to approving (June 11, 1958) a Swedish resolution to send observers to Lebanon so that there would be a halt to the illegal infiltration of the Lebanese frontiers. The small group of observers, whose probings were apparently not well informed and neither intense nor extensive, did not document Lebanon's charges.

Early in June President Eisenhower and Prime Minister Macmillan met in Washington and publicly announced their agreement to give increased support to Lebanon, Jordan, and Iraq. In Lebanon the fighting continued, but the flash point of the expanding crisis came in the new Arab Union. Early in July the King of Jordan discovered a military plot against himself, the King of Iraq, and their governments. Hussain attempted to warn Faisal without effect and, though the plot was barely headed off in Jordan, it erupted in Iraq.

There the ground had been long prepared.[10] The revolt was republican, Arabist, pro-Nasser, anti-Western and anti-British, and, in particular, anti-Nuri es-Said. The latter had some influential supporters but after the Baghdad Pact and notably Suez, the base of his support had become narrower. Occasionally even he, with all of his talent for maneuver and stratagem, realistically lived with a weary sense of time running out on all his expedients. But more often complacency was the somewhat irresponsible companion of his old age. The military, abetted by supporters of Nasser's Arabism and the smaller group of communists, took the initiative in the rebellion. It broke out, sparked by the rising of troops in Baghdad on their way to the Lebanese frontier in response to an appeal from Chamoun.

The revolution (July 14, 1958) was notably bloody. In its brief course the King, the Crown Prince, the former Regent, and Nuri were killed with almost painstaking brutality. Attacks on British subjects and property were the external sign of the ending of the major and direct British influence in Iraq.

For the moment, there was uncertainty as to the reaches of the revolution and it was in the brief and hectic time of uncertainty that British and American policy decisions had to be made. If the revolution were to rage forth as a Nasser pan-Arab force, most of the Western interests in the Middle East, as well as the Israeli-Arab truce, might be jeopardized. The tremors reached Washington, London, and Ankara, but immediately the danger spots were Lebanon

[10] Benjamin Shwadran, *The Power Struggle in Iraq* (New York, 1960).

and Jordan, where the King had to struggle with a real sense of
desperation embittered by the unwillingness of King Saud to render
any assistance. Thus, on July 15, 1958, American Marines landed in
Lebanon at the request of Chamoun's government, and British forces
and American supplies went to Jordan in response to Hussain's plea
for aid.

At the United Nations, as Sir Anthony Eden noted, the outcry
over Suez was re-enacted with this difference: Anglo-American cooperation was firm and the Anglo-American forces were in Jordan and
Lebanon at the request of those governments. That these forces either
preserved peace in the Middle East or, at any rate, deterred from war
and momentarily contributed to moderation and stability, was not
admitted by the Soviet Union, the former colonial nations, many
socialists, and those who had adopted the cause of Arab nationalism.

The effectiveness and the legitimacy of the intervention, however,
did not make the consequences less difficult. Initially, the diplomacy
of the American Deputy Under Secretary of State, Robert Murphy,
made possible an arrangement in Lebanon, whereby that country
under its new General President withdrew from a strict Western
orientation, and a recognition that the Revolution did not necessarily
mean Iraq's inclusion either in Nasser's camp or the Soviet world.

The inevitable appeal to the United Nations became embroiled in
perplexing and menacing efforts of Khrushchev to promote a summit
meeting. In spite of heightened mistrust of him, even on the part of
Prime Minister Macmillan who in principle favored a summit meeting—though not a summit meeting to be concerned with Middle
Eastern affairs—with persistence the Soviet leader might have forced
such a meeting in the General Assembly. But he changed his mind
after a conference with Mao Tse-tung and called for a summit meeting elsewhere on terms unacceptable to the major powers involved.
Finally, the immediate tangles were disposed of by the Middle
Eastern states. The Arab League states, with the assistance of Dag
Hammarskjöld, sponsored a resolution which the United States and
the Soviet Union found themselves unable to oppose. The landing
of the Anglo-American forces was not condemned, but their speedy
withdrawal was urged. The Arab states resolved in favor of the territorial integrity of member states, although Egypt and Syria had
certainly violated the injunction against interference in the domestic
affairs of other states. Nevertheless, the Arab League solemnly resolved and affirmed that its members discountenanced intervention of

one member in another's affairs. This fairy tale was allowed to do the healing work of peace.

The British and American forces were withdrawn, and the Arab states were left largely unimpeded to confront and promote their own stalemate.

10: BRITAIN AND THE CONTEMPORARY MIDDLE EAST

When the Revolution of 1958 destroyed the Iraqi monarchy as well as the political ascendancy of Nuri es-Said, Iraq also terminated her pro-Western orientation and her special relationship with Britain. The latter's tie with Iraq had been based on calculations of interest that appealed primarily to the monarchy and a small circle, who had feared Soviet influence and had seen in this fear and Western dependence on Iraqi oil the shared interests making possible and desirable Western-Iraqi cooperation. British tutelage and, later, British influence had supplied Iraq with the skeleton of government. The sinews were provided by the local landowners and the revenues accruing to the government from the operations of the oil company. The Iraqi version of Arab nationalism looked to a unity based upon an initial union of Jordan, Syria, and Iraq. But the Iraqi variant shared Arab nationalism's unrelenting hostility to Israel and to the remnants of foreign influence. By 1955 Britain had veered to the left in Iraq until she had nothing further to offer apart from the surrender of such influence as the Baghdad Pact afforded. On Israel, as well, Britain had nothing to offer Iraq except restraint. The mutual interests in oil exploitation and income were substantial but were insufficiently appreciated in Iraq to tame the nationalists and those aggrieved or slighted by the power of Nuri. His government, based on mistrust of the consequences of the free play of Iraqi political processes, was paternalist: it assumed that Nuri knew best. It is easy to argue that he did know best, that he was right to mistrust Iraqi politics, and to prolong his tenure of office in order to provide a necessary continuity in developing his country. But his government failed to secure the general consent of Iraqis, a necessary support in an age of nationalism. His adherence to the Baghdad Pact gave Nasser the opportunity to appeal to Iraqi nationalist discontent and to foster an already existing revolutionary temper.

While Suez had popularly discredited Nuri's pro-British association, the foundation of the United Arab Republic not only appeared to vindicate Nasser's claim that the Arabs could take care of their own defense against communism but further undermined Nuri's position and British influence in Iraq. As evidence of the strength and direction of Arab nationalism, the Revolution, in ending the older sources of British influence in Iraq, also posed a threat to governments charged with being under Western influence, for example, Lebanon, and to governments created and maintained by Western influence, for example, Jordan.

Empire by Treaty had all but been eroded away. There remained Aden and the Persian Gulf sheikhdoms. These involved either British dominance or an imperial position based on a treaty. But these positions were also under challenge and they could not be readily maintained, as in the days of their origin, by the display and movement of British power. Suez and the aftermath of Suez were warnings against the menacing processions of proconsular and imperialist strength. In 1957 and 1958 the tensions of the post-Suez period resulted in the reappearance of a limited form of gunboat diplomacy, American style. The British government had publicly supported the American actions and had sent British forces to Jordan in July 1958. Soviet retaliatory threats, as well as the Middle Eastern reaction to these deployments of Western forces, made it unlikely that similar landings would soon be repeated if the Soviet Union observed the restraint that the Lebanese and Jordanian missions of Western forces had been designed to foster.

If American initiative in the Middle East was inhibited, British policy had to be almost demure. On October 28, 1958, when the British House of Commons was debating the Queen's Speech which set forth the government's policies as well as its proposed subjects of legislation for the new parliamentary session, Hugh Gaitskell, then leader of the Labour Party, noted a contrast between the spectacular actions recently undertaken and the part of the Queen's Speech dealing with Middle Eastern policy. The latter, Gaitskell noted, was curiously mild, subdued, and detached.[1] Gaitskell's characterization of the policy advanced in the speech was quite accurate and the words might fairly describe the government's general approach to the area in this period, for the British government, so far as the Middle East was concerned, was a weakened, shorn, and chained Samson.

Prime Minister Macmillan had had to sweat out the consequences of failure at Suez. His slogans for that period, "Europe and Power,"

[1] *Parliamentary Debates*, Commons, 5th series, Vol. 594, col. 17-18.

expressed his sense that Britain by herself did not have the power that would permit his country to take Middle Eastern initiatives in any major way. The melodrama of 1957-1958, moreover, was rather too blunt and dangerous for the exercise of British diplomatic talents. Reduced British power and Britain's small island space made for an awareness of vulnerability that in turn discouraged any atmosphere of threats and the calling of bluffs. For Britain, there was necessary a time with at least the appearance of quiet. Situations would be fluid enough, at the very best, to permit future gains to be won by deft pragmatic policy. Behind any appearance of quiet, all would be in the ordeal of rapid change: Britain's defense policies, her relations with Europe, her economic position, and her relations with the Middle Eastern oil countries. Meanwhile, the great rollback of imperialism had begun in Africa.

Quiet, then, would be at best an appearance, a setting for a bourgeois pastoral of consultation of interest and negotiation rather than the *Heldenjammer* of the superpowers and Arab states. The Arab-Israeli feud remained unresolved, the major source of tension in the Middle East. To contain that tension the British government supported the Truce Supervisory Organization of the United Nations, established after the Arab-Israeli armistices, and the United Nations Emergency Force placed in Gaza after the Suez attack. Further, Britain reiterated the Tripartite Declaration of 1950 by which France, Britain, and the United States promised to assist an Arab state or Israel against aggression across the armistice lines. France and the United States, however, had on various occasions qualified their endorsement of this Declaration, and the British government recognized that it did not apply to Egypt, which had firmly indicated her unwillingness to have the Declaration apply to herself. Britain, in the interest of promoting an Arab-Israeli peace treaty, had insisted that the precise frontiers of the armistice were not the subject of an ironclad guarantee. The Arab refugee problem also continued without solution. Finally, the supply of Soviet arms to Egypt, Syria, and Iraq deprived the Western powers of a decisive check on Arab aggression.

A further difficulty was created by Soviet espousal of the Arab side in the dispute. To the British argument that the Arab-Israeli feud was the chief source of tension in the area, Khrushchev had replied with the pro-Arab contention that the cause of tension was the Western attempt to use Israel for colonialist politics.

The Baghdad Pact was also transformed. The Iraqi Revolution meant that the Pact had lost its only Arab member as well as the capital city that gave the Pact its name. The loss of Iraq reduced the Pact's attraction for Britain, which found in the Pact's new form as CENTO a commitment, in part embarrassing, of honor. Indeed, the Pact's sustaining force became American. At Ankara in 1958 Secretary Dulles had argued that the Eisenhower Doctrine, backed as it was by a Congressional resolution, was as effective as American membership in the Pact. At the Pact's Council meeting in London, Dulles signed a declaration that assumed for the United States the same obligations as the Pact's members had mutually undertaken.[2] Thus, the United States in 1959 also entered into bilateral agreements for the support of Pakistan, Turkey, and Iran, and these agreements constituted the major deterrent influence of the CENTO states.[3] For the rest, Britain and the United States encouraged the Pact's members to emphasize its regional character as an association to prevent subversion and to promote defense. Nevertheless, the Pact, now restricted to the "Northern Tier," had limited military capacity and, more important, its members, notably Iran, were not sturdy fortresses against subversion. The Pact's members, however, pressed for a more formidable military organization that on a reduced scale would have made their organization somewhat comparable to NATO. While Britain and the United States opposed this pressure, the CENTO Council agreed in 1961 to the establishment of a Military Staff Commander. The following year saw the project stalled, because the CENTO's Asian powers called for an American Commander whereas arrangements had been made to supply a British Commander.

The British approach to Kassim, whose regime received speedy British recognition, was certainly subdued until the Iraqi dictator

[2] *The Times,* July 29, 1958.

[3] The CENTO organization permitted joint planning and some cooperation. But the American guarantee to the three countries was the major deterrent influence of the CENTO organization. The Treaties, finally, went beyond American offers. Originally, President Eisenhower did not wish to go beyond the Eisenhower Doctrine. Turkey, however, urged the rapid conclusion of the Treaties. Iran, meanwhile, dissatisfied that it was not in NATO, as Turkey was, and not in SEATO, as Pakistan was, sought larger American guarantees and promise of more economic and military aid. The Soviet Union, in opposing the Iranian bilateral military pact with the United States, sent a mission to the Iranian Shah. This mission and rumored negotiations hastened the completion of the Treaty with the United States on terms more acceptable to Iran. *New York Times,* February 12, 13, 1959.

menaced Kuwait in 1961. Kassim in his few years as Iraqi leader expressed the more negative phases of Arab nationalism. He originally drew his government from the range of those opposed to Nuri and Faisal, excepting the communists. In September 1958, however, he learned that his deputy, the future Premier after the Revolution of January 1963, Colonel Ab al-Salam Aref, was working with other pro-Nasser forces to overthrow the new Iraqi government. After February 1959, when conservative and some army forces had revealed continuing hostility to Kassim, the Iraqi leader found it necessary to look to local communist support. But in mid-July 1959 he was driven to disband communist, semi-military forces, who had organized a massacre of anticommunist groups. Subsequently, the Soviet Union and the communists gave support to a movement for Kurdish autonomy led by Mustapha al-Barzani. By September 1961 this movement had become an armed rebellion. Kassim, thus, was increasingly dependent on the loyalty of the army and security forces, for he had not been able to acquire a political following and organization that in his eyes would have warranted an election.[4]

Iraq's initial pro-Soviet orientation gave Khrushchev a wider range of Middle Eastern influence, now in Iraq, as well as in Egypt and Syria. Indeed, in spite of later quarrels with the communists, Kassim's isolation made him dependent on Khrushchev. But this position also brought the Russian leader into the midst of Middle Eastern rivalries. Here, as in Egypt, the communists had influence, not control; and, as a result, their endeavor and commitments occasionally evoked Arab criticism. Thus, the Soviet Union also fell afoul of the Iraqi-Egyptian rivalry that had posed so much difficulty for the Baghdad Pact.[5]

This rivalry still affected Anglo-American cooperation, for Britain continued to send arms to Iraq, and the United States appeared to have greater hopes from Kassim's rival, Nasser. With an eye to Iraqi oil, the British government argued that to allow the Soviet Union to have a monopoly as Iraq's arms supplier was dangerous. But Kassim boasted: "Whenever I meet the oil companies, I ask for more." [6]

[4] Vito Priestly, "The Political Situation in Iraq," Middle Eastern Affairs, XIII (May 1962), 139-145.

[5] Khrushchev affirmed the continuity of good relations with Nasser but indicated that "our sympathy with Iraq is greater," for Iraq had a more progressive order. Time, March 30, 1959, p. 17. Here, the liberty of the local communist party is clearly Khrushchev's criterion of a more progressive order.

[6] Christian Science Monitor, August 17, 1961.

Under his pressure the Iraq Petroleum Company gradually yielded claims and concessions involving large areas of Iraq. Soviet technicians took over from British and other foreign companies in such tasks as widening some Iraqi railways and surveying for minerals and oil.[7]

Iraq's Development Board, to which before the Revolution 70 per cent of Iraq's oil revenues had been assigned, received far less under the revolutionary government. The decline in Development funds was mainly the result of the regime's instability and ineptitude, although Iraqi expectations of revenue declined in 1960 with the lowering of oil prices on the world market. The effect of marketing conditions on the revenues received by oil-producing states encouraged the formation of the Organization of Petroleum Exporting Countries. This was established after delegates from Iraq, Iran, Kuwait, Saudi Arabia, and Venezuela met in Baghdad (September 10-14, 1960). The organization, the outgrowth of earlier Arab League meetings concerning oil, generally functioning on a technical and expert level, did not at first attack concession agreements but protested instead against reduced price levels. Venezuela readily joined in an effort to raise the price of Middle Eastern oil, for success in that attempt would make Venezuelan oil more widely competitive.[8]

In general, Iraq's history under Kassim was markedly violent. He had no major source of power outside the army and the street mobs he used on occasion. He sought to maintain his control of the army by purges, as Nuri had done with less violence. He sought the aid of Iraqi communists, who gladly supported him in the purging of Baathists, members of a socialist, Arab-unity party of Syrian origin which acquired a following in a number of Arab lands and in Iraq became the first beneficiaries of the Revolution of 1963. He was challenged by several uprisings and repressed them with notable brutality. The show trials of his People's Court reveal a shocking crudity. He was unable to come to terms with the rebel Kurds, who still remain a threat to the Iraqi state. In foreign affairs he quarreled with Iran over claims to the Shatt el-Arab and he vainly laid claim to

[7] *New York Times*, June 11, 1962.

[8] This story contrasts with the activities of the Arab League itself. In its meetings it had proposed the building of a pipeline under Arab ownership. But when Lebanon proposed to the first Arab Petroleum Congress meeting in Cairo (April 16-23, 1959) that the Arab oil countries should advance 5 per cent of their oil revenues and oil companies operating in them should advance 5 per cent of their profits to the Arab Development Bank, no action was taken.

Kuwait when Britain recognized that sheikhdom as a sovereign state in 1961.

In maintaining an Iraqi state and its interests, he helped to maintain the divisions of Arabism. Although immediately after the Iraqi Revolution in 1958 he entered into a mutual defense agreement with Nasser and renewed Iraq's participation in the Arab League, the rivalry of the two leaders erupted sharply after the army revolt in Mosul, March 8, 1959. In short order Kassim, who received the public support of Khrushchev in criticizing Nasser, was denouncing Nasser. The latter, in turn, attacked Kassim for yielding the Arab cause to foreign, that is, communist influence. Kassim pursued the conflict aggressively. On several occasions during November 1959 he urged the union of Iraq and Syria and, including Jordan, endorsed the Greater Syria proposal.[9] As Kassim's actions had made other Arab leaders doubtful of him, he turned to exploit the Palestine issue as a proof of Arabist orthodoxy. On December 15 he proposed the creation of a Palestine state drawn from the areas taken by Israel, Jordan, and Egypt. On March 15, 1960, he announced the formation of a Palestine Army in Iraq. Meanwhile, for a year Iraq had boycotted the Arab League and it resumed its boycott when in 1961 Kuwait was admitted to the Arab League. The latter had long served as an unwilling claque for President Nasser, whose influence in it began to diminish in this same year. Nasser's pan-Arabism did endanger other Arab rulers. He expressed it in strange historical perspective, against the communists and Kassim on the occasion of the Mosul revolt: "The Communists, who think they can march against us from Baghdad, will, with the help of Allah, be the losers. The banner of Arab nationalism will be raised over Baghdad also, as it was when the Tatars were routed." [10] Kassim's Arabism, except in respect to Syria and Jordan, was less unitary: "Nationalist sentiment will dominate every other emotion. Since July 14 all Iraqis are pledged to work for Iraq and for no other country. . . . Iraq is a member of the Arab nation, but she is a completely independent Republic." [11]

[9] November 6, 16, and 20; *Christian Science Monitor*, November 29, 1959.

[10] Nasser was using warnings against the communist threat, here looked on as something foreign, for his conception of national and Arabist purposes conflicted with Russian policy as well as Kassim's policy. *New York Herald Tribune*, March 14, 1959.

[11] Interview with J. B. Slade-Baker, *Sunday Times*, March 8, 1959. Both Nasser's and Kassim's statements are so pragmatically motivated that they cannot be gravely taken as expressions of long-range intent.

The liquidation of Suez and the British approach to the Middle East in this new situation made imperative the resumption of diplomatic relations with Nasser. Restoration of full diplomatic intercourse, however, involved as a necessary preliminary the outlines of a settlement of many claims and counter-claims. Britain maintained the freeze on Egypt's sterling balance, estimated at £72,700,000, and Egypt demanded payment for damage inflicted in the Suez War. At that time Egypt had seized British military supplies in the Canal Zone and had nationalized or sequestered British businesses and property in Egypt. These British losses prompted large counter-claims against Egypt. On January 1, 1959, Eugene Black, President of the International Bank, visited Cairo and in the aftermath of his visit the two countries agreed to negotiate. By January 17, 1959, earlier preliminary exchanges and new negotiations had resulted in the initialing of a new agreement.

The agreement, formally signed early in March, provided that Egypt should pay compensation of £27,500,000 from the frozen sterling balances and between £8 and £10 million as two installments due to the Suez Canal Company under an agreement signed in July 1958. About 511 English businesses in Egypt had been sequestered. Of these about 430 had been liquidated or disposed of in some way. Some forty-seven of the remainder (banks, insurance companies, and factories) had been Egyptianized. The Suez War damage was balanced against the Egyptian seizure of British supplies in the Canal Zone base. On the British side, Prime Minister Macmillan, eyeing a prospective election, delayed the agreement in vain efforts to secure the release of two British prisoners held in Egypt.

The agreement, which soon fell afoul of a dispute caused by rival interpretations, did not mean the re-establishment of diplomatic relations. Beyond the immediate dispute was the conflict involved in Nasser's continuing "anti-imperialist" attack on British positions in Southern and Eastern Arabia. But the persistence of Nasser's pan-Arabism, as well as his continuing hostility to Kassim, also provided an argument for attempting to establish the means of influence with Nasser. The *Sunday Times*, March 15, 1959, insisted that the Mosul revolt and other events in Iraq had demonstrated the necessity of resuming diplomatic relations with Egypt. Even though Nasser's terms were expected to amount to a hard bargain, the word "bargain" could still be used. The bargain would provide a chance to open trade relations and regain diplomatic influence. "At present we lack the essential diplomatic mechanisms to conduct a policy towards the Arab world." [12] On December 1, 1959, Britain and the United Arab Republic exchanged *chargés d'affaires*. Finally, on January 16, 1961, the United Arab Republic announced that it would exchange ambassadors with Britain. The new British Ambassador was Harold Beeley, who had been the target of Zionist criticism for his alleged pro-Arabism when he served as Secretary Bevin's advisor. Beeley had also been an Assistant Under-Secretary at the Foreign Office during the summer of 1956.

Upon the resumption of full diplomatic relations with the United Arab Republic, *The Economist* noted that while Cairo was "no longer the crossroads of world strategy," it was "the indispensable listening-post for both the Middle East and Africa, and it has been a serious disability to have but half an ear there." [13] At any rate, the low estate of Britain's fortunes in the Middle East is revealed in the fact that for several eventful years British diplomatic relations with Egypt had been severed. Moreover, the major initiative in restoring relations came from Britain.

In 1961 Nasser's Arabist influence receded with Syria's peaceful withdrawal from the United Arab Republic. Nasser blamed this setback on the intrigues of reactionaries, especially King Saud, with whom he coupled the Imam of Yemen. Against them Nasser launched a new campaign of Arab socialism. Nasser had inaugurated his socialist program before Syria's secession. In his early policies Nasser had borrowed from the ideology of the Syrian Baath Party and in his later socialism was influenced by the example of Tito. His socialism of 1961 and afterwards won the acclaim of imitation in other Arab states. Indeed, 1961-1962 marks a new stage in the serious concern of Arab states with social welfare.[14] While Saud sought to rally Islam

[12] Later, *The Economist*, December 5, 1959, 947-948, sounded the same note: "Without diplomatic relations with the United Arab Republic, the British Government had either to do without a Middle East policy, or to try to frame one that took only indirect account of the most significant state in the region."

[13] *The Economist*, January 21, 1961, "Diplomatic Status." Michael Adams, a correspondent of *The Guardian*, January 13, 1961, writing in the playful and irresponsible Little England vein that forms a part of that radical journal's tradition, described the British Embassy in the center of Cairo as a "white elephant," a pretentious and unsuitable memorial to the past, and thought that it was a pity that it had not been burned as the British Embassy in Baghdad had been.

[14] Oded Remba, "The Middle East in 1962—An Economic Survey II," *Middle Eastern Affairs* (May 1963), pp. 30-145.

to his side and against secularist socialism, Nasser ridiculed the
Imam for writing a poem against socialism and asked: "If there were
social justice and the laws of justice and God were observed, how
then would King Saud accumulate his fortune?" [15]

Later *coups* and revolutions in the Arab world, in Yemen (1962),
in Syria, (in 1962 and 1963), and in Iraq (1963), reveal both the
strength and the limits of Nasser's Arabism. In Yemen the Imamate
was overthrown and a Republic, at first, largely limited to the low-
lands, was established with the help of Egyptian armed forces. The
old Imam Ahmed had quarreled with the British and had sought to
head off Nasser's hostility by association with the United Arab Republic. This policy failed and the Imam became mistrustful of the
consequences of associating with Nasser, whom he then attacked.
The Egyptian dictator replied by dissolving the association of Yemen
with the United Arab Republic (December 26, 1961). The revolution
following the Imam's death in August 1962 revealed the strength of
Nasser's appeal and was an ill omen not only to Saudi Arabia but
also to Britain's efforts to arrange for the future of Aden and the
Protectorate states.

In the aftermath of the Syrian *coups* and the more bloody Iraqi
coup (February 8, 1963), Arabism was proclaimed and gestures of
close fraternal association of Egypt, Syria, and Iraq were made. But
these gestures have been accompanied by power struggles in Syria and
Iraq and have been followed by Nasser's criticisms of Baathists in
Iraq and Syria for hampering Arab unity.

A number of Arab leaders were beginning to state publicly that
while unity should be the ultimate goal of the Arab people, a rapid
and sweeping political unity was impractical for the immediate
future. Dr. Hashim Jawad, Iraqi Foreign Minister under Kassim,
had attempted to moderate the tone of Arab exchanges and to replace
the projects of unity with forms of Arab cooperation. His endeavors
met with some success until Kassim himself, in June 1961, laid claim
to Kuwait. Nasser's new emphasis on Arab socialism involved a certain
lessening of hopes for immediate Arabist goals. In a long interview
with a British journalist, Nasser implied that the political struggle for
liberation must now merge in the tasks of social revolution. This
Arab socialism, however, provided Nasser with appeals to Arab peo-

[15] Speech at Port Said, Dec. 23, 1961, quoted in a leader "Nasser's New
Quarrel" of *The Times*, February 5, 1962.

ple against their reactionary rulers; and, more than occasionally, Nasser equated opposition to himself with reaction.[16]

The rivalries of Arab states, which along with the rivalries of Arab groups justify the judgment that the Arabs are the principal obstacle to Arab unity,[17] appeared strikingly in the controversy that attended Britain's recognition of Kuwait as an independent state.

Kuwait, a small sheikhdom, supplies Britain with more than 40 per cent of her oil. The profits of Kuwait's oil business largely go to British and American companies, and a considerable share of the ruler of Kuwait's revenue has been invested in British securities. Wealth for Kuwait has meant a welfare state and general education. This, in turn, has been accompanied by the growth of Arab nationalism. The sheikh himself has begun to face the problem of providing for popular participation in his paternalist government. To assure its oil supplies and provide against the more stormy future that past experience portended, the British government decided to take the gamble of removing all imperialist reins from Kuwait.

On June 19, 1961, the British government announced that the Agreement of 1899, placing Kuwait's foreign relations under British control, had been abrogated. To replace it, a sovereign Kuwait and the United Kingdom had negotiated a Treaty of Friendship. In foreign affairs Britain was to act on Kuwait's behalf until the new state had established its own foreign service. Britain was also to come to Kuwait's aid, upon request, if Kuwait were menaced by aggression. The ruler of Kuwait, Sheikh Abdullah al-Salam al-Sabah, proclaimed the independence of his Sultanate on June 26, 1961. But modern anti-imperialism has such indefinitely flexible resources that Kassim was able to denounce this development as an anti-Arab imperialist stratagem, with the backing of a reactionary ruler, to create a state out of oil wells.

Both Saudi Arabia and Iraq had territorial claims to Kuwait, and Nasser's Arabism provided him with the hopeful title of ambition to control the wealth of that oil-enriched principality, where oil produc-

[16] "My Revolutionary Life," Part III, told by Nasser to David Wynne-Morgan, *The Sunday Times*, July 1, 1962. A sympathetic account of Nasser's socialism by Patrick Seale exaggerates, I think, the withdrawal from Arabism that went with it. "Syria, Egypt, and Arab Nationalism," *The Listener*, April 5, 1962, pp. 585-587, 597.

[17] This judgment was made by a former British diplomat, Sir William Hayter, after a visit to the Middle East in 1962. See, *The Observer*, May 6, 1962.

tion had multiplied more than 100 times between 1946 and 1960. Kassim's claim that Kuwait was part of Basrah province was so threateningly advanced that King Saud offered support to Kuwait. Nasser, concerned for his own version of Arab unity, expressed opposition to any attempt to take over Kuwait. By June 29 British forces had been sent in response to the Sultan of Kuwait's request for military aid. Saudi forces also entered Kuwait.

The British government supported Kuwait's complaint concerning Iraq to the Security Council. But the presence of British forces as a deterrent to Iraq was a source of embarrassment to Saudi Arabia and Nasser. The British forces in Kuwait gave plausibility to Kassim's argument that the Arab world was being exploited by the rapacity of feudal sheikhs and imperialist powers. In embarrassment at the British presence Nasser and his government urged that the issue be settled in the Arab League, which met on July 12. Iraq, however, opposed Kuwait's admission to the League and Kuwait's ruler, though eager for Arab acceptance and protection, was fearful that the replacement of British troops by Arab League forces would leave him with the United Arab Republic's forces as the controlling presence in his territory.

The Soviet veto halted a conciliatory British Security Council resolution (July 5) which took note of Iraq's profession of peaceful intent and the fact that British forces were at the disposal of Kuwait's sultan. The resolution had also favored the Arab League's initiative and asked all states to respect Kuwait's independence. After the failure of the United Nations, the Arab League (July 20) adopted an amended Moroccan resolution. The Arab League solution involved giving offence to Iraq, which withdrew from the League session in protest against Kuwait's admission. This strange withdrawal actually permitted Kuwait to be admitted to membership by unanimous vote as the League's constitution required. For her part, Kuwait was to ask for the departure of British troops, who were to be replaced by League forces. British forces completed their departure on October 10. As evidence of its serious interest in Kuwait's independence, British forces were placed on an alert concerning Kuwait in late December when Syria defected from the United Arab Republic and Nasser consequently withdrew his forces from Kuwait.[18]

Nasser, however, had his own problems with the Arab League.

[18] For the Kuwait story see two articles by Benjamin Shwadran, "The Kuwait Incident," *Middle Eastern Affairs*. XIII (1962), 2-13, 43-52.

Syrian charges (August 1962) of Nasser's intervention in Syrian affairs precipitated the walkout of the United Arab Republic's delegate from the League Council's sessions and a withdrawal (September 1962) of its contribution to the League's budget. For the moment, the principal gainer in prestige was Saudi Arabia, which had taken successful initiative in the Kuwait affair. On August 29, 1962, Jordan's Hussain and King Saud announced that they would merge their military forces and coordinate their economic activities.[19] But this Hashemite-Saudi concord was short-lived.

The independence of Kuwait represents a British coming to terms with the nationalist forces in the Middle East. Many considerations impelled Britain to this move, including an unwillingness to be caught in local Arab struggles, as had happened in the Muscat-Oman rebellion. Recognition of Kuwait's sovereignty is a gamble but a gamble that has so far paid off. Kassim had continued his pressure on the Iraq Petroleum Company. The Company had found negotiations difficult because it believed that one concession would simply be made the occasion for extended demands. Kassim himself—refusing arbitration of the dispute over the Company concession—and his Minister for Oil gave every indication that the Iraqi pressure on the Oil Company would be unending.[20] Thus, the British government had to face the prospect that Kassim might have pressed Iraq's claim to Kuwait anyhow. As the security of Kuwait's oil was a necessary support of Britain's resistance to Kassim, the decision to recognize Kuwait's sovereignty was taken. In the light of these considerations it is a fair inference that the British government was not entirely surprised by Kassim's immediate claim to Kuwait and the subsequent conflict. Here, at any rate, British intervention, while not publicly welcomed by Nasser, was in behalf of a course which he then favored.

A significant aspect of Kuwait's continued independence is her provision of substantial capital for the economic development of the Middle East. The Kuwait Fund for Arab Economic Development was established in 1961. Its capital is £100,000,000 and it may borrow up to £200,000,000 more to finance Arab economic development projects on a government-to-government basis. Later, arrangements were also made for a private company, drawing on private capital in Kuwait and concerned with medium-range investment, to promote

[19] *New York Times*, August 30, 1962.
[20] *The Economist*, January 6, 1962, "The Sorry-go-round," and November 4, 1961, "Qasim's Bequest."

the investment of private capital in productive activities. The smaller
company has a staff of architects, engineers, and economists, and is
prepared to cooperate with Western enterprises, to invite the participation of the World Bank, and to be associated even with the
socialized economy of Egypt.[21] The Fund itself has not (as of mid-
1963) made large loans, for it operates on rather rigid financial
standards. So far it has approved projects in Lebanon, Jordan, and
the Sudan.

The Kuwait incident may provide an indication of the future
following Britain's withdrawal from the Middle East. As the former
imperial power and foreign enemy (and thus, in part, both the conscious and involuntary abettor of Arab union) withdraws, the
rivalries of the region are expressed with particular sharpness in keeping with the region's own autonomy.

Britain had been reduced to two principal bases: Cyprus on the
approaches to the Middle East; and the Headquarters of the British
Middle East Command at Aden. Where in 1954 Cyprus was denied
the prospect of independence and sovereignty because the island base
was necessary for the maintenance of British influence and positions
in the Middle East, the loss of influence and positions in the period
between Suez and the Iraqi Revolution made possible a wider offer
to the Cypriotes. In 1959 and 1960 long, uneasy, and frequently interrupted negotiations culminated in the independence of Cyprus (July
29, 1960). The issue, then, was not settled by *enosis*, union with
Greece, as many Greek Cypriotes had demanded. The settlement included detailed provisions to guarantee the rights of the Turkish
minority. Britain also retained the military use of two enclaves as
bases in Cyprus, which became a member of the British Commonwealth.

From the protracted and bloody Cypriote dispute Britain emerged
with a new settlement resting on a pluralist, popular foundation, and
with bases that may serve, mainly for aerial action in the Middle
East. But even Britain's remaining major base at Aden is menaced by
the growth of Arab nationalism among the workers and trade
unionists of the port city. Evidence of the growth of Arab influence
may be found in the city's increasing observation of Friday as the
day of rest.

To maintain British interest in Aden, Britain has followed a two-

[21] Article by "Our City Editor," *The Times*, July 5, 1963.

fold policy: the promotion of a Federation of the Eastern and Western Protectorate states, along with Aden, in the Federation of South Arabia; and the acceleration of Aden self-government, to be extended to the Federation. The first part has been only partly successful, for some of the rulers of the states are reluctant to lose power to a federation, especially where they have hope of oil discoveries in their territories. Others have played the game of discounting Britain's future and of seeking aid from Yemen or Egypt. The port of Aden itself is the seat of an Arabist national movement among the trade unionists, and many of the workers are Yemeni immigrants. Here, Britain is likely to face a stern challenge. As the last major base, Aden has been the object of British pledges that the base and port with its bunkering facilities and large oil refinery will be sternly defended. It is also likely enough that, if Aden ceases to be a British base, the economy of the port will decline. But it is already clear that Britain's twofold policy has encountered severe difficulties, made more formidable by the Yemeni Revolution of 1962. Thus, it is probable that Britain's Aden policy, made in London and taking some local interests into account, may not long be viable in the contemporary Middle East.

The history of the years since 1945 and Britain's difficulties in maintaining a mobile reserve of military forces at home suggest that the outposts of empire have frequently become a "wasting asset." [22] The Kuwait operation displayed the value of bases at Aden and Bahrain, allowing the rapid movement of forces. But Britain's intervention in Kuwait was successful because the occasion of British intervention attracted important Arab support. Behind that was the lesson that a base held in defiance of substantial popular wishes only too often became an end in itself—as Suez was in danger of becoming—that is, a base garrisoned by forces which were largely occupied in maintaining the base. In spite of the 1957 Defense White Paper and the resolve to cut overseas commitments, in 1961 about one half of the effective strength of the British Army was scattered around the globe. This was testimony to the world interests of Britain and to the difficulties Britain faced even in attempting to curtail commitments. Nevertheless, British policy can be effective and enduring only if it

[22] The phrase used to headline an account by the Defense Correspondent of *The Times*, August 23, 1961. See also, "Is Showing the Flag Worth the Cost," *The Times*, August 22, 1961.

recognizes "the changing threat and the part which Britain, beset by economic pressures and shortages of manpower, must play in meeting it." [23]

British policy in the Middle East is now primarily concerned with security of transit and, particularly, with the security of oil supplies. Apart from Aden and the naval base at Bahrain, the British government is concerned to bargain for the oil with the present leaders of the Middle East. In this approach British policy, in general, has received the support of the American government. The Soviet Union, however, continues to exploit the Middle East's political temper against the Western oil-producing companies. But Soviet selling of oil abroad reveals the Soviet Union as a competitor of Middle Eastern oil states.[24] British policy, then, is to emphasize Britain's common interest with the Arabs.

The problem is, as in the past, to gain Arab recognition of this community of interests. The Arab leaders are now as a rule, not the figures under British power and influence with whom Britain sought treaties and agreements to avoid the burden of direct empire. The Arab leaders now are representatives of states, nations, and an aspiring nation, that of the Arabs.

But even when an Arab leader recognizes the thread of interest with Britain, Arab nationalism's heritage of suspicion means that the leader's followers may turn to his rival when the latter turns against the leader for bargaining with Britain.

Britain, then, continues to struggle with the suspicion that attended the bargains of her period of Empire by Treaty. The proper making of a Middle Eastern oil agreement will involve protracted negotiation. But it is a little dismaying for a business-like, bargain-ready British representative to encounter the suspicion that this approach may be the cleverest and slyest mask of imperialism.[25]

The British, like most Western imperialists, brought revolution with them to the Middle East. This, of course, was not usually their explicit intention. For Britain the Middle East was originally a middle

[23] *The Times*, August 23, 1961.

[24] Leon M. Herman, "The Soviet Oil Offensive," *The Reporter*, June 21, 1962, pp. 26-28.

[25] Sir William Hayter observed this Middle Eastern reaction in 1962 and wearily hoped that as the area developed economically and in confidence, "sense may come at last to the Middle East." *The Observer*, May 6, 1962. *The Economist*, January 13, 1962, argued that for five years Britain has been "trying to make the best of existing situations, not to overturn them."

ground, an area prized because of its proximity to India. Later it was prized as a transit area, because of the newly-constructed Canal, and because from Egypt it provided access to the imperialist tournament in Africa.

The First World War saw the end of the European checkmate, the balanced considerations that had forestalled the dismemberment of the Ottoman Empire. The Middle East was dismembered, in part to meet the imperialist interests of victorious France and Britain, but also in the name of Arab nationalism. In the interwar years the British government sought to maintain its Middle Eastern ascendancy and its increasing oil interests by establishing a kind of half-way house of imperialism, Empire by Treaty.

The maintenance of this half-way house required its acceptance by an Arab elite of policy-makers. This acceptance, in turn, involved a continued British presence in force unchallenged by other major interested powers and an accompanying Arab recognition that the association with Britain was a source of profit and protection. The Second World War briefly extended British dominance, although the ordeal of war eventually made inevitable the roll-back of British power.

This inevitability was admitted in the postwar recognition of India's independence, a decision that not only deprived Britain of a major source of her power in the Middle East but memorably signalized for the Middle East the dwindling of British power and British unwillingness to maintain the dominion of imperialism.

In planning for the postwar Middle East, the British government looked to a continued close association with the Arab world. This association, it was recognized, might be jeopardized by Britain's mandatory responsibility in Palestine.

Palestine posed an impossible problem to the Mandatory, which therefore surrendered the Mandate to the contending local forces. No practicable solution for Palestine could have been squared with Britain's interests. The latter, of course, included Britain's relations with the United States, one of the superpower protagonists in the Cold War. Here Britain's freedom of action was limited by her dependence on American aid and by the growth of American interest in the Middle East.

The surrender of the Mandate marked the failure of Britain's policy of close association with the Arab world. Middle Eastern and Arab nationalists pressed for larger concessions from Britain, all the more in that they might look for American and, later, Soviet support. Nationalists passed from defiance to revolution and in Nasser's Egypt created a powerful center from which to oppose Britain and her Arab associates.

Thus, paradoxically, the American role in the Middle East, as well as the growing Soviet influence there, made for the freer play of autonomous Middle Eastern forces. Since frequently their play was destructive of British interests, the American role on occasion became ambiguous; American policy both supported the *status quo* and sought to adapt itself to the forces likely to be victorious. British policy, meanwhile, seeking to prevent the existing order from crumbling, attempted to maintain the dwindling positions believed necessary to uphold it. The Suez crisis represented an effort to regain the past. Its failure hastened the process of imperial diminution.

Today Britain is prepared to make business deals with Middle Eastern states. But at Aden and along the Persian Gulf Britain holds the remains of imperial positions. These positions involve commitments to Arab rulers that cannot simply be waived. There is the further fear that the abandonment of these positions might mean the loss of significant levers of power for the immediate future. This is so obvious that there is the additional fear that the abandonment of these positions may be followed by a dangerous inter-Arab struggle for their possession.

The British approach to the Middle East has been largely dictated by her statesmen's reading of Britain's interest.[26] In serving British interests, British representatives in the Middle East have left an unusual tangle of anti-imperialist suspicions. The British impact has had the revolutionary effect of modernizing the Middle East, a process that might have taken a more violent course in other hands. Inevitably, there is little recognition of this in the contemporary Middle East. Nor have the Arabs readily, as yet, learned from the British to think of politics in limited terms as the art of the possible.

The formulation of interests in a limited manner appears in the contemporary British approach to the Middle East. There, Britain holds on to positions that may become less tenable. The British approach still is more favorable to Iraq and her present approach to Arab unity than to that of Nasser. The American government apparently looks to the triumph of the Egyptian dictator's view of Arab

---

[26] This judgment may also be found in Elizabeth Monroe's able and recently published, *Britain's Moment in the Middle East* (Baltimore, 1963).

unity on the grounds that he alone gives promise of having the power to forge a Middle Eastern order and of having the assurance to make a settlement with Israel. This American hope ignores the traditional and British caution against the temptations that growing power engenders. This caution appears to be justified by Nasser's intervention in Yemen and the related attacks of his forces on Saudi Arabian territory.

Each policy has its dangers; and each involves a kind of gamble. What is certain is that the Arab aspirations to unity and to socialism will continue and will make Middle Eastern politics lively for many years. A large part of Britain's relations with the Middle East have become matters of history. The passing of British influence and the loss of British positions may prompt a judgment of ultimate failure on British policy. But in spite of Suez rebels and a minority of imperialists with a strong sense of British mission in the Middle East, there was usually a sense of the temporary and the provisional in British Middle Eastern arrangements. Though the temporary reached its term more sternly and earlier than British leaders were able or ready to recognize, those who study the details of British-Middle Eastern negotiations are likely to be less surprised at the ending of British influence and more impressed by the fact that for so long a time it remained formidable beyond the magnitude of its supporting power.

INDEX

A

Abadan, 85
Abbas II, 28
Abdulgani, 169
Abdullah, 27, 27n, 69, 69n, 70, 71, 72
Abu-Dhabi, 117
Aden, 18, 220-221
Allen, George V., 78, 140
Altrincham, Lord, 55, 94
Amman, 68
Anglo-Egyptian Treaty (1936), 31, 67, 98-99
Anglo-Egyptian Treaty (1954), 138, 140, 168
Anglo-Iranian Oil Company, 81, 84-85, 91
Arabi, Ahmed, 10, 28
Arab-Israeli War, 67
Arabism, 94, 98, 129, 197
Arab League, 46-47, 58, 69, 70, 70n, 71, 118, 123, 124, 131, 153, 205, 212n
Arab Legion, 27, 43, 66, 68, 70, 145
Arab nationalism, 14, 16-17, 36, 37, 43, 45, 46-47, 50, 56, 57, 126, 191, 193, 216-217
Arab refugees, 65, 66, 71

Arab Revolt, 15, 17
Arab Union, 207
Aramco, 84
Aref, Colonel Ab al-Salam, 211
Asquith, Henry, 23n
Aswan Dam, 130, 142-143, 158-160, 162
Attlee, Clement, Labour Party leader, Prime Minister, later Lord Attlee, 49-50, 53, 59, 113-114, 190
Austin, Senator Warren, 65
Azerbaijan, 78

B

Baath Party, 201
Baghdad Pact, Chapter 6, *passim*, 144, 145, 153, 162, 193, 196, 210
  Ankara meeting, 199
  Britain's role, 126-127
  first conference, 133
  Karachi meeting, 200
  Teheran meeting, 154-155
  and United States, 117. *See* CENTO
Bahrain, 6, 6n, 186, 222
Balfour Declaration, 15, 33, 58

al-Barzani, Mustapha, 211
Basra, 78
Bandung Conference, 132
Bayar, Celal, 145
Beeley, Harold, 215
Ben-Gurion, David, 48, 59, 138
Bevan, Aneurin, 155n
Bevin, Ernest, 50, 53, 54, 57, 59,
    61, 63, 64-67, 74, 75, 77, 94-
    96, 98
Bevin-Sidky Agreement, 94-96
Biltmore Program, 48
Black, Eugene, 143, 214
Bricker Amendment, 150
Bulganin, 149, 153
Buraimi Oasis, 7n, 117, 118n, 127n
Byrnes, James F., 77
Byroade, Henry, 160

C

Cadogan, Sir Alexander, 97
Caffrey, Jefferson, 107, 110-111,
    137n
Cairo Conference (1921), 25, 27,
    68
Cairo Radio, 199
Capitulations, 16
Carey, R., 45
Catroux, General, 38
CENTO, 210
Chamoun, 202, 203
Churchill, Randolph, 184
Churchill, Winston, 25, 25n, 38,
    39, 39n, 40, 41, 42, 47, 48, 49,
    50, 54, 60n, 62, 86-87, 102,
    106-107, 109, 114, 156n
Clayton, Brigadier, 71
Condominium, 95
Congress of Berlin, 5, 5n
Conservative Party (British imperi-
    alists), 86
Containment policy, 52
Convention of 1888, 114
Crimean War, 4-5
Cromer, Lord, 11, 30
Crete, 40, 42

Curzon, Lord, 6n, 7, 8, 8n, 10, 10n,
    18-19, 19n, 21, 29
Cyprus, 5, 116, 148, 155n, 165,
    182, 220
Czechoslovakia, 138-139

D

de Gaulle, 38, 39, 40, 44n, 187
Dardanelles, Straits of, 19
Dhahran, 51
Ed-Din, Salah, 101
Disraeli, 5n, 9
Dulles, John Foster, 118n, 119,
    136, 139, 196, 210
    Arab-Israeli relations, 140, 140n
    Eden, 149-150
    Egypt and the Aswan Dam, 148,
        158, 159, 160
    new approach to Middle East,
        120-121, 121n
    neutralism, 159-161
    pre-Suez policy, 166, 170, 171,
        172, 173, 175, 175n, 176, 177,
        179, 181, 185
    view of Baghdad Pact, 134-135

E

East India Co., 6, 6n
Eastern Question, 11n, 14, 19
The Economist, 74, 215
Eden, Sir Anthony, 86, 114, 115,
    117, 118, 118n, 126, 136, 161-
    192 passim, 193
    Anglo-Egyptian Agreement
        (1954), 119
    Baghdad Pact, 126-127
    bases overseas, 148, 157
    Churchill, 106n
    consequences of Suez policy, 184-
        188
    decision to topple Nasser, 164,
        170, 171, 179
    domestic criticism of, 146-147,
        147n
    Dulles, 149-150
    Egypt's arms' deal, 148

Guildhall Speech, 140-141
imperialism, 148
Israel, 149
joins Suez and Arab-Israeli dispute, 186
Jordan, 145, 152
judgment of American diplomacy, 108
judgment of hostility of Nasser, 156, 157
judgment of Nasser, 148-149
judgment of Nasser's Canal policy, 163, 169-170
Mansion House Speech, 48
possible use of force against Nasser, 163
primacy of responsibility in the Middle East, 107
Prime Minister, 112, 146
Sudan, 106n
Suez as vote of no confidence in American leadership, 187
supports Arabism, 45
and United States, 128, 147, 149, 150-151, 154-155
Egypt, 40, 43, 44, 161-192 passim, 221
Anglo-Egyptian Treaty (1954), 112-113
appeal to U. N. Security Council, 96-97
armed forces amalgamated with Syria and Jordan, 181
Aswan Dam, 142-143
Bevin-Sidky Agreement, 94-96
blocked sterling balances, 92
Britain recognizes sovereignty, 29
Britain supports Sudanese self-determination, 95-96
British occupation, 5, 10-11, 28
British pressure in summer (1956), 164-165
British Protectorate, 24, 28-29
Cairo Radio, 199
communist arms deal, 136, 138-139
Concession to Canal Company, 9, 9n

cotton, 139, 139n
Council for the Revolutionary Command, 103
effect of Wafd nationalist agitation, 93-94
forms United Arab Republic, 201
Greater Syria Plan, 69n
Israel, 137-138
Milner Commission, 29
nationalist demands, 95
negotiations to revise Anglo-Egyptian Treaty, 98-99
neutralism of, 97
Palestine War, 70-71
resumption of diplomatic relations with Britain, 214-215
Revolution, 102-103
rioting in Cairo, 102
Sudan, 11, 29, 104-106
Suez Canal Base negotiations, 108-113
Treaty (1936) with Britain, 31
Unity of Nile Valley, 96
Wafd Party, 25n, 28-29
Second World War, 42, 44-45, 46, 93
Eisenhower, 118n, 120, 120n, 142, 143, 149, 156n, 163, 167, 171n, 176, 178, 190
Eisenhower Doctrine, 195-197, 198, 199, 201, 202

F

Faisal, King, 22, 26, 68
Faisal (Iraq), 204
Faisal, Prince (Saudi), 201
Farouk, 43, 44, 46, 93, 101, 103
Fawzi, Mohammed, 177
Federation of South Arabia, 221
Fedayeen, 138, 139, 144, 148
Fertile Crescent, 45, 123
Foreign Office (British), 54
Forrestal, Secretary, 52
France, 23, 36, 37, 38, 39, 68, 137, 179, 183
rivalry with Britain, 27-28
sale of planes to Israel, 158

Tripartite Declaration, 67
Turkey, 4-5
Free French, 38-39
Fuad, 32
Full Circle, 165
Fund for Arab Economic Development, 219

G

al-Gailani Rashid Ali, 43, 73
Gaitskell, Hugh, 164, 208
Gallman, Ambassador Waldemar J., 134
Gaza, 138
General Syrian Congress, 24
Geneva "Summit," 146
Germany, 28, 36, 37, 38, 39, 40, 42
Gladstone, W. E., 5, 11, 14
Glubb, John Bagot, 17, 144, 145, 145n, 151-152
Grady, Henry, 83
Granville, Lord, 6n
Greater Syria Plan, 69
Greece, 36, 38, 40, 42, 51, 52
Grey, Sir Edward, 8, 8n

H

Hammarskjöld, Dag, 158, 178, 185, 205
Hardinge, Sir Arthur, 7, 7n
Hart, Liddell, 184
Haykal, M., 131
Head, Anthony, 114
Henderson, Loy, 154
Henriques, Colonel Robert, 187
Hinchingbrooke, Lord, 190
Home, Lord, 190
Hoover, Herbert, 22
Hussain, Sharif of Mecca, 15, 22
Hussain (of Jordan), 72, 144, 151, 152, 198, 199, 204, 219

I

Imperialism, 1-2, 11-12
India, 2, 3, 6, 6n, 8, 8n, 53, 54, 87

International Bank for Reconstruction and Development, 82, 143
International Court of Justice, 89
Iran, 42, 43, 210, 210n, 212
Agreement of 1921, 87
Appeal to United Nations, 77
bargain with Soviet Union, 78
Britain mistrustful of Soviet exclusion from Iranian oil, 78
British policy after Iran's nationalization of oil fields, 89-90
British policy in, 81, 85
civil service, 79-80
distressed conditions in 1950, 85
effect of presence of United Nations' forces in Second World War, 76-77
influence of nationalization experience on British at Suez, 92
loan refused by International Bank, 82
Majlis, 78, 79
Majlis reject Soviet oil concession, 78-79
nationalism, 80, 83
negotiations with Britain after nationalization, 87-88
parties, 80, 81, 81n
settlement of oil dispute, 90-91
Seven Years' Plan, 82
sources of political extremism, 81
Soviet breach of Teheran Agreement, 77
Soviet Union, 51
supplementary oil agreement, 84
Tudeh Party, 54, 78
U.S. policy to, 81, 82
Iraq, 12, 22, 40, 43, 46, 145, 186, 193, 199, 201-202, 216, 217, 218
agreement with U.S. (1954), 122
approves Nasser's nationalization policy, 162
ascendancy of Nuri es-Said, 76
attempted Treaty (1930) revision, 74-76

Baghdad rioting (1948) and sources of dissatisfaction, 76
British effort to secure participation in regional defense, 75
British interests in, 73
British Mandate, 24-27
British sterling balances, 74
Cold War, 73
end of mandate, 26-27
nationalism, 72
Revolt (1958), 204-205, 207
split of Regent's and Rashid Ali's supporters, 73
Treaty (1930), 73, 123
Treaty of Portsmouth (1948), 74-75
treaty with Turkey, 124-125
and Turco-Pakistani Agreement, 122, 122n
Iraq Development Board, 212
Iraq Petroleum Company, 22, 212, 219
Ismail, Khedive, 10
Ismailia, 102, 183
Israel, 65, 131n, 137, 140, 161-192 *passim*
British-American divisions, 65-67
British Spitfires shot down, 67
Eden, 148-149
effect on British position in Middle East, 65-67
Egypt, 138-139
France sells planes, 158
negotiations with Jordan, 71
occupies El Auja, 139
origin, 58
United Nations, 65
Italy, 28, 36, 37, 38, 39, 40

J

Jackson, Basil, 88
al Jamali, Mohammed Fadhil, 124, 125
Jawad, Hashim, 216
Jebb, Sir Gladwyn, 86
Jewish Agency, 61
Johnston, Ambassador Charles, 198

Jordan, 144, 151-152, 181, 186, 193, 201-202
approves Nasser's nationalization, 162n
Baghdad Pact, 145-146
British forces arrive in (1958), 205
consequences of annexing West Bank, 71-72
Emirate of Transjordan, 27
negotiations with Israel, 71
terminates treaty with Britain, 197-198
treatment of Arab refugees, 71
treaty of 1948, 144-145
unification with West Bank, 71

K

Kassim, 210-213, 216, 219
Keightley, Sir Charles, 183
Khrushchev, 149, 153, 158, 187, 195n, 200, 205, 209, 211, 213
Kitchener, Lord, 28
Koprulu, 119n
Kirkuk, 40
Kurds, 211
Kuwait, 6, 6n, 91, 186, 217-218
Kuwait Fund for Arab Economic Development, 219

L

Labour Government (British), 53, 87-88, 89, Chapter 5 *passim*
Labour Party (British), 49, 60, 188, 189
anti-colonialism, 50
back-bench opposition to Bevin, 55
Bevin, 53
criticizes Eden's Suez policy, 164, 172, 174-175
United Nations, 50
Zionism, 50, 59
Lampson, Sir Miles, 44, 44n
Lawrence, T. E., 17, 22, 22n, 25n, 27, 27n

Lansdowne, Marquess of, 7n
League of Nations, 18, 22, 24, 26
Lebanon, 23, 36, 38, 39, 42, 46, 196, 202-204, 205
Liberation Rally (Eq.), 104
Libya, 118, 183n
Lloyd, Lord, 29
Lloyd, Selwyn, 147, 151, 152, 157, 165, 179, 180
Lyttleton, Oliver, 40-41

M

Macmillan, Harold, 109, 187, 204, 205, 208, 214
Mafrak, 70n, 197
Mandates, 22
Majlis (Iranian), 78, 79
Malik, Charles, 202
Malta, 165
Mao Tse-Tung, 205
Marshall, Secretary of State, 52
Mehmed Ali, 95
Menderes, Adnan, 119, 124, 129
Menzies, Robert, 170
Middle East Command, 100-101
Middle East Office, 55, 71
Middle East Supply Center, 39, 45-46, 55
Middleton, Drew, 155
Milner, Lord, 24-25, 25n
Milner Commission, 24-25, 29
Molotov, V. M., 51, 132
Mossadegh, Dr. M., 43, 54, 84, 86, 87, 87n, 88, 90, 91-92
Muscat, 6, 6n
Muslim Brotherhood, 94
Mussolini, 39
Murphy, Robert, 167n, 205

N

Nabulsi, Suliman, 197-198
Naguib, Mohammed, 103-104, 105, 112, 120
Nahas, Mustapha, 43, 44, 44n, 99, 101

Nasser, 103, 112, 115, 116, 124, 126, 127, 136, 161-192 passim, 193, 194, 199
  Arab nationalism, 195, 197, 198, 201
  Aswan Dam, 142, 143, 158-160
  attacks American policy as imperialism, 195
  attacks American support of British policy, 120n
  Baghdad Pact, 129-131
  Bandung Conference, 132
  at Brioni, 161
  communist arms deal, 136, 138-139
  course runs parallel with Soviet policy, 133
  Eden's desire to topple, 164, 170, 171, 172, 179
  Eden's Guildhall speech, 141
  forms United Arab Republic, 201
  gluts Canal with ships, 186
  nationalizes Suez Canal Co., 161, 168
  neutralism, 132, 136
  propaganda against Jordan and Iraq, 202
  The Philosophy of the Revolution, 131
  prelude to union with Syria, 200-201
  recognizes Communist China, 158
  restoration of diplomatic relations with Britain, 214-215
  Socialism, 215, 216-217
  supports Lebanese rebellion, 202
Nessim, Tewfik, 32
National Front (Iran), 84n
National Iranian Oil Co., 91
NATO, 118
Nehru, 132, 161
Neutralism, 133, 136
Nicolson, Sir Harold, 95n
Al-Nokrashy, 70n, 96, 97
Nutting, Anthony, 113
Nuwar, Ali Abu, 156

O

Oman, 7, 202
Organization of Petroleum Exporting Countries, 212

P

Pahlevi, Mohammed Reza Shah,
21, 42, 83
Pakistan, 122
Palestine, 15, 51, 58-67, 223
Anglo-American Commission of
Inquiry, 61
Arab refugees, 65
Britain consults U. N. about
Mandate, 64
Britain contemplates yielding the
Mandate, 64
British mandatory responsibility,
56
British White Paper policy on
Jewish migration, 60-61
Mandate, 68
partition of, 35
Report of Anglo-American Com-
mission, 63
West Bank, 68
White Paper, 45, 46
Palmerston, Lord, 9
Paris Peace Conference, 18, 22, 29
Peel Commission (1937), Report
of, 34-35
Persia, 7
Britain, 20-21
Germany, 20
Russia, 21, 21n
Soviet Union (Treaty of 1921),
20, 20n
treaty negotiated with Britain
(1919), 21, 21n
Persian Gulf, 6, 6n, 12, 54
Petain, 38
Peterson, Maurice, 32
Philby, Henry, 17
Philosophy of the Revolution, 131,
165

Pineau, Christian, 163, 180, 180n,
181
Port Fuad, 183
Port Said, 183

Q

Qatar, 6n
Qavam-es-Sultanah, 77, 78

R

Razmara, Ali, 84, 86
Red Line Agreement, 22
Richards, Ambassador James, 196
Rommel, 40
Roosevelt, Franklin D., 42, 48, 82,
82n
Rose el Youssef, 156
Royal Dutch Shell, 91
Russia, 1, 4-5, 14

S

Al-Sabah, Sheikh Abdullah al-
Salam, 217
Sacher, Harry, 62
Salem, Salah, 124
Salih Jahr, 75
Salisbury, Lord, 6n, 8n, 9n, 190-191
Salisbury, Marquis, 190-191
es-Sadat, Anwar, 142
es-Said, Nuri, 45, 76, 122, 122n,
123, 124, 125, 129, 130, 131,
141, 141n, 155n, 162, 169,
171, 186, 193, 204, 207
San Remo Conference, 22, 33
Saud, Ibn, 15, 22
Saud, King, 144, 194, 196, 199,
202, 215-216, 218, 219
Saudi Arabia, 12, 17, 23, 46, 51,
69n, 91, 118, 118n, 150, 198,
217
Shawcross, Sir Hartley, 179
Shepilov, 153, 177
Sidky, Ismail, 94, 96
Slim, Sir William, 99n, 100

South Arabia Federation, 221
Soviet Union, 2, 19, 27, 36, 37, 38,
    40, 42, 43, 142, 153, 159, 180,
    184, 193, 195, 209, 210, 210n,
    211, 222, 224
    Agreement of 1921, 87
    Arab nationalism, 50
    bargain with Iran, 78
    Berlin Blockade, 66
    breaches Teheran agreement, 77
    change of Middle Eastern policy,
        132-133
    designs on Iran, 76, 77
    Egypt, 137
    Greece, 51
    influences of Iranian experience
        (1951-1953), 133
    Iran, 51, 91
    Persia (Treaty of 1921), 20, 20n
    post-Second World War advan-
        tages in the Middle East, 50-
        51
    Turkey, 51
Spears, General E., 39
The Spectator, 151
Stalin, Joseph, 42, 48, 51, 132
Stark, Freya, 42
Stevenson, Sir Ralph, 98, 187n, 191
Sudan, 29, 95-96, 143, 159
    Britain supports self-determina-
        tion, 95-96
    Egypt, 11
    Egypt's Demand for Unity of
        Nile Valley, 96
    Naguib, 104-105
Suez Canal, 8, 9-11, 40, 44, 92, 138
Suez Canal Co., 9, 9n, 161, 167-
    169, 182
Suez Canal Conference (London),
    170-171, 176
Suez Canal Convention, 10, 167,
    168, 172
Suez Canal Zone, 31, 64, 102, 111-
    113
Suez Canal Users' Association, 172-
    173, 175, 176
Suez Rebels, 113, 114, 147, 165
Sunday Times, 214

Sykes-Picot Agreement, 21
Syria, 23, 36, 38, 39, 42, 46, 68,
    124, 181, 186, 200, 201, 216

T

Teheran Declaration, 42, 81-82
Templer, Sir Gerald, 145
Thompson, Sir G., 43
Tito, 132
Transjordan, 56, 68, 69, 70n
Tripartite Declaration, 51, 67, 98,
    137, 138, 140, 149, 150, 180,
    209
Truman, President Harry, 60-61
Truman Doctrine, 52
Tudeh, 54, 87, 133
Turkey, 4, 14, 19, 36, 37, 38, 113,
    200
    Agreement with Britain (1953),
        118n
    Agreement with Pakistan, 122
    Britain, 4-6, 14-15
    Britain discontinues support of,
        52
    France, 4-5
    key to Middle East defense, 118-
        119
    Russia, 4-5
    Soviet Union, 51
    treaty with Iraq (1955), 124-125

U

United Arab Republic, 201, 215
United Nations, 50, 59, 64-65, 66,
    67, 77, 89, 96-97, 118, 172,
    176-178, 183, 184-185, 200,
    203, 218
United Nations Emergency Force,
    209
United States, 2-3, 27, 42, 43, 48,
    223, 224
    Agreement with Iraq (1954), 122
    American Marines to Lebanon,
        205
    Aswan Dam, 142-143, 158-160
    Baghdad Pact, 117, 128, 150-151

Britain and Palestine, 64-67
Britain's primary responsibility in Middle East, 51, 108
Britain seeks cooperation of, 51
Britain seeks cooperation in relation to Palestine, 61
colonies and British colonialism, 3
British imperialism, 51, 120-121, 121n
containment policy, 52
Eden, 147
Egypt, 136
Eisenhower Doctrine, 195-197
gunboat diplomacy, 208
Israel, 119
judgment of British Suez policy (summer, 1956), 166, 170, 171, 172, 175-176, 179, 184
Libya, 118
Middle Eastern policy, 142-143, 149-151, 154-155
military aid to Iran, 82
Nasser attacks American imperialism, 195
Palestine, 64-65
policy to Iran, 81
post-Suez Middle Eastern policy, 194-195
Saudi Arabia, 51
Sixth Fleet to Lebanon, 199
Suez Canal Base negotiations, 108, 109

supports Britain against Mossadegh, 92
Tripartite Declaration, 67
Truman Doctrine, 52

V

Venezuela, 212

W

Wafd Party, 28-29, 43, 44, 46, 93, 100
Wahhabis, 117
Waterhouse, Capt., 113
Wavell, General, 40
Weizmann, Chaim, 34, 48, 62
Wheelus, 118
Williams, Paul, 190
Wilson, Sir Henry Maitland, 43

Y

Yehia, Abdul Fettah, 32
Yemen, 23, 23n, 201, 216
Yugoslavia, 38

Z

Zahedi, General Fazlollah, 90
Zaghlul, Saad, 25n
Zia-ed-Din, Seyyid, 21n
Zionism, 33, 37, 45, 47, 48, 50, 56, 57, 58, 59, 60-67